Communicating
for Managerial
Effectiveness

Dedicated to my parents, Dr. Bert and Betty Clampitt, who provided all the physical, psychological, and spiritual support a son could ask for.

Communicating for Managerial Effectiveness

Phillip G. Clampitt

 SAGE PUBLICATIONS
The International Professional Publishers
Newbury Park   London   New Delhi

For information address:

SAGE Publications, Inc.
2455 Teller Road
Newbury Park, California 91320

SAGE Publications Ltd.
6 Bonhill Street
London EC2A 4PU
United Kingdom

SAGE Publications India Pvt. Ltd.
M-32 Market
Greater Kailash I
New Delhi 110 048 India

Printed in the United States of America

Library of Congress Cataloging-in-Publication Data

Clampitt, Phillip G.
    Communicating for managerial effectiveness / Phillip G. Clampitt.
        p.   cm.
    Includes bibliographical references and index.
    ISBN 0-8039-3759-8. — ISBN 0-8039-3760-1 (pbk.)
    1. Communication in management. I. Title.
    HD30.3.C52   1991
    658.4'5 — dc20   90-15581
                                                               CIP

SECOND PRINTING, 1991

Sage Production Editor: Diane S. Foster

Contents

Foreword

The communication that takes place in an organization is an important influence in the success of that organization. Therefore, a good book on organizational communication can be a valuable resource for all kinds of students—managers who want to be effective communicators, as well as academic students who want to understand how organizations work. Phil Clampitt has written such a book.

Over the years I have evaluated a number of manuscripts offered to various publishers, and many of them have good coverage of rather standard materials that are commonly covered about organizational communication. What Phil Clampitt has done, however, is to write a book that is original and interesting.

What strikes me most about his work is its freshness. The quotations with which he begins each chapter are not typical organizational literature; they demonstrate how well read he is and how this breadth of resources have led him to think about organizational life in some innovative ways. He also demonstrates great originality in the way that he uses metaphor to explain how communication works. For example, while I love to dance, I would never have thought of using dance as a metaphor for the way organizational communication works. Yet, Clampitt does so in a convincing way. Furthermore, he is able to coin new phrases that are rich in explanatory power.

I also like the way Clampitt makes this book a statement of his theory about organizational communication. It is not merely a report on the research about a topic. He includes basic propositions and clarifies some of his basic assumptions. He makes a major addition also by describing some common problem areas and then telling his reader "what to do" about them. Finally, he adds some important areas that are often overlooked. His work with communication audits has prompted him to add major discussions of inter-team communication.

One of the great rewards of being a university professor is being able to watch exceptional graduate students become major contributors to one's discipline. Phil Clampitt is doing this with his book. There are many gems in these chapters, and I am delighted to recommend it.

—Cal Downs
University of Kansas

Acknowledgments

C. S. Lewis once said, "Two heads are better than one, not because either is infallible, but because they are unlikely to go wrong in the same direction." I have had the benefit of many heads trying to steer me in the right direction. Without the guidance of many friends and colleagues this book would not have taken the shape it has. First, there is Ann West of Sage Publications who put faith in the kernel of an "exciting idea" in spite of all the other crazy notions originally associated with the manuscript. Paul Feingold was equally encouraging about the general thrust of the book, while suggesting some excellent reorientations. Lois Lemke, Jeannette Terry, John Gregg, Karen Gregg, Brent Hussin, Pat Lidwin, and Angela Laird-Brenton patiently read drafts of the manuscript and made many useful suggestions. Carol Polacek and Brent Hussin did all the graphic work. Any visual appeal this book has is largely due to their efforts. Mary Beth Stradal, Joan Spaite, Andrew Zinkl, Melissa Hall, Kimberly Clark, and Marie Garot provided excellent technical support for this project. Dr. Mary Ann Hazen of the University of Detroit carefully critiqued the final draft and helped tighten the conceptual foundations. Her comments were invaluable.

Dr. Cal Downs was my major professor at the University of Kansas. He has continued to shape my thinking by providing extremely useful and specific guidance for the "final draft." His wit and encouragement helped me make it through the rough times. Finally, there is Laurey Berk. If there is a coauthor of this book, it is Laurey. She read countless drafts with an unfailing eye for detail and a relentless dedication to the cogency and clearness of expression. She also provided the encouragement and support necessary to complete the task. It was in her condominium in Door County that I often listened to strains of Vivaldi's Concerti and received my final source of inspiration.

Introduction

"The first principle is that you must not fool yourself . . . and you are the easiest person to fool," wrote the Noble Laureate, Richard Feynman. Physicists are not the only ones who must guard against self-delusion—managers must as well. And the temptation of self-deception proves almost irresistible when it comes to the elusive business of communication. The purpose of *Communicating for Managerial Effectiveness* is to enable managers to clearly view their communication abilities, dilemmas, and challenges.

This is not an easy task for two reasons. First, our knowledge of the communication process is still unfolding. New and exciting theories have recently appeared on the horizon that allow us to see communication in a light never before possible. Only in the past few years have we started to discern the implications of these ideas. For instance, some scholars have challenged the traditional assertion that "understanding" is always the goal of communication. Sometimes managers are purposefully ambiguous. What are the implications of this notion for managers? Can misunderstandings be useful in an organization? These are the types of questions addressed in these pages.

Second, there is what I call the "Everybody/Anybody phenomenon." Translation: since *everybody* communicates, *anyone* can hold a seminar on the subject. Hence, what gets passed off as training for "communication excellence" is often nothing more than warmed-over platitudes or rehashed pop psychology. That is unfortunate not only because it misrepresents a rich field of scholarship, but also because managers encounter a host of communication challenges that are not addressed by the "Everybody/Anybody" speakers. They treat ideas like they are cotton candy: something fluffy and sweet, but not the staples of organizational life. Nothing could be further from reality. Ideas have consequences. Bad ideas have bad consequences. When the communication system breaks down, tragedy often is the result. A case in point: the space shuttle *Challenger.*

The impetus for this book was research conducted in over 25 organizations (see Appendix A). The methodology consisted of administering surveys and conducting interviews with employees (see Appendix B). As I conducted communication assessments, often in conjunction with students, I discovered a group of concerns that emerged as common themes in these organizations.

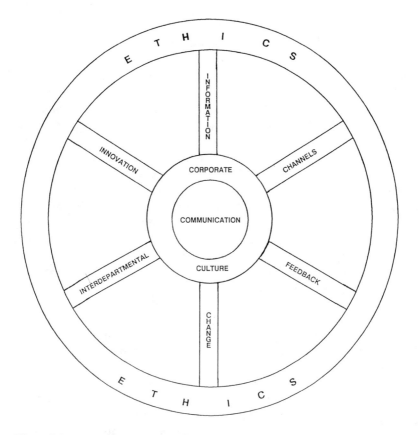

Figure I.1 "Wheel" of Communication Effectiveness

For instance, executives often were dismayed at the seeming impossibility of getting departments to communicate effectively with one another. Employees often were frustrated by the lack of useful feedback from their managers. So the book took shape around these kinds of concerns.

The illustration featured in this Introduction (Figure I.1) provides the framework for the book. At the hub of managerial effectiveness lies communication and culture. The first two chapters are devoted to explaining the complex process of communication. The third chapter concerns the core issue of corporate culture, which has a pervasive impact on the communication climate. The spokes represent six critical communication challenges most managers face. In each case, I begin by analyzing the challenge and close with practical recommendations based on actual cases. The corresponding six chapters discuss how to

- manage information
- select appropriate communication channels
- develop an effective performance feedback system
- communicate about organizational changes
- foster interdepartmental communication
- create an innovative spirit

The final chapter is on ethics, which is the rim that holds an organization's communication system together. The wheel is a symbol of wholeness as well as movement. My hope is that the book will provide a more complete picture of managerial communication effectiveness, while presenting an image of the ever-changing nature of that quest.

Examples are drawn not only from the business world but also from a wide range of arenas including politics, history, science, and art. The rationale: communication is a concern in almost every area of life. Many examples are drawn from my consulting experiences. Unless otherwise noted, I have changed the names and slightly altered the background in order to "protect the guilty." When particularly illuminating, I have discussed the findings of key scholarly studies. The focus, however, is on the practical implementation of the material in the organization. It is my hope that managers, potential managers, training personnel, and students of business communication will find in these pages a way to abide by Professor Feynman's "first principle."

1

How Managers Communicate

> Human communication permeates the human condition. Human communication surrounds us and is an inbuilt aspect of everything human beings are and do. That makes any effort to explain, predict, or to some extent control human communication a pretty big order. How does one get a handle on the totality of human communication?
>
> Frank Dance

If, by a wave of a magic wand, managers could communicate perfectly, how would organizations change? Would the company be more productive? Employees more satisfied? The wand presents an intriguing dilemma for the manager. On the one hand, managers know that their success largely is a function of their communication skill. On the other hand, they are often unclear about what "perfect" or effective communication really is. Some argue, for example, that if employees completely understood their managers, organizations would function smoothly. Yet the misunderstandings may prove useful, as in the case of an employee who misinterprets a manager's sarcastic criticism as a legitimate suggestion. Such a misunderstanding may temporarily preserve "the peace." How managers might use this magic wand proves revealing: It creates the illusions and reality of their world. Typically, managers choose to wave the wand in one of three ways. The Arrow, Circuit, and Dance approaches are discussed in detail below.

Arrow Approach

Mr. Taylor almost perfectly, though unwittingly, articulated the Arrow philosophy during a presentation to a management team about communication problems in his organization. He managed the data processing department and he asked the consultant numerous technical questions about how the data were analyzed. With each response he increasingly appeared more uneasy and antagonistic. When the consultant suggested that his employees were less than satisfied with certain aspects of the communication system, his technical questions assumed an almost acidic quality. The tone of the conversation became increasingly combative. Finally, he exploded with a 15-minute diatribe. As frequently occurs, the technical questions masked his actual concern. His remarks went along these lines:

> Why should I take my time to ensure that people understand? I spend my time putting the information together. I send memos because then I know that I've communicated my message. Then I don't have to worry about it. I've done my duty. They got my message. These meetings you propose for our company may make people feel good but I just see it as a waste of my time and the company's.

After this rather illuminating soliloquy there was a profound but understandable change in the atmosphere. An uncomfortable silence prevailed for a moment. Yet there was also a sense of relief because Mr. Taylor had laid all his cards on the table. His comments had some merit. He had clearly pointed out one of the greatest challenges in organizational communication: providing efficient methods of communication. But there were significant flaws in his thinking.

First, he assumed that if a message is sent via company mail it will be received at the proper time. In some organizations, this is a dubious presumption at best. In fact, during a training session at a hospital, one participant revealed that in some cases it took two weeks to get mail from a seventh floor office to one on the eighth floor. Second, Mr. Taylor assumed that if the message was received, it was read. With information overload one of the facts of organizational life, this assumption may be suspect. Finally, he assumed that even if the message was read, it was understood in the way intended. This is probably the most tenuous of all his premises. Yet these are exactly the kinds of assumptions that all Arrow managers make.

Arrow managers tend to be straightforward and results oriented. They view communication rather like shooting an arrow at a target. Like the marksman, the speaker seeks to embed an intact message into the receiver so as to achieve the desired results, to hit the bull's-eye. Communication is seen as a one-way activity based primarily on the skills of the sender. The targets may move, but they never interact with the communicator. Hence, the aim of communication for the Arrow manager is to select the proper words and organize the

Table 1.1 Evaluation of Arrow Managers' Assumptions

Communication Effectiveness	Underlying Assumptions
Being able to clearly and precisely put my thoughts into words.	What is clear and precise to one person is clear and precise to another.
Speaking with credibility and authority.	Credibility is something the speaker possesses and not something given to the speaker by the audience.
Getting the results I want by talking to my people.	Communication is primarily a one-way activity.

ideas effectively in order to hit the target. The focus of arrow thinking is on the speaker or sender of the message.

Effectiveness

Nowhere is this orientation more evident than when managers are asked about the meaning of effective communication. These are typical responses:

- "Being able to clearly and precisely put my thoughts into words."
- "Speaking with credibility and authority on topics I know about."
- "Getting the results I want by talking to my people."

Certainly managers should seek to speak clearly, concisely, and with credibility in order to achieve results. Yet, reexamination of each of those statements in light of the underlying assumptions is revealing (see Table 1.1). In short, the underlying premise is that managers are responsible for accurately encoding their thoughts into language; rather like selecting, aiming, and firing arrows at a target. Receivers of messages are viewed as passive information processors that react appropriately if the words are on the mark. Thus, feedback not only is improbable, it is unnecessary.

Explaining Communication Breakdowns

The problem is that inevitably communication does break down, in spite of "proper" encoding. Yet many managers tenaciously hold to the Arrow approach with explanations like:

- "Why didn't they just follow my instructions?"
- "Why can't they get it right? If I told them once, I told them a thousand times."
- "How could this project get so fouled up? I told the idiots exactly how to do it."

In each case the receiver is at fault for the foul-up. Hence, for the Arrow manager, lack of performance is caused primarily by the receivers' ignorance of the language or even, in some cases, a result of a malicious intent to undermine management objectives. After all, the meaning of the words is self-evident and fixed; therefore, everyone should understand the message similarly. And certainly the workers heard what was said because management repeated it a "thousand times." This type of reasoning inevitably leads some managers to the conclusion that their employees are inherently ignorant, lazy, or subversive.

But what if the manager fails to understand someone? Curiously, the onus of fault shifts from the receiver to the sender. The Arrow manager's likely responses: "I should have been notified," "Why didn't you just say that?", or "You've just got to say it in plain English." In these cases the sender clearly failed to "hit the target" because the "proper" words were not uttered. In sum, communication breakdowns are always the fault of the sender *or* the receiver. Arrow managers never think that the problem, and hence the responsibility, might be mutual. They fail to see that effective communication is a shared commitment between *both* the sender and receiver.

Origins

Why would a manager adopt this orientation? It is probably not the result of a conscious decision. Rather, through countless individual experiences, an unconscious pattern is formed that becomes the modus operandi. There are three major factors that appear to contribute to the process.

First, the technical training of many managers reinforces a stimulus/response orientation. On a number of occasions I have had the opportunity to speak with engineers who have recently assumed managerial responsibilities. Many experience problems in managing people. For years they have been trained to use precise formulas that exactly predict certain outcomes. If the design is developed according to standards, then it works and performs as expected. All competent engineers use basically the same formulas. Colleagues learn to interpret the drawings and specs similarly. Since the entire emphasis is on proper design and development, the results are inevitable.

Transferring such logic to management is as natural as it is problematic. Simply stated, the communication effort is seen as a problem of proper design. After all, like the specs, everyone should interpret the message in the same way. Thus communication is expected to be akin to engineering. Choosing the right language, as in selecting the proper materials, should lead to effectiveness. Of course, the problem is that people do not react like they are "supposed to" and human beings are not passive objects like girders, cable, and concrete. It requires great intellectual dexterity to get rid of these conceptions, built up literally through years of training and countless daily experiences.

The second contributing factor, strangely enough, comes from "speech teachers." The very term, "speech teacher," implies a one-way view of communication. Why not "speaking and listening teacher," or just "communication teacher"? Historically, teachers of public address have been profoundly influenced by Aristotle's remarkable work, *The Rhetoric*, which was one of the first truly systematic treatises on the spoken word. His genius was most fully realized in his penetrating discourse and explanation of the three canons or provinces of proof: ethos (the credibility of the speaker); pathos (the use of emotion); and logos (the use of logic). The canons have stood the test of time, for the system continues to be taught.

Aristotle (1960) applied his passionate inquisitiveness to the issues of his day and so naturally he was concerned with how to persuade others, how to influence the masses, and how to achieve the greatest amount of good for the largest number of people:

> But the art of Rhetoric has its value. It is valuable, first, because truth and justice are by nature more powerful than their opposites; so that, when decisions are not made as they should be, the speakers, with the right on their side, have only themselves to thank for the outcome. A proper knowledge and exercise of Rhetoric would prevent the triumph of fraud and injustice. (p. 5)

Note that the Aristotelian emphasis is on the speaker, or the orator, arranging an appropriate message in accordance with general principles. If the communicator is effective, justice and good triumph. Then the speaker takes the credit. The hearers are passive and reactive rather than active and interactive. In short, communication is a one-way act of influence.

More recently, communication theorists have taken to model building in an attempt to represent the communication process. One of the classic and most influential models was developed by Claude Shannon, an engineer at

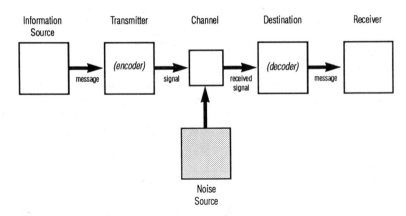

Figure 1.1 Shannon & Weaver Model

Bell Telephone Company. This model, shown in Figure 1.1, was developed to help engineers decide how to most efficiently transmit electrical impulses from one place to another. Other models having a more social-psychological emphasis were developed based on Shannon and Weaver's (1949) basic premise (c.f. Lasswell, 1948, or Gerbner, 1956). As fascinating as these models are, my purpose is not to provide a thorough exegesis on them. Rather, the point is that in this class of models, communication is not only visually represented as a one-way activity but also conceptually proclaimed to be so, just as Aristotle claimed.

Finally, certain people may have personality predispositions to communicate in this way. Treating communication as a one-way event allows an individual to avoid the complexities, ambiguities, and paradoxes of human behavior. There is an illusion of permanence and finality in all that is spoken. Dynamic contexts, unique individuals, adjustable styles of discourse and multileveled conservations can prove not only bewildering but deeply troubling to those who tenaciously cling to a simplistic world view. The Arrow manager avoids complexity, with seeming efficiency and total control. Thus the origins may be a result of some sort of functional necessity for a manager's personal psychological makeup. After all, a world in which all elements are dynamic can be profoundly unsettling and deeply disturbing.

Evaluation

The Arrow approach has both strengths and weaknesses. These are examined below.

Weaknesses

The fundamental flaw of this approach lies in the belief that:

Effective Expression = Effective Communication.

The problem is that even if a person effectively articulates a position, this does not necessarily guarantee that it will be understood as intended, much less appropriately acted upon. Misunderstandings occur that may not be the fault of either party. Since feedback is not encouraged in this one-way approach, a corrective mechanism that might clarify a misunderstanding does not really exist. Ironically, Arrow managers may never know if they are "on target" or not. At the heart of the shortcoming are two critical assumptions that are simply inaccurate.

First, the receiver is seen as a passive information processor. Arrow managers typically communicate with people as information processing machines. The net result is a work unit devoid of interpersonal warmth and creative inputs from subordinates. The listener's role is trivialized. But communication does not operate that way. A sender's idea is transformed into a code and transmitted. Then, the receiver actively reconstructs messages based on the signals sent by the sender. This is an *active,* not passive, process that is fraught with potential points of breakdown.

Second, words are viewed as containers of meaning. The language we use subtly works against us in this respect. The expressions we use every day convey the notion that we put meaning into words and the words act as carriers of meaning: "Capturing ideas in words," "Put that idea into writing," or "I have difficulty putting my thoughts into words." In fact, Professor Reddy (1979) has made extensive studies of the metaphors used to describe the communication process. He conservatively estimates that about 70% of the English language is directly, visibly, or graphically based on metaphors that stress this perspective on communication. For example, "I didn't get the meaning out of the memo," "just read what it says," or even, "read my lips," create the illusion that meaning resides in the words themselves. Such is not actually the case. Rather, meanings are developed in a unique vortex that includes the words used, the context of the utterance, and the people involved. There is abundant evidence that people develop unique meanings for words and that words do not so much act as containers of meaning as they act as useful, although usually sloppy, stimulators of meaning.

Strengths

The fundamental weaknesses in the Arrow theory should not obscure the benefits.

First, the Arrow approach encourages managers to clearly think out their ideas, accurately articulate their directives, and provide sufficient specificity in their instructions. This emphasis on sender skills is certainly healthy for many a manager. One of the common complaints of corporations hiring college graduates is their universal lack of basic communication skills. These skills include how to make presentations, write a memorandum, and develop an agenda for a meeting (e.g., Golen et al., 1989). Arrow managers tend to excel at such one-way communication tasks.

Second, the Arrow approach implies a strong link between communication behavior and action. Arrow managers discourage idle chatter, discussions of personal problems, and unnecessary information sharing. Thus high productivity is encouraged because potential time-wasting communication activities are eliminated. Provided that subordinates do understand directives and management knows what's best, the Arrow approach may actually encourage maximum performance.

In short, while the Arrow approach is flawed in a number of significant ways, there are some redeeming aspects. The next approach reviewed attempts to rectify a number of the difficulties while emphasizing a new set of communication skills.

Circuit Approach

If the language of the Arrow manager involves "targeting an audience," "attacking arguments," and "firing a volley of commands," then the discourse of the Circuit manager involves "networking," "going with the flow," and "making connections." The Circuit approach represents an evolution from the arrow to the circle. Circuit managers stress feedback over response, relationship over content, connotations over denotations, and understanding over compliance. Communication is seen as a two-way process involving a dynamic interplay of an active sender and receiver.

Nowhere is this interaction style more fully evident than in conflict situations. In a communication assessment for a car dealer we found a strange split of opinion over the performance of the CEO, who had recently taken over the company from his father. Those in the sales department loved the new management style. Elton, as he liked to be called, believed in participative management and wanted to make sure that everyone was satisfied. Yet, employees in the service department had little or no respect for him. One service technician, nicknamed Bronco, explained that he was "elected" by his colleagues to confront the CEO about a problem. He did so. Elton was "delighted" with the chance to talk about the issue. But nothing changed. So Bronco went back. Bronco received the same enthusiastic reception and predictable results. Since the CEO seemed so open to these meetings, Bronco went back for one "final try." Bronco reported:

> He seemed like a nice enough guy. Then he starts questioning me about why I "really" came to see him. He started saying stuff like, "you don't really like me." He kept pushing. Finally I got so mad that I told him that he was a lazy bum and he never would have gotten this job without his daddy. I thought that was it. You're history bub. Pack your bags. But you won't believe what he did. He patted me on the back and said: "I knew we could get to the bottom of this issue." It was over. Problem solved. He didn't have the guts to fire me.

I asked the CEO about this incident. He explained: "I am proud of that. Now my employees know that they can say anything to me and have no fears whatsoever." The employees may have had no fears, but problems were never solved either. Indeed, within a year, the organization was in such disarray that Elton's father, a classic Arrow manager, took over again. Elton went on to "bigger and better things." He is now a management consultant.

Judging Effectiveness

Views of effectiveness prove to be so revealing because they expose individuals' goals and desires. To be effective, a manager must bring about a desired result. The critical question is: What are the desired results? Indeed, Circuit managers' responses to the effectiveness issue expose their ultimate aims:

- Communication effectiveness is actively listening to my workers, so as to know what makes them happy.
- I'm effective as a manager when I am sensitive to employees' needs and concerns. Then I try to communicate that sensitivity to them by adapting my message to each individual.
- My communication is effective when I am open to my employees' ideas and suggestions. I want them to feel included and understood by me.

Table 1.2 Evaluation of Circuit Managers' Assumptions

Communication Effectiveness	Assumption
Listening to employees, in order to make them happy.	Job satisfaction is the goal of organizational communication.
Being sensitive to employees, in order to adapt messages to each individual.	Messages are exclusively interpreted in the context of interpersonal relationships.
Being open and understanding.	Openness is useful in all circumstances. Understanding is always more acceptable than ambiguity.

As shown in Table 1.2, there is an implicit perspective of the communication process in these comments. Circuit managers make conceptual leaps from communication behavior to job satisfaction to productivity. The research suggests that these leaps, particularly from job satisfaction to productivity, are dubious at best (Locke, 1976). And the probability of successfully completing these leaps is about the same as one athlete completing the high jump, the broad jump, and the pole vault in one bound.

Explaining Communication Breakdowns

Unlike the Arrow manager who assumes that communication should always work, the Circuit manager recognizes the unavoidable certainty of communication breakdowns. According to this approach there are four primary reasons for the breakdown.

First, the most frequently cited cause of communication breakdowns for Circuit managers is that people just "don't connect." That is, people's values, ideas, or feelings are so dissimilar that they have difficulty in relating to one another. Circuit managers are fond of saying, "meanings are in people, not in words," which suggests that everyone has a unique interpretation for each message. Hence, huge amounts of time must be invested in "reaching an understanding." For example, the ODS Corporation of Japan is a research, consulting, and advertising organization that seems to take the Circuit approach to the limit. There are meetings about everything, including a companywide meeting in which individual salaries are negotiated. In one instance this process lasted an entire work week. Employees typically spend seven hours a week in meetings in which they may confess to treating clients inappropriately or critique other employees' wardrobes. Although the corporation is a booming success, there is a price — high turnover (Ono, 1989).

Most organizations are not willing to go that far. Thus Circuit managers explain breakdowns by complaining about the amount of time available. Their underlying premise is that understanding is always possible because everyone shares the same basic needs and desires.

Second, Circuit managers often cite poor listening as the reason for communication difficulties. Circuit managers often encourage their employees to develop active listening skills such as paraphrasing others' remarks, giving feedback, and asking the appropriate probing questions. These skills help employees think about possible misinterpretations of their remarks as well as check for unintended messages. Therefore, employees involved in a misunderstanding are frequently reminded of the maxim, "You cannot not communicate."

Third, conflicts are explained in terms of "hidden agendas" or unarticulated goals. Circuit managers might seek to dissolve a tense situation with comments like: "Are you sure you are being completely honest with us?" or "You have got to share your true feelings." The obvious inference is that someone is hiding something or has a "hidden agenda." Circuit managers believe that trust comes from employees revealing their true motives which, in turn, fosters an atmosphere of open and honest communication. Only then does the Circuit manager believe that conflict can be truly resolved.

Finally, like electrical circuits, the Circuit manager suggests that communication relationships can operate only under certain conditions. Circuit managers believe that many communication breakdowns occur because a proper climate has not been developed. Specifically, a defensive as opposed to a supportive climate inhibits communication effectiveness. Defensiveness is a result of evaluative comments, a dogmatic demeanor, and an attitude of superiority—the J. R. Ewing approach to communication. Supportiveness is fostered through sensitivity to the connotative meanings of words, an emphasis on spontaneity, and a development of a climate of equality. When all other reasons fail to explain a communication breakdown, the Circuit manager suggests that there is a defensive climate. Ironically, it is rather perplexing to attempt to respond to the command, "Quit being so defensive." Either attempting to justify your behavior or an outright denial only proves your interlocutor's assertion. Perhaps a heartfelt laugh is the only appropriate response.

Origins

Managers develop a Circuit orientation to communication for a wide variety of reasons, but three tendencies in particular appear to be noteworthy.

First, in the not-too-distant past, business schools stressed a human relations orientation to management that harmonized with the Circuit approach. The well-known Hawthorne studies often provide the key arguments used to build the human relations case. These studies began as an attempt to investigate the relationship between the levels of lighting in the workplace and worker productivity. Employees at Western Electric's Hawthorne plant increased their productivity in all instances: in the test group when lighting was improved as well as made more dim, and even in the control group where there were no changes in illumination. Therefore, it was determined that factors other than lighting influenced performance. The mistaken interpretation of the research often passed down in folklore was that employees thought management was interested in them, so they continued to increase their production regardless of the physical conditions. Hence the axiom, "Satisfied Workers are Productive Workers." Therefore great care is shown in keeping workers satisfied, and that means communicating in proper ways. The problem with these extrapolations is that the evidence shows that a satisfied worker can be a very lazy one (e.g., Downs & Picket, 1977). In fact, there is a fundamentally incorrect inference in the folklore. The key reason for the productivity increases was not the managers' behavior but the *interpretations* made by employees. That is where the emphasis should be placed — employee interpretations — not managers' soothing communication style. These mythical interpretations of the Hawthorne studies tend to encourage a Circuit orientation to communication.

Second, some communication teachers encourage a Circuit approach. Courses in interpersonal communication have been quite popular on campuses and typically they focus on receiver listening skills, giving appropriate feedback, and relationship building. Sometimes these courses are jokingly referred to as "touchy-feely 101," which is one way to characterize the emphasis on getting in touch with one's own feelings as well as others'. Even the models of communication used stress the circularity of the communication process. The Schramm (1954) model in Figure 1.2 is one of the classics of this type. It looks like a circuit diagram and depicts the feedback portion of the communication event. Thus such models lend theoretical justification to the Circuit perspective of communication skills.

Finally, some people seem to have a natural predisposition to viewing communication like a circuit. They tend to focus on people's feelings and interpersonal relationships. People are naturally attracted to those who are sensitive to their feelings. It is one way to avoid controversy, build up self-esteem, or meet affiliation needs. Hence, the Circuit manager may have a deep need to keep peace and harmony.

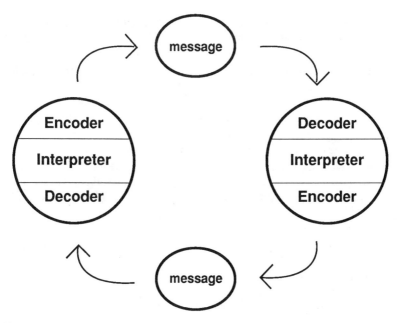

Figure 1.2 Schramm Model

Evaluation

The fundamental assumption of Circuit managers is that:

Understanding = Effective Communication.

But there are two flaws in this view.

First, there is an implicit belief that understanding will lead to agreement. Most problems between managers and employees are cast as "communication problems," which means that the parties do not understand one another. But the problem may be that they understand one another all too well, but they simply disagree. The Circuit manager will often plead that the parties involved do not "*really* understand one another." Yet, in this strange logic loop, the thought is never entertained that people could actually disagree. Unlike the Arrow manager, the Circuit manager acknowledges that people do not always understand a message in the same way. Therefore, it seems logical to assume that two people might not agree. Ironically, such thoughts are rarely entertained because Circuit managers will spend countless hours trying to ensure that their messages are "really understood."

Second, there is an error in assuming that understanding should be the singular goal of communication. People communicate for a wide variety of reasons. Effective managers, like politicians, may equivocate in order to induce creativity or give themselves room to change. Making sure that subordinates clearly understand everything is not always feasible or desirable. "Ambiguous missions and goals allow divergent interpretations to coexist and are more effective in allowing diverse groups to work together" (Eisenberg & Witten, 1987, p. 422). There are instances in which a manager may not have time to explain, just as a physician gives orders during an emergency. A sincere love of mutual understanding does not necessarily yield the best decisions. Accommodation strategies, while useful at times, do not guarantee solutions to difficult problems. Chris Argyris (1986) perceptively notes:

> The ability to get along with others is always an asset, right? Wrong. By adeptly avoiding conflict with coworkers, some executives eventually wreak havoc. And it's their very adeptness that's the problem. The explanation for this lies in what I call skilled incompetence, whereby managers use practiced routine behavior (skill) to produce what they do not intend (incompetence). (p. 74)

Paradoxically, an organizational culture in which "understanding" is the norm often breeds a reticence to bring up areas of disagreement. Employees become afraid to clearly articulate their views for fear of exposing how deep the gulfs really are. Hence, differences — important and meaningful ones — often are glossed over in the name of "understanding."

Third, in spite of these shortcomings, there are some valuable insights that can be gleaned from the Circuit perspective. The emphasis on the relational aspect of communication and the importance of feedback are two noteworthy issues highlighted by this approach. Research has shown that competent communicators do pay attention to these aspects of interaction (e.g., DiSalvo, 1980). And these are precisely the kinds of issues the Arrow manager is oblivious to.

The proposition that messages can be interpreted in many ways is equally important. The Arrow manager focuses on constructing the best possible message, but the Circuit manager looks at the meanings imposed by listeners. This shift in perspective is enlightening and useful. Even though the link between job satisfaction and productivity has proven tenuous at best, the Circuit approach has persuaded many that job satisfaction is an important variable in its own right.

There is much to be learned from Arrow and Circuit approaches. Yet there are gaps in both viewpoints. It is not so much that these approaches are wrong, but that they are incomplete. The lens of each perspective creates a somewhat distorted view of the communication process. There is a better point of view. I call it the Dance perspective on communication.

Communication as Dance

Some have argued that dance was the first form of communication. There are so many similarities that it is hard to disagree. Dance involves patterns, movement, and creativity. It can be enjoyed by participants as well as observers. There are as many styles as people. Tastes vary. Standards differ. Styles change. Trends come and go. But dance has been and will always be part of the human community. Once a dance is performed it can never be recaptured in the same way again; it is unrepeatable and irreversible. Even the simplest of dances involves thousands of intricate and complex maneuvers. It may well be one of the highest and most unique forms of human expression. So, too, is communication. The list of similarities could be quite lengthy indeed. A few of the more important ones are highlighted below.

(1) Communication is used for multiple purposes.

People dance for a wide variety of reasons: to entertain, to inform, to persuade, to incite, and even to seduce. Some dance for themselves — a form of self-expression — while some dance for others. Tne same can be said of communication. The famous physicist and poet, Leo Szilard (1961), once commented:

> When a scientist says something, his colleagues must ask themselves only whether it is true. When a politician says something, his colleagues must first of all ask, "Why does he say it?"; later on they may or may not get around to asking whether it happens to be true. A politician is a man who thinks he is in possession of the truth and knows what needs to be done. Scientists rarely think they are in full possession of the truth, and a scientist's aim in a discussion with his colleagues is not to persuade but to clarify. It was clarification rather than persuasion that was needed in the past to arrive at the solutions of the great scientific problems. (p. 25-26)

Herein lies a problem. The scientist, the politician, the teacher, the salesperson, the philosopher, and the preacher all use the same language. It is like blurring the lines between entertaining dances and lewd ones; the purpose of communication is not always clear. In fact, communicators often have multiple goals for a single message. The effective teacher seeks to enlighten and motivate, the salesperson to inform and persuade, and the philosopher to clarify and question. In fact, effective managers at one time or another must perform each of these roles.

Therefore, communication effectiveness cannot be limited to either the "results" or "understanding" criteria as characterized by the Arrow and Circuit perspectives, respectively. Effectiveness only can be determined in light of the communicator's goals — whatever they may be — including obfuscation, confusion, or deception. Whether these are legitimate goals is an ethical question, just as there will always be questionable forms of dancing. Hence, there is no single measure of communication effectiveness, just as there is no one criterion to evaluate all dances.

(2) Communication involves the coordination of meanings.

Dancers have to learn to coordinate their movements with one another regardless of the type of music. They must learn how to move together even though they do not necessarily share one another's reality. That is, dance partners see the situation differently but they know their appropriate roles and responses. Communicators do, as well. It is not always necessary or even desirable to totally share meanings to communicate, as long as participants know how to respond in their roles or according to the "rules of the game." In fact, there is a theory of communication called the Coordinated Management of Meaning that is based on this very premise. These theorists argue that

> communication is the process by which persons cocreate, maintain, and alter patterns of social order, but . . . the coordination of talk through which patterns of order emerge is not necessarily based on mutual understanding or a shared social reality. (Pearce, Harris, & Cronen, 1982, p. 157)

Subordinates may not know why the boss asks, "How are things going?", but in time they learn how to respond. The boss's question may be interpreted as "intrusiveness" on the part of the subordinate and "concern" on the part of the boss. But, despite the vastly different interpretations, social order is maintained. Meanings are not necessarily shared but they are coordinated.

So what? The point is that in order to understand the communication process, there is a need to look beyond the interpretations of messages. How messages facilitate social order, maintain structure, and set up patterns is of prime importance. The issue is: How does communication help or hinder the process of coordination in an organization? Couples who dance are evaluated, in part, on the degree to which their actions are coordinated with one another. The evaluation of communication effectiveness is judged similarly. Clumsiness, whether self-inflicted or induced by others, is not rewarded in organizations or dance studios.

(3) Communication involves coorientation.

In order to coordinate actions, dancers must learn to coorient. They must be able to sense one another's cues, anticipate their partner's possible actions, and know the appropriate responses. So, too, do communicators. When communication breaks down, it is not always the result of misunderstandings, per se, but rather that people have failed to coorient; they have no adequate predictive capacity. Effective communicators are able to forecast with some accuracy the actions of others, their responses, and interpretations. For example, the CEO of a paper manufacturing firm was bewildered by rampant rumors circulated about layoffs and plant closures after his brief announcement about forthcoming pay freezes. In his speech he had specifically noted that these measures were *not* considered to be alternatives to cope with an industry slowdown. When asked if he ever had a meeting like this before, he said, "I never had the need to." Even though over a 20-year period he had personally hired most of these workers, he was so out of touch with their reality that he could not anticipate these possible reactions to his announcement. He did not effectively coorient.

The seeming ease with which professional dancers whirl, pirouette, and leap into one another's arms is deceptive. With long hours of practice, they can do this even when improvising because they are responding to one another's subtle cues. What is astonishing is that they can do all of this while *both* are constantly in motion. It is not like trying to get oriented while lost in a forest by calculating your position in relation to some fixed object. Rather the "objects" are both moving, and they must simultaneously be orienting with one another. And this is precisely the complex and difficult challenge facing communicators who must simultaneously orient to each other while both are constantly changing. As the aforementioned CEO found out, people can change considerably over a 20-year period. It takes time and energy to coorient, and there inevitably will be spills and mishaps along the way.

(4) Communication is rule-governed.

How can dancers cope with the tremendous range of possible movements? How can all the possibilities be mastered? Communicators, like dancers, develop rules of thumb to cope with the uncertainties. In almost every style of dance there are rules of some sort, whether written or unwritten. Joan Lawson (1980), who for 17 years taught at the Royal School of Ballet, wrote:

> Principles and rules should all be studied by aspiring dancers and choreographers if they are to create the style and qualities of movement necessary to communicate the mood, emotion, theme, and story of classical dance. (p. 1)

Years of excellence are distilled in these rules which, in turn, allow the dancers to coorient.

Communicators, as well, develop a wide range of implicit rules that govern conversations. There are rules concerning who has the right to initiate or terminate a conversation, and what topics are appropriate to speak about and under what conditions. The list could go on, but the point is that the rules affect the conversation in much the same way that rules of dance constrain movement. Conversational rules, too, are a way to handle all the uncertainty and distill the essence of learning into a few easily manageable units. It is by enacting these rules that people coordinate their actions in the organization.

Basically there are two types of rules at work in conversations: interpretation rules and regulative rules (Pearce & Cronen, 1980). Interpretation rules are the communicator's rules for abstracting the meaning out of a message.[1] For example, during a meeting about a new proposal, a manager might say, "Tell me more," to an employee, which is interpreted as, "You have a great idea, I want to hear the details." On the other hand, the same manager who says, "Tell me more," after an employee gives an unacceptable explanation for being late to work, is communicating a very different message. The interpretation is, "This excuse is unacceptable, shape up." Even though the same words are used, the context has changed and different interpretation rules apply. Regulative rules are those that regulate or guide the ongoing action of the communication event. Effective listeners, for example, often have these kind of regulative rules:

- Initiate conversations with questions about unrisky topics.
- If a person's comments are unclear, then ask for clarification.
- If a person appears defensive, nod head.
- Terminate conversations by summarizing the conversation.

Note that in each case these rules help guide the conversation in a particular direction.

The rules vary from setting to setting just as the conventions of dance change from the ballroom to the clubroom. To be an effective communicator, one must learn the special rules that apply in different settings. They, of course, vary from person to person, department to department, and organization to organization. But that does not mean that a whole new set of rules needs to be learned when experiencing a new situation. There are some common rules regardless of the situation, just as there are fundamental dance steps. But effective communicators also learn the special rules of each setting. The rules do not exist on some unseen tablet waiting to be discovered. Rather, people are actively engaged in negotiating the rules, particularly during the first stages of relationships. This is why the orientation of new employees is so important. Negotiating over the rules, although usually implicit, is a fascinating process. There even are rules about making the rules — metarules. The important point is to recognize that the rules exist and determine how they affect managerial effectiveness.

(5) Communicators develop a repertoire of skills that may pass from the level of consciousness.

Beginning dancers have to consciously think about each movement in executing a pirouette, for instance. Over time they no longer think about how to execute each movement; they become concerned less with body mechanics and more with artistry. The apparent naturalness and ease of execution comes from years of practice, as movements that were once conscious now merge into the subconscious. Communicators learn in much the same way. When we learn a foreign language we have to think more consciously about syntax and semantics. But over time, through trial and error, we learn the rules and can speak with apparent ease by relying on subconscious processes.

The same can be said of pragmatic rules of conversation. When first interacting with people, we may have to consciously think about appropriate behaviors, just as when we go to a first job interview. But over time we no longer consciously focus on such concerns. Frequently communication problems are the result of an unconsciously used rule, long ago "forgotten." For example, one manager reported that she was often accused by her employees of being a poor listener. She had difficulty understanding their perceptions. During a lull in a social conversation with her, I mentioned being involved in a minor car accident. Her response was, "Yes, but did I tell you about my new car?" Clearly, such episodes might cause her employees to infer that she was uninterested in them and lead to the "poor listener" assessment. This manager apparently never learned the regulative rule: "When someone mentions an unusual event, probe for further information." Effective conversationalists utilize this rule all the time without any conscious thought of it. Unfortunately, this manager did not, and the result was that her employees were uncooperative. The manager's operative rule was: "When someone mentions an unusual event, talk about something that interests me." Even though these rules are unconscious, there are consequences for having them. In this case, the manager was eventually asked to step down and assume a lower paying job.

When training employees to become better negotiators, most individuals' existing set of rules needs to be refined. For example, it is important to know that concessions should be offered slowly, not all at once (Gilchrist, 1982). At first, consciously trying to do this seems awkward, but with practice it becomes natural. The same kinds of procedures are effective in teaching interviewing, public speaking, and motivation skills. And this is precisely the technique used by dance instructors when they point out a motion that should be consciously attended to in order to execute a graceful maneuver.

(6) Communication can be viewed as a patterned activity.

Choreographers map out patterns for their dances, a kind of circuit diagram drawn with arrows. Even with improvisational dances, a map can be drawn of the dancer's movements. Likewise, there are patterns of interaction in a conversation. The patterns are a by-product of the rules of interaction used by the communicators. In other words, the patterns are the net result of the way the enacted rules interlock with one another. The interaction rules are viewed through a telescopic lens, while the patterns are seen through a wide-angle lens.

Expert chess players who are familiar with an adversary's style of play (i.e., personal rules) frequently are able to sense deep but recurring patterns to their opponent's games, not move by move but in a more general sense. Communicators, like amateur chess players, may not be aware of their own patterns but perceptive observers, kibitzers, can see them. For example, a manager may jokingly insult an employee: "Hey, Pat! Has your golf game improved yet?" The employee may respond by placating: "I haven't been golfing lately." The manager could react to the placating with even harsher insults, to which the employee responds with more placating responses. The pattern repeats itself until either someone else steps in or the employee gets angry.

In this case, the manager's regulative rule is: "Respond to placating with playful insults." The employee's regulative rule is: "Respond to insults with a placating reply." These rules interact to form a pattern in which the manager sees the employee as the problem and the employee feels the manager is the problem (see Figure 1.3). Such problems technically are known as punctuation difficulties in which each party sees the other as the source of the conflict (Watzlawick, Beavin, & Jackson, 1967). Neither the manager nor the employee sees the overall pattern resulting from their personal rules of interaction. This is a simple example; think about the complexity of group communication. Part of the challenge of an organizational communicator is to ferret out the destructive patterns while setting up constructive ones.

(7) The beauty of communication is a function of the degree of coordination.

The truly awe-inspiring dances are the ones in which the dancers flow as one with the music and each other. One dance that comes to mind is the "bottle dance" in the movie *Fiddler on the Roof,* in which the dancers begin by placing bottles on their heads. Slowly they start to move to the music, then the beat picks up with an ever-increasing level of intensity. Step by step, beat by beat, the dancers move to the music and one another. The tempo and spirit of the music picks up even further, as does that of the dancers. The bottles waver but do not fall. One marvels at how everything can be so perfectly in balance and in step. The music beats faster still. And then precisely at the moment the music climaxes, the dancers flip the bottles off their heads and whirl into a rousing frenzy.

The aesthetic appreciation of the dance flows from the intricate patterns of coordination, the way in which it all fits together. So, too, with communication. The greater the coordination between communicators, the more effective it is. They learn to anticipate one another's reactions and possible meanings. They are able to coorient. They know the way in which the environment affects communication. This is what communicators aim for in organizations.

To be sure, there are some communication situations that require more specialized skills than others. Learning to negotiate effectively, for instance, requires more coorientation than does giving a speech. Employees have different levels of skill. For some, communication is easy. But as with

Manager's Interpretation (meaning rules)	Manager's Regulative Rules	Actual Conversation	Employee's Regulative Rules	Employee's Interpretation (meaning rules)
Greeting.	Initiate conversations with playful reparteé.	**Manager:** Hey, Pat— Has your golf game improved yet?		Insult. Manager doesn't care about me or my game.
Employee is ignoring me.		**Employee:** I haven't been golfing lately.	Respond to insults with placating reply.	Factual reply to a question.
Playful question.	Try to reestablish conversation with another playful comment.	**Manager:** Well, how's that clunker of a car running?		Another insult. What kind of game is the Manger playing?
Employee is catching on, but still takes the conversation too seriously.		**Employee:** I sold it.	Respond to insults with a placating comment.	Another factual reply.
Joke.	Continue conversation with another playful insult.	**Manager:** I hope you didn't buy another lemon.		Another insult. Now the Manager is questioning my decision-making ability.
What is the Employee so upset about? I'm just trying to build some rapport. **The Employee is a poor conversationist.**		**Employee:** Why don't you just get off my back and mind your own business!	If placating doesn't work, then stand up for yourself.	My only alternative was to be assertive. **The Manager is insensitive and unprofessional.**

Figure 1.3 Conversation Analysis

dancing, anyone can refine and improve his or her skills. Even natural dancers become more proficient with practice and training. The aesthetic thrill of an illuminating discussion or a scintillating meeting may prove elusive and rare, but there are few experiences more pleasing and fulfilling.

Conclusion

The anthropologist Mary Catherine Bateson (1989) said, "there are few things as toxic as a bad metaphor" (p. 347). The Arrow and Circuit approaches mask the complexity of the communication process. Managers who view communication as a dance have a more vivid metaphor with which to analyze organizational situations. They see the complexities in the apparent simplicity of communication. They are concerned with patterns and unwritten rules. They look at the degree of coorientation between employees as well as departments. Unlike the Circuit managers, they are not exclusively concerned with what is best for relationships but what is best in a particular situation. Unlike Arrow managers, they are not focused solely on immediate results, but seek deeper patterns of sustained success. They do not expect to be understood at all times and do not always see that as the goal of communication. Their communication style and choice of medium vary according to the goals and context. They do not share the Arrow manager's belief that humans are basically lazy, but neither do they believe that all are good. They recognize the organizational realities but seek the ideal. Finally, they take comfort in the fact that there appears to be no relationship between their ability to communicate and their ability to dance.

Note

1. Pearce and Cronen (1980) call these constitutive rules. They also have an elaborate system that explains how meanings are abstracted at various levels.

References

Argyris, C. (1986). Skilled incompetence. *Harvard Business Review, 64*(5), 74-79.
Aristotle. (1960). *The rhetoric of Aristotle* (L. Cooper, Trans.). New York: Meredith.
Bateson, M. C. (1989). An interview with Mary Catherine Bateson. In B. S. Flowers (Ed.), *Bill Moyers: A world of ideas* (pp. 345-357). New York: Doubleday.

DiSalvo, V. S. (1980). A summary of current research identifying communication skills in various organizational contexts. *Communication Education, 29,* 283-290.

Downs, C. W., & Pickett, T. (1977). An analysis of the effect of nine leadership-group compatibility contingencies upon productivity and member satisfaction. *Communication Monographs, 44,* 220-230.

Eisenberg, E. M., & Witten, M. G. (1987). Reconsidering openness in organizational communication. *Academy of Management Review, 12*(3), 418-426.

Gerbner, G. (1956). Toward a general model of communication. *Audio-Visual Communication Review, 4,* 171-199.

Gilchrist, J. A. (1982). The compliance interview: Negotiating across organizational boundaries. In M. Burgoon (Ed.), *Communication yearbook, 6* (pp. 653-673). Beverly Hills, CA: Sage.

Golen, S., Lynch, D., Smeltzer, L., Lord, W. J., Penrose, J. M., & Waltman, J. (1989). An empirically tested communication skills core module for MBA students, with implications for the AACSB. *Organizational Behavior Teaching Review, 13*(3), 45-57.

Lasswell, H. D. (1948). The structure and function of communications in society. In L. Bryson (Ed.), *The communication of ideas* (pp. 37-51). New York: Harper & Row.

Lawson, J. (1980). *The principles of classical dance.* New York: Knopf.

Locke, E. A. (1976). The nature and causes of job satisfaction. In M. D. Duppette (Ed.), *Handbook of industrial and organizational psychology* (pp. 1292-1350). Chicago: Rand-McNally.

Ono, Y. (1989, September 12). Sick of meetings? Then ODS is not the place for you. *Wall Street Journal,* pp. A1, A11.

Pearce, W. B., & Cronen, V. E. (1980). *Communication, action, and meaning.* New York: Praeger.

Pearce, W. B., Harris, L. M., & Cronen, V. E. (1982). Communication theory in a new key. In C. Wilder & J. H. Weakland (Eds.), *Rigor & imagination* (pp. 149-194). New York: Praeger.

Reddy, M. J. (1979). The conduct metaphor: A case of frame conflict in our language about language. In A. Ortony (Ed.), *Metaphor and thought* (pp. 284-324). Cambridge, MA: Cambridge University Press.

Schramm, W. L. (1954). How communication works. In W. Schramm (Ed.), *The process and effects of mass communication* (pp. 3-26). Urbana: University of Illinois Press.

Shannon, C., & Weaver, W. (1949). *A mathematical theory of communication.* Urbana: University of Illinois Press.

Szilard, L. (1961). *The voice of the dolphins.* New York: Simon & Schuster.

Watzlawick, P., Beavin, J., & Jackson, D. (1967). *Pragmatics of human communication.* New York: Norton.

2

What Is Communication, Anyway?

> It requires a very unusual mind to make an analysis of the obvious.
>
> Alfred North Whitehead

> Understanding seems to be a very complicated notion.
>
> Roger Schank

To use dance as a metaphor to describe communication can be illuminating. Yet, it is a more right-brain, holistic kind of illumination. The left-brain, linear orientation demands more precision. What actually happens in the mind of the sender? What happens in the mind of the receiver? Why do problems occur? Can communication breakdowns be described more specifically than to say that two people are not coordinating their actions? These are the issues considered in this chapter. Ten propositions about communication are presented and the practical implications of the notions are explicated.

Propositions

Proposition 1: Language is inherently ambiguous.

The inherent ambiguity of language can be seen in the words we use, the sentences we utter, and in the countless communication breakdowns we experience. One researcher says that for the 500 most frequently used words in the English language there are over 14,000 definitions (Haney, 1979). Take, for instance, the word "run." A sprinter can "run" in a race. Politicians "run" races, but not exclusively with their legs. Although a horse "runs" with legs, it uses four of them, which is still a little different than a sprinter. A woman can get a "run" in her hose, which is troublesome, but having a "run" of cards is good. However, having a "run" on a bank is bad. For a sailor, "running" aground is not good at all, but a "run" with the wind can be exhilarating. To score a "run" in baseball is different than a "run" in cricket. Hence one "runs" into the ambiguity of language at every turn even with a simple, everyday word like "run."

The argument could be made that the context helps clarify the precise meaning of the word, and in some cases that may be true. Yet, in the long "run," even the context of a sentence cannot guarantee precision. The seemingly innocent statement, "I'm going to run down to the bank," can be interpreted in at least two ways. Does the speaker mean a financial institution or a river bank? A comment such as, "the Chancellor ordered the professors to stop sleeping in class," can have a number of different meanings. Are students or professors the ones who are sleeping? Even the location of a pause in a conversation can radically alter the meaning of an utterance. Compare the following statements:

(a) People from Kansas who are industrious are well off.
(b) People from Kansas, who are industrious, are well off.

In the last sentence all people from Kansas are considered well off, but in the first only those who are industrious are deemed to be well off. All of these examples could be seen as amusing little observations about the human plight, the kind of routine Andy Rooney does on *60 Minutes*. Yet, the ambiguity of language has deep implications that are right at the heart of understanding the communication process.

Proposition 2: The communication process can be best described in terms of probabilities.

Given that language is inherently ambiguous, then it is reasonable to assume that the various interpretations can be assigned probabilities. The statement, "I am going down to the bank," when stripped of all contextual clues, could be seen as having a 50% chance of being interpreted as a financial institution and a 50% chance as a river bank. Therefore, communication can be viewed as uncertainty reduction in which the probabilities of one interpretation are increased and other decreased. Context is the major implicit modifier of the probabilities. If the person is deep in the woods on a hunting trip, the chances are that the speaker is thinking of a river bank. But it is not always that simple. In fact a number of implications flow from this probabilistic view of communication.

Implication A: Typically the message
sender sees only one possible interpretation.

Yet, for a receiver, there are three different options. First, the receiver may see the same possibility, in which case the two individuals have understood one another. Second, the receiver may see a different possibility, which may go unnoticed or even be found amusing (as in the case of an unintended pun). Third, the receiver may be unable to determine the correct possibility. At this point, a clarifying question may be asked. Or the receiver may not choose to inquire as to the precise meaning because the risk level may be too high. Fears of losing prestige, being ridiculed, ignored, or thought incompetent often stifle further understanding. In most large group situations, for example, the pressures not to ask for clarification can be immense.

Perhaps the most serious situations are those in which the communicators fail to grasp the fact that there are, indeed, different possible interpretations. The following case provides an intriguing insight into the difficulty. A young woman from Green Bay, Wisconsin, was taken to the emergency room of a hospital at 7:00 p.m. on a Friday night for a minor injury. After the usual name and address part of the intake process the conversation continued:

Stage 1

Nurse: How much did you drink?
Patient: I haven't been drinking at all tonight.
Nurse: No, no I mean liquids.

Stage 2

Patient: Oh well, I'm not really sure. Normal, I guess.
Nurse: Okay.

Stage 3

Patient: Why did you need to know about how much I drink?
Nurse: (caustically) I don't care how much you party! That's your business. But I see the results of you kids who drink and drive. It's not fair to those who don't.
Patient: I didn't mean alcohol. I meant fluids, I meant. . . .

The nurse walked away in disgust. The patient limped away in pain.

What is intriguing about this case is how the probable interpretations started out one way, flip-flopped, and reversed again. In the end, neither person recognized the true source of the conflict.

Table 2.1 Using Probabilities to Diagnose a Communication Breakdown

Meaning for "Drink"	Theoretical Probability	Stage 1		Stage 2		Stage 3	
		Nurse	Patient	Nurse	Patient	Nurse	Patient
Alcohol	50%	0%	100%	0%	0%	100%	0%
Fluids	50%	100%	0%	100%	100%	0%	100%

NOTE: In every stage the perceived probabilities remain at 100%. There is nothing said in the dialogue that clarifies which probability is operative.

In the beginning (Stage 1), both people had different meanings for the question, "How much did you drink?" The nurse was referring to liquids (100% probability), the patient to alcohol (100% probability). Theoretically, both are plausible interpretations. The term "obviously" meant liquids, in the normal context for the nurse. After all, the amount of liquid in the human body is a crucial medical factor. But there is another context at work here, as well. For many people on a Friday night, the term "drink" typically means alcohol. This is particularly true in Green Bay, Wisconsin, which has one of the highest bar-to-person ratios in the country. Nevertheless, eventually each person recognized the "mistake" in the other's interpretation.

The relevant information was abstracted in Stage 2 with the patient adjusting to the interpretation of the nurse. Then, in Stage 3, each assumes the other's interpretation, still at a 100% probability, as the operating rule for the conversation. On the surface, this switch appears to be the source of the conflict. But the real source of the problem is that neither the nurse or the patient recognizes that "drink" has a probability of meaning *either* fluid *or* alcohol consumption. In essence, only one possible interpretation, a 100% probability, is considered throughout the entire conservation, as can been seen in Table 2.1. Hence, the communication totally breaks down in Stage 3, resulting in frustration for both nurse and patient.

Implication B: The sender of a message
may purposely use language that has multiple interpretations.

Speakers can use a kind of verbal Rorschach in which a phrase is used that can have many possible meanings. In the famous Rorschach psychological test, the subject is presented with an ambiguous graphic, an inkblot. Then a question like, "What do you see in this picture?" is posed. Theoretically, the interpretation of the inkblot reveals the subjects' intellectual and emotional orientation. In the same way, statements can be designed that elicit different interpretations depending on the receiver's orientation.

Politicians provide a plethora of examples. Consider a statement like, "Our party wants to take the offensive on the drug war." The meaning of this statement is practically opaque because there are so many possible interpretations. But it sounds good! Corporate executives are not above using such tactics and may use statements like, "We are trying to develop a strong organizational base," or "People are the key to our success." Again, the precise meanings of these statements are difficult to ascertain. But that does not imply that such statements are void of meaning. On the contrary, such language can be extraordinarily powerful if the sincerity of the speaker is unquestioned. Even though every person who hears such a statement may have a different meaning for the message, the ultimate impact may be favorable. The receivers read their own meanings into the statements. Yet none of the private interpretations can be confirmed, so, for the speaker, they are deniable.

Even less abstract language can be used in this manner. Sarcasm and jokes often are used in this manner to test how an individual may react. A disreputable salesperson who says, "Hey, you make this purchase order for your company and there will be a little something for you," may be coyly testing the waters. The receiver has to decide if this is indeed a bribe or a joke. The onus of interpretation lies with the receiver. If the receiver reacts negatively to the comment, then the salesman can say it was only a joke and thus deny a clearly possible interpretation. The debate on whether some rock music should be given ratings, like movies, is another example. Some musicians have claimed that the "dirty" interpretation of some lyrics is only in the minds of adult fanatics and that kids don't think about them.

Is this kind of strategic ambiguity ethical? The question is, in a sense, moot. Ambiguity, whether we acknowledge it or not, is a part of the language. People who are both ethical and unethical use such tactics. Ambiguity can stir creative ideas, allow people to save face, or resolve a conflict. For example, there is evidence that employees deemed effective do not have to *actually* agree with their managers on the regulative rules guiding conversation. But they must be *perceived* by their managers as agreeing with these rules (Eisenberg, Monge, & Farace, 1984). Hence, ambiguity may serve to create the perception of unity, if not the reality. On the other hand, the unscrupulous do use such tactics for deception, power plays, and fraud (see Table 2.2). While managers should assess their own personal ethics on this matter of strategic ambiguity, it is equally important to detect such ploys

Table 2.2 Assessing the Value of Ambiguity

Potential Benefits	Potential Liabilities
• Induce creativity	• May not be useful with those desiring specific direction
• Allow people to save face	• May be used to deny personal responsibility
• Resolve conflict through different interpretations of one message	• May allow unwanted misunderstanding
• Allows stalling	• Creates ethical concerns
• Enhance credibility in a conflict	• May gloss over meaningful differences
• Allow diverse groups to work together	• May delay conflict resolution
	• Allows plausible deniability

when they are being used to achieve illegitimate ends. The final chapter of this book deals with this question in more detail.

Implication C: The receiver may purposely misunderstand.

In some circumstances, receivers exploit the probabilistic nature of communication in order to meet their goals. In short, they have a need to misunderstand. My favorite example is the artist who sculpted figures to adorn the top of a building in London. There was a problem. When city officials saw that the building was rimmed with statues of nude males, they ordered the artist to "cut off the offending parts." The artist complied, but in his own special way. He lopped off the heads of all the statues.

Employees often have a similar need to misunderstand communication they may find "offensive." For example, an employee was sent the following memo from his boss on Wednesday afternoon: "I need the report first thing Monday morning." Then Monday rolled around and, lo and behold, no report. The angry boss confronted the employee, at which point the employee remarked: "I thought you meant the following Monday." Sure enough, that is one possible interpretation. In fact, the memo could have been referring to any future Monday. Of course, the employee's interpretation conveniently fits in with his schedule. No doubt, the employee understood precisely what Monday the boss was referring to. But the extra week of preparation met his needs at the time. The employee needed to misunderstand. The probabilistic nature of communication allowed him to legitimately argue that there was a "communication breakdown."

Proposition 3: Context can best be thought of as solidified interpretations — the default assumptions — that shape the probabilities.

If communication is inevitably wrapped up in uncertainties, then how is it possible for two people to ever understand one another? Some scholars might argue that it is indeed impossible to fully understand another person, that there can never be 100% understanding. And in many ways that is true. However, people do seem to be able to understand each other well enough to get tasks done, communicate intentions, and effectively function in an array of situations. How? In part, the answer lies in the role that context plays in the communication process. The context freezes or predisposes certain probable interpretations.

For instance, the acronym, IRA, has a multitude of possible interpretations. It could stand for the Irish Republican Army, Individual Retirement Account, International Rugby Association, or even a person's name. Usually, it is not necessary to clarify how the acronym is being used. In a discussion on banking, IRA stands for Individual Retirement Account. Likewise, two politicians on a subcommittee on British foreign policy can regularly use the acronym to stand for the Irish Republican Army. The exquisite ease and simplicity with which we understand the various uses of an acronym or term are astonishing. What happens is that the context of the discussion increases the probability of some interpretations while decreasing others (see Figure 2.1).

One of the great challenges for researchers working on artificial intelligence (AI) has been attempting to get a computer to "understand" human language. This has proved to be exceedingly difficult. Initial attempts sought to use the brute power of the computer by teaching it the meaning of a multitude of words. But this proved practically useless because of the ambiguous nature of even the most concrete words. Douglas Hofstadter (1979) put it this way: "It is probably safe to say that writing a program which can handle the top five words of English — 'the', 'of', 'and', 'a', and 'to' — would be equivalent to solving the entire problem of AI, and hence tantamount to knowing what intelligence and consciousness are" (pp. 629-630). The difficulty is that the precise meaning of those words depends heavily on unspoken assumptions that are part of the context.

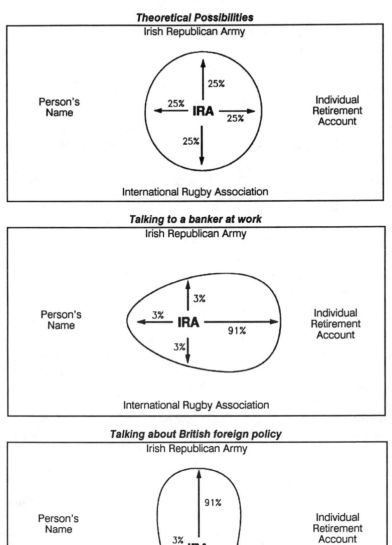

Figure 2.1 Probabilities Altered by Context

What has proven more useful is constructing fairly restricted "scripts." Certain meanings and assumptions in specific situations, such as in a restaurant or hospital, are specified in advance. Thus clearly specified interpretations are preprogrammed into the computer. For instance, one rarely says, "I want to eat," when ordering a meal in a restaurant. That is part of the context and must be programmed into the computer. When someone orders "chicken" in a restaurant, the context dictates that the chicken should be in an edible form, not live with wings flapping and feathers flying. Hence, the computer can interpret the meanings of various phrases based upon assumptions about the context. Indeed, the context can be thought of as a series of hidden assumptions that go unspoken and often unnoticed.

When the assumptions are not shared — that is, the context is not shared — then the receiver fails to understand the sender's meaning. My favorite example of this occurs in a Peter Sellers movie. Sellers, as Inspector Clouseau, is standing at a street corner with a dog at his side when a stranger approaches him. The stranger asks, "Does your dog bite?" The always forthright Clouseau responds, "No." Then the dog at Clouseau's side promptly chomps on the leg of the bystander. The astonished man replies with justifiable anger, "I thought you said your dog does not bite." Clouseau calmly replies, "It's not my dog." The humor of this episode lies in the incongruity between Clouseau's context of interpretation and the other man's. The obvious assumption implied in the context is that the dog standing by Clouseau is *his* dog, which in this case proves inaccurate. Normally, one would assume that the "dog" being referred to is the dog that is in plain sight, even if the person standing next to the dog is not the owner. That is, the probabilities are shaped by the context to exclude references to all other dogs in the world and focus on the dog in sight.

Yet all incidents of this type are not so easily chalked up to a comic's antics; some are quite serious indeed. For example, a bidding deadline may be missed because the bidder assumes a different time zone than what was intended; or a party may assume the "final offer" is only a "firm offer," not the actual last offer that will terminate the negotiations. In both cases, the hidden assumptions — the contexts of the sender and receiver — differ just enough so that different meanings are assumed. The results are unintended but very real and disturbing. The unspoken and the assumed can, by shaping the context, alter the probable interpretations in such a way that senders and receivers do not share one another's meaning.

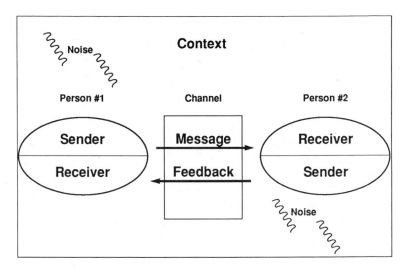

Figure 2.2 Typical Communication Model

Proposition 4: A context is developed through the dynamic process of individuals interacting.

One of the great myths about context is that it is something "out there." Typical models of communication look like the one seen in Figure 2.2. Note that the context is pictured as an element outside the communicators. The implication is that two people share and operate in the same context. It is as if the context is like air: breathed by everyone, walked through by everybody, and existing independent of anyone's presence. This is wrong. There is not one context, there are many. A context is not walked into, rather it is carried around in the minds of individuals. Context is not some kind of ever-present ether but a function of complex interactions between people and the setting. Our culture clearly shapes our perceptions, but fundamentally each individual has a personal and uniquely configured context. In short, context is a self-constructed image of the world.

Greeting behavior is one of the best examples of how contexts are dynamically developed. There are a limitless number of possible responses to questions like, "What's happening?" or "How ya doing?" In fact, the greeter is faced with an intriguing dilemma when someone actually proceeds to discuss in some detail "what's happening." Fortunately, most of the time we are spared such burdens. Past experiences in the "greeting context" make virtually certain that the responses will be quite limited. In fact, the only really important duty is to respond in some way because ultimately all responses are interpreted as a simple acknowledgment. In some cases, the context is so rigid that the greeter does not even listen to the actual response:

Greeting: "How's it going?"
Response: "Not so good. My dog just died and I got my foot run over by a car."
Salutation: "Oh great. Good to talk to you."

Creating a common context in the minds of communicators is a product of repeated exposure to people in certain roles, under similar circumstances, and in comparable settings. Through repeated experience, a series of probable interpretations are highlighted and others deemed less likely. "What do you want?" is a statement that means something dramatically different in a restaurant than in an argument. "It's all your fault" can be a joke between friends or an accusation by a foe. One usually does not clarify such remarks. Indeed, the humor of a sarcastic comment is removed when explained. Rather, that secondary message, "This is a joke," is assumed from the context, which has been dynamically built up through numerous interactions.

This process of building contexts is a marvelously efficient way to communicate. All comments do not have to be clarified in precise detail in order for two people to effectively interact. As a result of certain interpretations being pushed into the foreground and others being pulled into the background, people can reasonably assume that meanings will be shared, except perhaps when talking to Inspector Clouseau. Hence, there is rarely a need for a banker to fill in the IRA acronym or for two friends who are kidding around to clarify, "This is a joke." In short, the dynamic nature of context building allows for a highly flexible but efficient method of reducing the interpretative probabilities.

Proposition 5: The context can become so powerful that it acts like a black hole.

Astronomers as well as science fiction buffs have a fascination with black holes. These are places in space in which the heavens collapse into a concentration of supergravity that warps space-time to such a degree that light can not escape from it. Celestial objects that get too close to a black hole can get sucked in and never return. Nothing, not even light, escapes from a black hole. In a similar but perhaps less dramatic way, a context can exert such a strong force that probable interpretations can become severely warped. Indeed, meanings that are inferred can have little or no relation to the actual realities of the situation or the intentions of the sender.

The proverbial tale of the boy who cried "wolf" once too often is a case in point. The first time he cried wolf everyone came running, only to find that it was a ruse. The second time, the same story. When an actual wolf appeared, no one believed him. The boy is gobbled up by the real wolf and the real contextual "black hole" he created. The context created by the previous incidents implied that the probable interpretation of "wolf, wolf" should be that of a "joke." The shift of probable interpretations from the first incident to the final episode shows the powerful role that context plays in the communication process. In fact, any other comments made by the boy would have been tainted with doubts about their authenticity. The irony, as well as the moral, is that in the end the boy actually was being truthful, but, because the context was so strong, he had no means to communicate his message. In essence, a black hole can destroy the capability for communication.

Unfortunately, the simple lesson of this child's tale goes unheeded in too many corporations. The situations vary in the particulars but not in kind. Past communication builds a powerful set of contextual cues. For example, the manager who continually criticizes and berates employees and then suddenly praises them may be seen as trying to placate or appease employees. His motives are suspect, when in fact he is giving honest praise.

The woes of E. F. Hutton provide a more grim example. Robert Fomon became CEO of Hutton in 1970 and promptly led it to great success. Fomon seemed to love power and the trappings of power. He was known for his personal excesses, including a penchant for young women and fine wine (Stevens, 1988). He also set up a management system that simply was too unwieldly for one individual to handle, even Fomon. There was a price to be paid for such carelessness (Carpenter & Feloni, 1988). Three devastating blows hit E. F. Hutton in the mid 1980s:

- The company pled guilty to 2,000 counts of mail and wire fraud. They agreed to pay a fine of $2 million as well as reimburse those cheated. Fomon claimed he knew nothing about the practice.
- Through a complex check-kiting scam one customer bilked Hutton out of $48 million.
- An unwise promotional campaign of tax-exempt bonds resulted in a $55 million loss.

To instill some organizational discipline and cope with these problems, Fomon hired Robert Rittereiser as his second-in-command. But Fomon undermined Rittereiser at every turn, which eventually led to a nasty skirmish before the board of directors. Fomon was replaced by Rittereiser but stayed on as chairman. Fomon became so difficult to deal with that he was asked to move his office, and eventually he resigned. One of the ironies of the story is that Fomon and Rittereiser had negotiated a deal to sell the company to Shearson Lehman in 1986 for $50 a share. The board rejected the deal only to sell a year later, after the crash, for $29.50 a share.

This sad tale shows in vivid strokes how a black hole develops. Each debacle acts as the interpretive context for the next incident. There is such inertia that all judgments, even legitimate ones, are questioned. This is exactly what happened when Fomon recommended sale of Hutton for $50 a share. That is, the force of the context became so constraining that every recommendation by Fomon was interpreted as "yet another ill-advised move." But events proved otherwise. Yet, for the board, the implication was always the same, Fomon had to go. The context, the "black hole," so warped or shaped the possible meanings that there was no escape from the past. To be sure, other factors may have influenced the board's decision as well. Yet, the lesson is simple and fundamental. As Jacob Marley warned Ebenezer Scrooge, the chain that binds is forged link by link, day by day, and act upon act. So too, the context that binds; it is built one incident at a time. The past lives in the context utilized in the present.

All contextual black holes are not always negative in nature. Success breeds success in part because useful meanings are accentuated by the context, the "halo effect." In many ways the reputation of IBM acts as a positive black hole. Almost every action is positively interpreted by outsiders. The corporate philosophy, past successes, and image all serve to skew meanings in a positive way, regardless of more objective interpretations (e.g., Fombrun & Shanley, 1990). In sum, the black hole may act positively as in the case of IBM. Or it may function negatively as with Robert Fomon. Now, like the boy who cried wolf, when E. F. Hutton speaks, only the wind listens.

Proposition 6: Context construction is uniquely sensitive to time sequencing.

The message in Figure 2.3 appeared outside a church on its marquee. If these two statements are read as question and answer, sequentially, then this church had a rather unusual approach to piety. Indeed, the humor comes from the fact that the first line was not intended to form the context for the second line. If the statements on the marquee were reversed, the faux pas no longer exists because the context did not necessarily suggest a sequential reading of the sign (see Figure 2.4). It is not always that easy to discern the lines between one message and another.

Figure 2.3 Church Marquee A

Figure 2.4 Church Marquee B

Assumed links between events or comments may imply interpretations that are at odds with reality. Unfortunately, the receiver is not always able to discern this. Rosalyn Turek, the extraordinary pianist and harpsichordist, related a particularly delightful story that illustrates this principle. She tells of a famous, though unspecified, pianist who recorded Chopin's C minor étude in 3,000 takes. "What he did was to play four measures at a time about

20 or 30 times. And when he finished the four measures all that many times, then he went to the next four measures" (Southern Educational Communication Association, 1985, p. 10). In this way he insured he performed each measure of the piece to perfection. Then the sound engineer had to find the best measures and sequence them properly. The supreme irony was that the recording was critically acclaimed and the critics noted that the pianist's "endurance was phenomenal." In this case, the critics, like most people, naturally assumed that the piece was played in a complete sequence. Linkages were assumed that, while reasonable, were actually fictional.

The timing of the messages can have a tremendous impact on the ultimate interpretations made by people. For example, one major airline boarded passengers on Flight 666. Fifteen minutes out of O'Hare Airport officials found out that half of the passengers had tickets to go to New York City and the other half to Los Angeles. All was not lost. Passengers got to "vote" on whether they wanted to go to Los Angeles or New York. In the airspace over the plains of Illinois, democracy triumphed, and passengers raised their hands to vote on where they would spend the next 24 hours. So the plane flew to Los Angeles and the New York passengers immediately boarded another aircraft bound for Chicago, where they boarded yet another plane that actually did arrive in New York.

Most business travelers accept certain delays and mishaps as a normal part of the "travel package." Most travelers could even understand that the same flight number might be assigned to two different routes. What makes this incident unique is that all the passengers, even those going to Los Angeles, interpreted the airline's antics as incompetence of the highest order. If the problem had been noticed on the ground, as it should have been, then passengers might have felt that "the computer screwed up" and not really have inferred anything negative about the airline. As it was, the problem was determined in the air and passengers interpreted the oversight as managerial incompetence. If there were any doubts, the vote alleviated them. Lunacy prevailed.

Such events are not unique. The manager who, while reading the *Wall Street Journal,* finds out about the organization's plans to restructure has a completely different perspective on the company than the manager who hears about the plans firsthand. Employees who depend on the grapevine first and the formal network second for accurate information come to different understandings than those who reverse the process. But the tangle can become even more complex when more than two messages are involved. And as the number of information sources and communication media increase, the problem of proper sequencing of messages will become more acute. Hence the wise manager is concerned not only about the messages employees receive but also their timing.

Each message forms the context for the next message, as one musical phrase does for the next. But it is not quite that simple. Some messages are seen as being connected to one another, while others are not. This, too, influences the interpretations. Why some messages are seen in the same context (as in the first church sign), and others are seen in different contexts (like the second sign) is still somewhat of a mystery. Why do people connect some events or messages and not others? Future communication researchers will have to answer that question. For now, it is important to note that those with whom we communicate will not always sequence the messages in the same way we do. A great many difficulties in communication can be traced to this very simple proposition. It is as if we all had the same musical notes but arranged them into distinctly different melodies.

Proposition 7: Meanings are a product of the interaction of content and context.

Content is considered to be the actual words or behaviors of senders. This is the "stuff" that is normally thought of when most people think of communication. As discussed above, the context basically functions as the background on which the content is placed, like the canvas for a painting.

Content alone cannot produce any meaning except in a very rudimentary sense. *"Ceci est un message de la part de cette société"* is certainly a message. It has content, but does it have meaning? That depends, of course, on whether you can read French. Only then is a sufficient context provided to allow interpretation. However, even if a translation is made into English can it necessarily be argued that there is "meaning"? Only in a narrow sense. The sentence translates as follows: "This is a message from the organization." That reveals a little more about the message, but still the "meaning" does not seem too apparent, not even in an ambiguous sense.

This sentence, in a certain context, can have a very precise meaning. For example, one manager was given a lateral move in an organization. The manager was faced with the task of determining if this was a message from top management. In some companies, a "lateral move" is the kiss of death; an indicator of poor performance. In other companies, like Japanese corporations, a lateral move is not a message about performance at all. It is a normal corporate event. Even in the same company a lateral move may or may not be a performance message. Hence, the manager given a lateral move must determine if this is indeed a message or not.

Douglas Hofstatder (1979) provides a deeply penetrating explanation. He postulated that there are three layers of any message. Layer one, the frame message, says: "I am a message; decode me if you can!" In the example above, the manager had to decide if a "lateral move" actually was a message. In some cases, a manager may be unaware that there is a message in the move, and hence, not get the meaning. On the other hand, if the manager determines that there is indeed a message in the move, then a layer two issue arises.

Layer two is the outer message, which tells how the message is to be decoded. What is the decoding mechanism for the manager? The corporate culture and the unwritten organizational rules determine how the message should be decoded. A manager may, however, be able to recognize that the lateral move is a message but not know how to interpret it. The situation would be similar to someone recognizing that French is being spoken but being unable to interpret the actual utterance.

The inner message, layer three, is the meaning intended by the sender. In this case, top management may be saying, "Your performance has been lackluster. You better shape up!" In essence, the top two layers provide part of the context so the actual meaning can be extracted.

Therefore, context provides two important pieces of information in order to reduce uncertainty. First, it designates what counts as a message and what does not. In one corporation, a "lateral move" may count as a message, while in other organizations it does not. Managers continuously are faced with some kind of ambiguity. Is being left off a circulation list an oversight or a message? What about not being invited to certain social events? Second, the context tells what decoding mechanism should be utilized. If, for example, an organization has gone through some radical changes to become "leaner and meaner," how should being left off a circulation list be decoded? Should the old interpretation rules be used or the new ones? Clearly the decoding mechanism significantly alters the interpretation. A message must have a context for interpretation to take place. Part of that context is provided by the message itself but the most significant part is provided by the unwritten organizational rules.

Proposition 8: Meanings may be constructed without any message at all.

The context can become so developed that the mere expectation of a message can "communicate" something. Take the case of 9-year-old Wendy Potasnik of Carmel, Indiana. She filed a lawsuit against Borden, Inc., because she did not get her free prize in her box of Cracker Jacks. She had written a complaint to the company but failed to receive a reply within 12 days. A Cracker Jack's spokesperson stated that a letter of apology and a coupon for another box was sent within 13 days but, by then, the suit had been filed.

In this case, the apparent "no response" created a meaning and no doubt an unsuspected reaction. The context exerted so much influence that the mere expectation of a message made certain that something would be "communicated to" Wendy. Unfortunately, these kinds of communication problems are not just cute little human interest stories that occasionally appear in the newspaper. Rather, such incidents occur with amazing regularity in most organizations. They have serious consequences and concern matters more critical than a box of Cracker Jacks. For example, how many valued employees leave organizations because management never gives them any feedback about performance? In most of these cases, the employees feel unappreciated and believe that they can find more desirable working conditions elsewhere — and that is precisely what they do.

It is somewhat disconcerting to come to the realization that, to a large extent, message senders are at the mercy of the interpretations of receivers. That is, regardless of the sender's actual intent, it is the receiver who will determine "the meaning" of any given utterance. Some communication scholars extend the argument further and claim that "you cannot not communicate." In practical terms that statement is nonsense. There are countless people with whom we do not communicate, with whom we do not intend to communicate, and who do not perceive an intent to communicate (Motley, 1990). Yet, rhetorically, this often-quoted maxim is quite useful. For every person can be seen as a walking grab bag of *potential* messages that *may* be interpreted. The type of clothing worn, the briefcase carried, the haircut, the accent, the rate of speech are just a few of the potentially interpretable messages.

A manager who does not respond to a written request from a subordinate, whether by design or carelessness, "communicates" a very important message. The marketing representative who fails to return a phone call from a client "sends" a potentially negative message. But is it really proper to use such words as "sends" or "communicates" in these instances? Does the manager or marketing representative actually transmit a message, as one who sends a letter does? Can "no communication" actually be "communication"?

At the heart of each of these questions is the role of intention in the communication process. A "no message" may actually be seen as a "sent message." The nonresponse to a subordinate's request may be an intentional strategy on the part of the manager to communicate the trivial nature of the request. But what if the manager simply forgot to respond? Is this nonresponse a "sent" message? But does it really matter? In either case, a meaning will be constructed in the mind of the subordinate because a response is expected. Therefore, "no communication," whether intentional or not, actually results in a communication of sorts. More precisely, *meanings can be produced if there is the mere assumption of intent.*

Even to use the term "receiver" implies that there was a kind of action on the part of some "sender." The term "receiver" only derives meaning in relationship to the term "sender." Therefore, even the language we use to communicate about communication obscures clear discussion of the issues. The point is that any action or nonaction can be thought of as having communication potential if there is a context present in the mind of someone. To extend the logic to the end of the line, employees could choose to attach any meaning they wish, to any act or nonact. Indeed, in every mental hospital there are those patients who suffer from just such delusions and seem to operate exclusively on this principle. The restraining force on this kind of linguistic meltdown is that our culture and language does, in fact, severely limit the probable interpretations and thus allow us to communicate with reasonable effectiveness. Two noted communication scholars, James Anderson and Tim Meyer (1988), discerningly point out that

> any piece of content limits the meanings that can be competently constructed from it. These limits are like the limits imposed in the phrase, "All the numbers between 1 and 2." Now we know that there is an infinite number of numbers between 1 and 2 (e.g., 1.000 . . . 00001, 1.000 . . . 00002); however, there is no 3. In a like manner, there is a large number of interpretations that can be given to any content, but there is an even larger number that can't. It's this larger number that makes communication work. (p. 26)

In short, even though there are limits on meaning construction, they are wide indeed. Meanings, in fact, may arise without any messages being sent at all; "something" can actually come from "nothing."

Proposition 9: There are secondary messages in every communication event.

The discussion thus far has implied that when a message is sent, it has only one meaning. Actually the process is much more complicated than that. With any given message there are countless secondary messages that can alter the context and change the interpretations. For example, to confirm a spelling for a name people will often say something like this: "Mr. Arrow: *a* as in alpha; *r* as in rover; *r* as in rover; *o* as in orange; and *w* as in wagon." A functional equivalent that could be given by the stereotypical flirtatious man to a waitress might be: "*a* as in adorable; *r* as in rich; *r* as in really rich; *o* as in obliging; and *w* as in willing?" To which the clever waitress might reply: "*N - O*; *N* as in never and *O* as in offensive." The secondary messages are quite obvious. The point is that the statements provide the same information on the surface — a redundant expression of the spelling — but carry vastly different secondary messages.

In a similar sense, it was no accident that the Arrow manager preferred to be addressed as *Mr.* Taylor and the Circuit manager went by his first name, Elton. When formal titles are used as a form of address, a more rigid and authoritative relational base is developed. The use of a first name implies a relationship of equality, openness, and flexibility. Peters and Waterman (1982) have perceptively pointed out that in the excellent companies, employees are called "associates," "crew members," and "hosts," as opposed to simply "employees" or "subordinates" or even "underlings" (p. 240). All of these names refer to the same basic role, but they express powerful secondary messages about the relationship between managers and employees. Forms of address are not the only ways to express secondary messages. For instance, the memo in Figure 2.5 was sent to all employees of a midwestern university by the recently inaugurated chancellor. A number of employees, particularly long-term ones, were offended by the last point in the memo, which implied that they needed to be reminded about how to take care of their basic responsibilities. It was as if a parent was talking to a child. Indeed, one graffiti artist added, "And be sure to brush your teeth every night." Employees do not warm to messages, intended or not, that imply a relationship of superior to inferior.

Most professional speakers are quite skillful at exploiting the impact of secondary messages. A management consultant addressing an audience of supervisors, trying to illustrate the usefulness of a particular appraisal system, might say: "When I worked at IBM, we used a similar system and we noted a 10% improvement in production over the next six months." Ostensibly her statement provides evidence for her claim that the appraisal system works. There are, however, other messages implicit in that comment as well:

(1) I have used this system.
(2) I have been a manager, just like you.
(3) IBM owes its splendid reputation, in part, to its appraisal system.

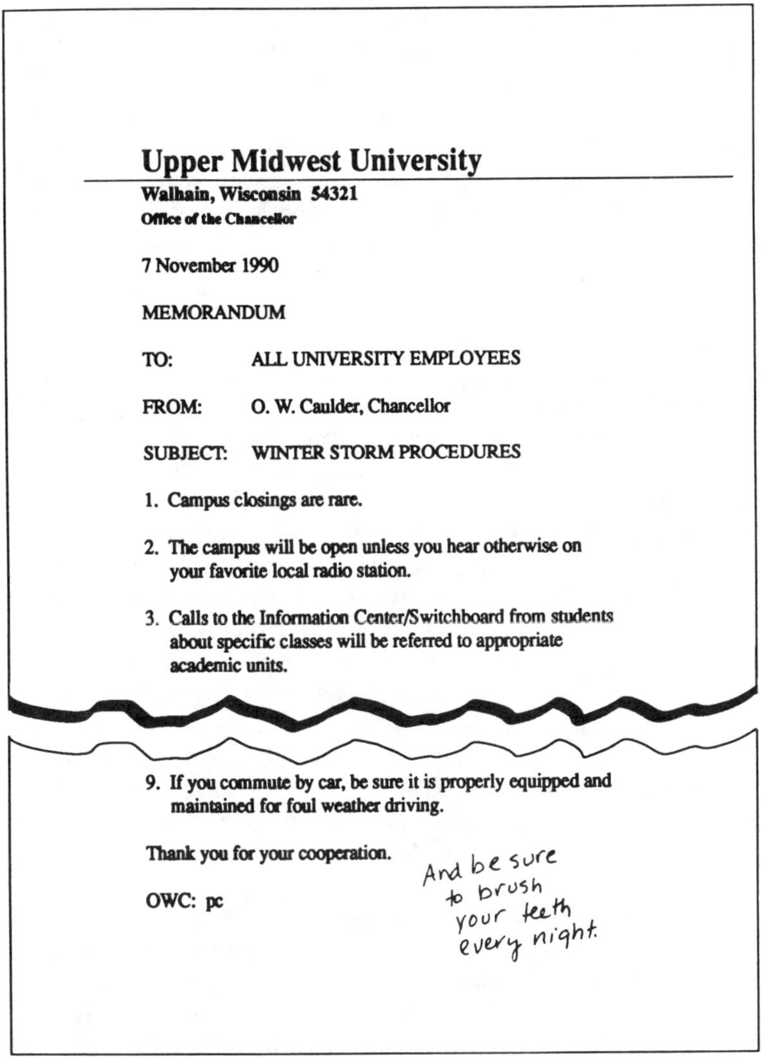

Upper Midwest University

Walhain, Wisconsin 54321
Office of the Chancellor

7 November 1990

MEMORANDUM

TO: ALL UNIVERSITY EMPLOYEES

FROM: O. W. Caulder, Chancellor

SUBJECT: WINTER STORM PROCEDURES

1. Campus closings are rare.

2. The campus will be open unless you hear otherwise on
   your favorite local radio station.

3. Calls to the Information Center/Switchboard from students
   about specific classes will be referred to appropriate
   academic units.

9. If you commute by car, be sure it is properly equipped and
   maintained for foul weather driving.

Thank you for your cooperation.   *And be sure*
                                         to brush
OWC: pc   *your teeth*
                                         every night.

Figure 2.5 Example of Unintended Message

Management consultants who use experiential examples to prove their points
are more likely to be successful than those who rely exclusively on theoretical
or statistical proof. The potent secondary messages provide a context – an
aura of credibility – that makes the consultant more believable to listeners.

In many cases people react as much to the secondary messages as they do to the primary message or, at least, the ostensive reason for the message. Ultimately, the secondary messages, intended or unintended by the speaker, act as elements in forming the context of interpretation. That is, the secondary messages push or pull certain probable interpretations into the foreground or background. Typically these secondary messages are not processed consciously, and speakers often are baffled as to why they are perceived in certain ways. Thus the effective communicator pays attention to both the primary messages as well as the secondary ones.

Proposition 10: Even though interpretations are relative, the process of meaning construction is not.

One of the frustrations associated with this probabilistic approach to communication is that everything seems hopelessly relative. Can managers ever completely be sure their words or actions will be interpreted as intended? In a word, no. Indeed, Angela Laird's (1982) pioneering research on communication rules found that in one company, close supervision was regarded as "checking up" on the employee, whereas in another corporation it was thought of as "concern" on the part of the supervisor. Does this mean it is impossible to predict how a person will probably interpret a message? Absolutely not, but a manager must always realize that it is possible for a message to be understood in different ways. A manager cannot look for total certainty of interpretation but rather must learn to live with the probable and plausible. There is middle ground between absolute certainty and total uncertainty. This is the arena of communication. It may not be all that comforting to deal with communication in this fashion, but it is the most realistic.

How can managers achieve reasonable certainty that their actions and words will be interpreted as intended? They do so by recognizing the unchangeable and total certainty of *how* people interpret messages. While the interpretations people make are relative, the process is not. Every dancer has a different style, but there are certain fundamentals that all dancers adhere to. The meaning construction process is the same for everyone; context and content interact to yield an interpretation. A manager achieves reasonable certainty by realizing that the context of communication is equally as important as the content of the communication. Inferring how the context and content will interact in the minds of the receivers is the heart of effective communication. The manager can be certain, totally certain, that both context and content will indeed interact to produce meaning. The more the manager knows about both facets of the communication process, the greater the chance of predicting the likely reactions to the messages. Likewise, the more a dancer is familiar with a partner's capabilities and the music, the greater the likelihood that she can predict the movements of her partner.

Implications of the Propositions

Woven into the fabric of the following chapters are the implications that follow from the basic propositions discussed above. However, three particular implications deserve to be highlighted at this point.

First, the more managers know about the context in which employees interpret actions and messages, the greater the likelihood that they can accurately predict the probable interpretations. Meaning is a product of the interaction of context and content. It logically follows that the more managers know about both variables, the greater the chance they will know how their employees will react to a communication episode. The mistake most managers make, especially the Arrow managers, is to assume that because they know what they mean, others will as well. That is, they assume that the context is stable and that knowledge of the content alone is sufficient. It is not. And, it is not surprising that Peters and Waterman (1982) found that the excellent companies often practice MBWA (Management by Wandering Around), because through the act of getting to know employee attitudes, environments, needs, and desires, the manager develops an understanding of the employees' context of interpretation. This kind of knowledge can help the manager implicitly, if not explicitly, structure communication that will be interpreted as intended. Perhaps William H. Peace (1986), the vice president and general manager of KRW Energy Systems, summarized it best:

> Perceptions form around tiny bits of data and become stronger as supporting evidence accumulates; they are never completely accurate, nor are they completely wrong. Staying in touch with others' perceptions is difficult, however, partly because these may not be wholly conscious and partly because only the tip of what may be a large threatening iceberg will be known to any one employee. So managers must piece together the overall picture for themselves by listening for the tone, or context, or shading that doesn't quite match their own perceptions. Moreover, managers (particularly those at high levels) must consider carefully how their decisions will be perceived. If a decision is right in some business sense but wrong (for whatever reason) from the employees' perspective, its implementation will be erratic at best. (p. 65)

Second, managers must learn to think in terms of the possible misinterpretations of their messages. Typically, managers only think about how to best structure their messages to get their points across. They rarely think: How might my message be misunderstood? Since communication is probabilistic in nature, it seems reasonable to try to lessen the possibility of likely misinterpretations. Osmo Wiio (1978), a former Finnish parliament member turned organizational communication scholar, put it this way, à la Murphy's Law:

- If communication can fail, it will!
- If you are satisfied that your communication is bound to succeed, it is bound to fail.
- If a message can be understood in different ways, it will be understood in just that way which does the most harm.

With tongue only partly in cheek, he makes the fundamental point that no manager can be 100% certain that his message will be understood as intended.

Third, one useful strategy for facilitating understanding is to use the "blackout" tactic. Occasionally a speaker will make a statement and follow it with, "I am not saying X; I am not saying Y." This may seem a bit odd, for certainly most speakers know what they are saying. Yet, upon closer examination, this tactic can be exceedingly useful for the audience because it clarifies the precise meaning of the speaker. In essence, the speaker has blocked out certain probable interpretations of his remarks. When the original remark is made, it is as though seven spotlights turn on to illuminate the stage. As the speaker says "I do not mean," each light is extinguished one by one until one light remains illuminated. This is the speaker's precise meaning. Of course this strategy could be modified to blackout only a few possibilities and still leave a number of possible meanings illuminated, like illuminating only a sector of the stage with several spotlights.

Conclusion

A probabilistic view of communication does not provide the certainty that most Arrow managers want. The propositions highlighted in this chapter point to a far more fluid and dynamic situation than may seem comfortable. Even Circuit managers may find it disconcerting to find that meanings are not simply the product of interpersonal relationships, but are influenced by a broader context that includes the organizational rules, and corporate environment and culture. Effective managers, however, are more comfortable with a realistic view of communication than a convenient one.

References

Anderson, J. A., & Meyer, T. P. (1988). *Mediated communication.* Newbury Park, CA: Sage.

Carpenter, D. S., & Feloni, J. (1988). *The fall of the house of Hutton.* New York: Henry Holt.

Eisenberg, E. M., Monge, P. R., & Farace, R. V. (1984, May). *Coorientation on communication rules as a predictor of interpersonal evaluations in managerial dyads.* Paper presented at the Annual Convention of the International Communication Association, San Francisco.

Fombrun, C., & Shanley, M. (1990). What's in a name? Reputation building and corporate strategy. *Academy of Management Journal, 33*(2), 233-258.

Haney, W. V. (1979). *Communication and interpersonal relations: Text and cases.* Homewood, IL: Irwin.

Hofstadter, D. R. (1979). *Godel, Escher, Bach: An eternal golden braid.* New York: Vintage.

Laird, A. (1982, April). *A rules approach as a supplement to organization communication research.* Paper presented at the Central States Speech Association Convention, Chicago.

Motley, M. (1990). On whether one can(not) not communicate: An examination via traditional communication postulates. *Western Journal of Speech Communication, 54*(1), 1-22.

Peace, W. H. (1986). I thought I knew what good management was. *Harvard Business Review, 64*(2), 59-65.

Peters, T. J., & Waterman, R. H., Jr. (1982). *In search of excellence.* New York: Harper & Row.

Southern Educational Communications Association. (1985, July 17). [Interview with Schuyler Chapin, Tim Page, and Rosalyn Tureck]. *Firing Line.* Columbia, SC: Author.

Stevens, M. (1988). *Sudden death: The rise and fall of E. F. Hutton.* New York: New American Library.

Wiio, O. (1978). *Wiio's laws—And some others.* Espoo, Finland: Welingoos.

3

Communicating the
Corporate Culture

> Culture includes the entire symbolic environment. Culture defines
> reality: what is, what should be, what can be. It provides focus and
> meaning. It selects out of the myriad of events and interactions in the
> world those we pay attention to. Culture tells us what is important; what
> causes what, how events beyond our lives relate to us. Culture gives us
> values and standards of value. What we may distinguish analytically
> (and at our peril) as fact, value, and goal is existentially integrated in
> culture — in identifications, expectations, and demands of individual
> persons.
>
> Jeane Kirkpatrick

As historians cull the artifacts of our culture and read the chronicles of our
times in an attempt to discern the myths of this century, they will come to
many startling conclusions. I believe one that they will expose is our
unadulterated faith in numbers and statistical reasoning. "The numbers don't
lie . . . ", "The polls predict that . . . ", "The stats show that . . . " are the
incantations of Western 20th century culture. Anything that can be measured
is measured. There is an implicit belief that everything that is really important
can be measured. But numbers cannot always tell the whole story. The easiest
distinctions to make are not always the most important. A number can do
many wonderful things but it cannot relay the beauty, the tragedies, the hopes,
and the dreams of a people. It cannot embody culture.

Companies, like societies, have cultures. Values, myths, rituals, heroes,
and devils are all parts of corporate life. As the former UN ambassador
perceptively suggested above, culture structures our view of reality. Hence,
employees are deeply influenced by corporate values. Managers ignore these

facets of corporate life at their peril. For they are as real and important as any profit and loss statement.

What Is Culture?

The origin of the word "culture" is revealing. The term has agricultural overtones, as in the word "cultivation." It meant to prepare the ground, to develop or foster a particular kind of growth. Weeds have to be destroyed and the soil tilled in order to refine or improve growth. To the early Christians, culture involved a kind of worship (Simpson & Weiner, 1989).

In a very real sense culture still embodies both of these definitions. Organizational cultures seek to foster certain types of growth, provide fertile ground for certain types of enterprises, and weed out other types of behaviors. While an organization's culture does not cause growth, it does cultivate the conditions of growth. Cultivation of the "organizational soil" allows for the reproduction of compatible and beneficial behaviors, practices, and policies. And in many companies there is a kind of zealous religious guardianship of the organizational culture. In some companies, "worship" may not be too strong a word to describe attitudes toward the culture. In some Japanese organizations employees ritually chant corporate slogans and certain employees are afforded an almost sacred status because they symbolize the beliefs, values, hopes, and dreams of the culture.

The *Oxford English Dictionary* (1989) defines culture as "the training, development, and refinement of mind, tastes, and manners; the condition of being thus trained and refined." Note that culture can be thought of as a process *or* a condition. Actually it is both. For an organization's culture is simultaneously somewhat stable but constantly evolving as new challenges are encountered. Deeply embedded within the concept of "culture" is the notion of judgment. Implicit or explicit decisions are made to encourage some values and discourage others. Jacob Bronowski (1978), a 20th-century Renaissance man, said: "For the values rest at bottom on acts of judgment. And every act of judgment is a division of the field of experience into what matters and what does not" (p. 132). These choices or "ways of being" become so thoroughly ingrained that other "ways of doing things" are precluded.

Organizations, like countries, have styles of action and typical patterns of thought that slowly evolve. If there is "an American way" then we also can say there is "Company X's way." To cut to the heart of the matter, culture consists of the fundamental values and beliefs of a group of people. Corporate culture, then, is the underlying belief and value structure of an organization collectively shared by the employees that is symbolically expressed in a variety of overt and subtle ways. Few organizations begin with the corporate leaders philosophizing over the "appropriate" values. Out of a host of individual practices emerges a company style, which ultimately reflects "how things are done around here" (Deal & Kennedy, 1982, p. 4). Faced with the frenetic pace of corporate life, few managers can take the time to contemplate what the organization has become and is becoming. While they may not be able to clearly articulate the values, they certainly function by them.

Why Do Organizations Have Culture?

Culture acts like music for dancers. It does not strictly determine movement but does constrain the options. In the long and intimate history of dance and music, there has evolved a symbiosis between the two, in which changes in dance result in changes in music and changes in musical traditions alter the structure of dance. For example, think about the impact of MTV on the music of the 1980s. One musicologist, Will Straw (1988), has forcefully argued that music videos have encouraged the "generic stabilization" of popular music. There is less musical experimentation now than in the past, and rhythms have become standardized to fit into the three- to five-minute dance format. Likewise, culture does not create the communication patterns but fosters certain types of interactions. The communication practices of employees contribute to and change the harmonies and rhythms of an organization. The driving beat of a march suggests a rigid cadence and a strict adherence to a rhythmic structure that the Arrow manager enjoys. Yet a melody can have such powerful emotive overtones that sentimentality almost drips off each note. Form becomes more important than substance. Such are the tendencies of the Circuit manager's culture. Furthermore, music can express discord, confusion, turmoil, or even randomness, and many employees stumble to the beat of an erratic culture. To harmoniously and creatively blend form and substance, rhythm and melody, is the cultural challenge for the Dance manager.

Regardless of the precise form of culture, what is abundantly clear is that all organizations have some kind of culture. Why? There are three basic reasons.

First, the human mind is capable of innumerable ideas and beliefs, and in order to function in society people must select a few to live by. The alternative is disconcerting. If individuals did not have some kind of semipermanent belief structure, their behaviors would be governed by randomness. Communication would be almost impossible because the context would be continually shifting, like talking to a person with an infinite number of personalities. Community, cooperation, coorientation, and coordination would all suffer. Chaos and anarchy are the likely results. In athletic leagues the "cellar dwellers" in the standings often are populated with teams in which players and coaches have different philosophies. Teams cannot function effectively when players have different beliefs about how the game is to be played. A semistable set of beliefs and values allows athletes as well as employees to develop a "role on the team," a unique self-identity, a self-"valuableness," if you will. The NBA's Detroit Pistons won back-to-back world championships. Center Bill Laimbeer credits the team's success to each person knowing his appropriate role. In brief, culture is a necessity because we must relate to others and to self in meaningful ways.

Second, culture is a necessity because it provides an efficient mechanism to coordinate the activities of employees. There are basically two ways to control behavior: inductive and deductive approaches. Inductive approaches outline the specific rules, regulations, and job descriptions for the employees with the expectation that they will conform to those stipulations. The problem is that it literally is impossible for any employer to specify every contingency that may occur, even in the most mundane of jobs. Even if the supervisor could be that specific, few employees could cognitively digest all the rules and regulations. The supreme irony is that managers try to use this approach with just those employees who have the least intellectual capacity to process the overload of information. This is not to argue that rules, regulations, and job descriptions are useless. Rather, the point is that the inductive approach must be balanced with the deductive.

Coordinated actions also can result from more deductive strategies in which general approaches or "ways of doing things" are specified. Policies like "treat the customer with respect" or "the customer is number one" are of this ilk. Of course a manager might specify certain rules like greeting each customer with a smile or finishing a sales transaction with a comment like "Thank you for shopping at our store." While useful, such rules are potentially innumerable and clearly do not allow employees to creatively implement strategies that achieve the same objective. In fact, a strict insistence of rule-governed behaviors can act as a psychological straitjacket on the employee.

Cultural approaches focus on teaching employees a few underlying values and why they are important. For example, Disney World has a legendary culture of customer service. Rick Johnson, who conducts seminars about the

Disney culture explains: "You can't force people to smile. Each guest at Disney World sees an average 73 employees per visit, and we would have to supervise them continually. Of course, we can't do that, so instead we try to get employees to buy into the corporate culture" (McGill, 1989, p. 4f). Then employees are expected to behave according to these general principles as unique situations occur. Employees usually prefer to work with a manager who has a set of values rather than a set of rules, who challenges others to share values instead of enforcing regulations, and believes in people over procedures. The cultural, or deductive, approach offers a unique and expedient method of coordinating activities within the organization.

Third, an organizational culture is a necessity because of the limits of managerial power. Ultimately all managers necessarily derive their power from their ability to control the livelihood of their employees. To put it bluntly, managers can fire employees and control the purse strings. But this power can only ensure conformity in the short run. With the level of litigation over wrongful firings running at a high level, even these traditional power levers are being eroded (Geyelin, 1989). There are only so many times a manager can threaten to fire someone. While rewards may be somewhat more motivating, even these have limitations. The challenge for the manager is to transform power into duty and conformity into desire. Indeed, culture is a necessity for this very reason; it allows workers to be self-motivated by a set of internalized beliefs and values. The culture holds the organization together in the absence of threats and rewards. Without a healthy culture we are merely beasts. Without the music there is merely movement.

In sum, all companies have some sort of culture but this does not mean that all corporate cultures are equally successful. Some corporations implicitly encourage too many conflicting values. Others seek to manage primarily with inductive techniques, and some even rule through the ruthless use of power. These strategies send their own brand of cultural messages to employees. Fundamentally, however, such approaches rob the company of the beauty, grace, and, yes, even the power of an evolving culture, rather like comparing some dull musical cadence to a stirring Tchaikovsky ballet.

How Can the Values Be Discovered?

First, deep and thoughtful reflection on the type of people in the organization is an excellent starting point. Employees, particularly those at the highest levels, are at once creators, carriers, and consequences of culture. The individuals who are hired, their backgrounds, biases, prejudices, and styles shape corporate culture. In turn, these people carry or embody culture. The daily rituals, the inside jokes, the "taken-for-granted" are all reflections of the values (Pacanowsky & O'Donnell-Trujillo, 1982). Employees are also consequences of the culture because even as they are shaping the culture, they are being shaped by it. The entire past, present, and future of the corporation are reflected in the employees like a broken corner of a hologram reflects the imagery of the entire picture (Smith & Simmons, 1983).

To be more specific, by questioning, probing, and observing the behavior of others, one can get a vision of the corporate values. Why were certain individuals hired, fired, or promoted? What makes a person successful in the organization? Unsuccessful? What does top management value in an employee? How are decisions made? Why?

The "why" questions are the most difficult and revealing, for the answers disclose the underlying thought patterns, beliefs, and values of the corporation. More often than not, the "whys" are implicit and unconscious. For instance, why do most organizations go through the ritual of asking for more information than they can possibly use? Many managers are abundantly aware of the practice, but the critical question is, why? The practice is in part a reflection that most companies want to believe they make informed decisions. Of course, the underlying assumption that more information equals more knowledge is a bit dubious. Why would a company take time to interview a number of people it has no intention of hiring? A silly practice? Perhaps. But it may reflect a corporate value of giving everyone "a fair chance." Thus a thorough examination of why people do what they do proves exceedingly useful in uncovering corporate values.

Second, being sensitive to corporate symbols can provide insight into the organization's culture. Corporate heroes frequently provide a rich source of information on organizational values. For example, during one seminar with employees of a savings and loan, the discussion turned to some typical difficulties tellers had in dealing with uncooperative clients. In the middle of the discussion the president of the company stood up and told a story. In a rather lengthy soliloquy, he told how he had handled a similar situation when he was a teller and went on to explain with great relish how he had become president from his modest beginnings. While I was a bit surprised, the employees were not. In subsequent discussions it became apparent that such an event was not without precedent. Marvin, as the president liked to be called, was one of the corporate heroes and those stories were common knowledge among employees. What purpose did Marvin's story serve? Fundamentally, the message reiterated the value that top management was "employee-centered" and that anyone could "make it." The president, whom they knew on a first-name basis, was a coworker who understood their difficulties and troubles — and, most of all, he cared. He communicated, consciously or unconsciously, the secret of this organization's success. For most employees at this seminar, the significance of this event was short-lived. After all, it was common knowledge. Yet the wise manager understands the deeper meaning of the commonplace and finds significance in everyday events. As the insightful scholar George Gerbner says: "The control of any culture is dependent on these who control the stories that are told" (personal communication).

Third, corporate slogans may be quite revealing. "All the news that is fit to print" has been the rallying cry for the *New York Times* for years. The Aid Association for Lutherans is a tremendously successful life insurance company with a corporate slogan of "Common Concern for Human Worth." The slogan reflects the beliefs of the founders that life insurance should be provided at a reasonable cost. Even the employee publication, *Common Concern,* in both name and editorial policy, reflects the corporation's values. Issues frequently contain articles describing how AAL meets the needs of members and how members show concern for their community. Concern is the consistent theme and rallying cry for the organization; it provides meaning and purpose. Slogans may appear to be simple-minded and trivial. Yet there is an elegance in simplicity; the farsighted manager never underestimates the power of the simple.

Fourth, corporate philosophies also can be clues into corporate values. They provide a brief and concise view of how the corporation views itself and its mission — a sort of corporate self-image. Imperial Incorporated is a nationwide telemarketing firm that has consistently grown despite economic fluctuations. Part of its secret lies in a clearly stated and easily internalized corporate mission, as seen in Figure 3.1. Not only are employees instructed on the philosophy, but customers are made aware of it through publication of the credo in the product manual. Therefore, internal and external pressures act to preserve the value of "customer service." Such practices must be having an effect. Between the years 1981 and 1989, Imperial increased the sales-per-employee ratio from $50,000 to $100,000 a year.

Fifth, there are more subtle indicators of culture as well. At Imperial, they use an intriguing rhetorical device to further transmit the value of "customer service." The organizational chart is "upside down," with the customer at the top as the "chairman of the board" (see Figure 3.2).

Company newsletters can be equally revealing, as we discovered in a study on employee publications. Of the 100 samples we gathered from various organizations, we noted the styles ranged from one-page photocopies to

---

MISSION

Through the development of our people;

Imperial, Inc.

intends to be the recognized national leader
in TeleServicing℠ that provides quality products
and is committed to unequaled customer service
and state-of-the-art distribution systems, while
meeting our profitability and growth objectives.

MAJOR CORPORATE GOALS:

Increase retention and penetration of current accounts.

Complete transportation and agriculture specialization.

Complete investigation and testing of industrial and
heavy-duty markets.

Figure 3.1 Imperial, Inc. Corporate Charter

elaborate magazines (Clampitt, Crevcoure, & Hartel, 1986). One of these,
from Champion International Corporation, had beautiful pictures and graphics that in photographic quality almost rivaled National Geographic. The

IMPERIAL'S ORGANIZATION CHART

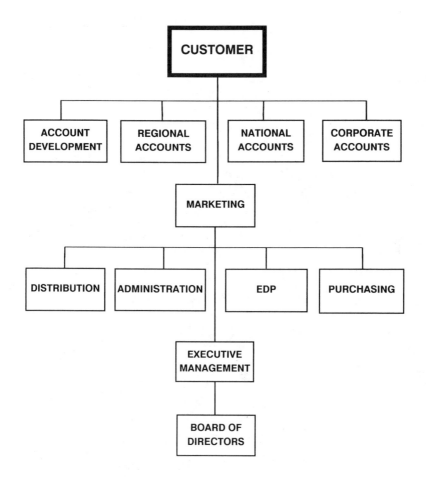

Figure 3.2 Imperial's Organization Chart

firm, an industry leader, produces high-quality paper products. This publication no doubt showcases their prowess. The implicit message is abundantly clear to employees and their families: Champion is a high-quality organization. One of my colleagues examined a publication from another business and remarked that it reminded him of a high school yearbook. Indeed, the proliferation of pictures of the company bowling team, softball teams, and company parties would tend to confirm such an evaluation. Discussions with

Table 3.1 Characteristics of Corporate Cultures

Healthy Cultures	*Unhealthy Cultures*
• Stated and unstated values are congruent.	• Stated and unstated values conflict.
• Employees are certain about what the organization stands for.	• Employees are uncertain about what the organization stands for.
• Employees are committed to the values.	• Employees are apathetic.
• Violations of values are treated seriously.	• Violations of procedures may be treated seriously.
• New values emerge by building consensus.	• New values only emerge during temporary crises.

several company employees revealed that top management wanted to develop a "family atmosphere." The newsletter was one vivid manifestation of the value.

In brief, there are a wide range of symbolic clues into corporate values. Some are more explicit, like corporate heroes, slogans, and philosophies. Others are more implicit, like symbols, graphic designs, and company newsletters. This is not to suggest that the culture exists in the symbols themselves. Rather, it is the way in which employees come to understand, react, and relate to symbols that create the culture. Through a dynamic interplay of symbols and reactions, culture evolves. In this way cultural symbols refine or cultivate certain values and beliefs.

What are the Consequences of Culture?

Since organizational culture is a given, why should a manager be concerned with it? Of what consequence is it? These are honest and important questions. The answers should be equally straightforward. There are healthy and unhealthy cultures (see Table 3.1). Corporate culture influences the organization in a variety of ways, but this section highlights four of the more notable consequences.

First, culture influences how an organization analyzes and solves problems. Few business activities have more significance on the profit/loss statement than how decisions are made and carried out. Paul Bate (1984), a noted scholar from University of Bath, England, writes in a thought-provoking article:

People in organizations evolve in their daily interactions with one another a system of shared perspectives or "collectively held and sanctioned definitions of the situation" which make up the culture of these organizations. The culture, once established, prescribes for its creators and inheritors certain ways of believing, thinking, and acting which in some circumstances can prevent meaningful interaction and induce a condition of "learned helplessness" — that is a psychological state in which people are unable to conceptualize their problems in such a way as to be able to resolve them. In short, attempts at problem-solving may become culture-bound. (p. 44)

His research confirms that culture can, and in fact does, restrain organizational thought.

Indeed, poor decisions can result from such cultural restraints. Meaningful alternatives are not explored because "that's not how things are done around here." For instance, one small but growing company had several problems with how various departments interrelated. The normal procedure was to forward all such problems to the company president and let him resolve the issue. After all, such procedures had worked well in the past and the president, a corporate hero, was legendary for his ability to solve problems equitably. The difficulty was that as the firm grew it became increasingly difficult for the president to know the necessary facts in order to make appropriate decisions. A simple and obvious solution was to have a middle manager's meeting to solve many of the problems and coordinate activities. Strangely, no one in the company had thought of this idea. Why? Because of the "way things are done around here" or, to put it another way, the value of respect for the chain of command precluded even thinking about such a solution. The culture had put perceptual blinders on the entire management team. The consultant who suggested the change did not have these particular blinders and was widely praised for this "revolutionary idea." Once the meetings began to take place, many of the problems were quickly and easily resolved.

In another company a manager boldly admitted during a meeting that she had not met her quarterly goals. The vice president's response was, "I would have lied." His statement set in motion a kind of "shoot the messenger" type of culture in which accurate information is not valued in the organization. Effective decision making no doubt was hindered from that point onward. Here is a classic example of how unhealthy culture results in poor decision making.

Second, culture impacts the quantity and quality of innovations developed within the corporation. Japanese car manufacturers routinely bring new cars to market in three years, while companies based in the United States typically take five years (Mitchell, 1989). One study revealed that Toyota

Motor company received an average of over 13 suggestions per employee per year. General Motors during the same time period averaged less than one idea per employee in spite of incentives of up to $10,000 (Nishiyama, 1981). Apparently money was not the prime motivator. Why the difference? In a word, culture. Most Japanese organizations actively cultivate cultures that emphasize corporatewide teamwork. Innovation develops out of a commitment to the task and corporation. In fact, over 90% of the suggestions of Toyota were implemented during the year of the study, while at GM less than 33% were (Nishiyama, 1981). The treatment of employee suggestions sends powerful signals about what is valued by the organization. At Toyota there is the synergistic interaction between the suggestion and implementation processes. Any organization's culture, Japanese or American, that encourages innovation will reap the benefits of greater productivity and employee satisfaction. Organizations that do not are destined to ignore "obvious" productivity improvements or pay huge fees to outside consultants to make many of the same suggestions. Either way, the corporation loses.

Third, culture influences how the company will respond to change. Culture can actively encourage quick and decisive change when conditions demand it. Many high-tech firms realize that to keep pace there is a constant need for change and development. Complacency means death. Apple Computer Company has a culture that actively fosters and encourages individuals to be creative and on the leading edge of technology. The revolutionary Macintosh computer is one manifestation of Apple's commitment. Few companies would take such a risky, costly, and bold step. Yet this is exactly what the culture demanded of its employees. On the other hand, the organizational culture can act as an impediment to change when it is needed.

Universities are almost legendary for such resistance. If the need arises to develop a program that crosses departmental boundaries, the budgetary and bureaucratic obstacles are almost overwhelming. Why? Because of the tremendous inertia of the system to maintain the traditional departmental structure. Fundamentally, it is an expression of the belief that knowledge should be compartmentalized. Hence, barriers are developed to ensure that this belief is not violated. In some ways, such barriers to change may be beneficial, but the benefits should be weighed against the costs. All organizations should closely examine the environment to determine how much change is actually needed. Then the question becomes: Does the culture foster the necessary degree of change? The answer has critical consequences for the organization's long-term survival.

Fourth, culture impacts employee motivation. There can be no greater motivation for employees than when they believe in what they are doing, what the company does and what the company stands for. Excellent companies are motivating because of their corporate cultures. When a company espouses one philosophy but practices another, employees become disheartened and disillusioned because they cannot believe in the company or even in themselves. An organization that has a corporate philosophy that says all employees should be respected but does not respond to employee inquiries and unfairly rewards employees is doomed to an unhealthy culture. The corporation that says it believes in offering a "fair pricing system" to its customers and then regularly deceives clients on the actual price of goods and services fosters disrespect among employees. When practice and belief are incongruent, the culture is not motivating. Hypocrisy has its price.

In short, culture does have consequence. George Gilder (1981) in his book, *Wealth and Poverty,* probably summarizes it best:

> Matters of management, motivation, and spirit — and their effects on willingness to innovate and seek new knowledge — dwarf all measurable inputs in accounting for productive efficiency, both for individuals and groups and for management and labor. A key difference is always the willingness to transform vague information or hypotheses into working knowledge; willingness, in Tolstoy's terms, transferred from the martial to the productive arts, "to fight and face danger," to exert efforts and take risks. (p. 26)

The I-We-Them-It Principle

As suggested before, culture is an irrefutable fact of life, and cultural values often are subtly expressed and not readily apparent. Generally, corporate values revolve around four central themes that can be conveniently summarized in terms of the *I-We-Them-It Principle.* There are variations from organization to organization, but fundamentally these four themes are the bedrock of an organization's culture.

The "I" theme refers to how individuals are regarded in the corporation. Is everyone a "winner" or is it "every-man-for-himself"? Do employees have to "earn their wings" or "know somebody who knows somebody"? In short, the "I" theme is concerned with the relationship of the individual to the corporation: What kind of people are valued by the corporation? Sometimes the theme is explicitly expressed through a policy statement or a corporate slogan. For example, the company slogan, "We are the best, because we hire the best," indicates that all employees are highly regarded. Other corporations take an opposite tack, stressing the competitive aspects with slogans like "Only the tough survive." Which approach is appropriate? There is no simple answer because what is successful will depend on the corporation's competitive environment, technology, the other corporate values, and the product or service offered.

The "I" theme also may be expressed through more subtle means. During one project, I asked the client to go out for lunch to discuss some proposals. He politely declined, explaining that all the managers and executives went jogging during the lunch hour. I was somewhat startled, since the temperature had been well below freezing for months. Upon further work with the corporation, the daily jogging ritual with the CEO made perfect sense. The CEO consistently stressed the importance of a lean and fit organization in which managers were self-motivated, nimble of mind and spirit, and had mental toughness and endurance regardless of the circumstances. The jogging ritual was a subtle and extraordinarily powerful expression of those values.

The "We" theme concerns how individuals relate to one another in the organization. How are coworkers treated? How are superiors spoken to? How do superiors relate to subordinates? These are the "We" questions. Often the language used by corporate heroes and others sets the values for interpersonal relationships. Using words like associate, colleague, or partners consistently communicates to employees a belief in harmony, commitment, and mutual respect. For example, employees at Disney World are called "cast members" (McGill, 1989). Conversely, labels like "boss," "subordinate," and "superiors" are indigenous to a culture emphasizing a hierarchical authority structure. Parking lots and lunch rooms also can be revealing. Do the bosses have labeled or special places? If so, this may indicate a greater distancing between the "elite" and the "rank and file." Where a company should be on the continuum, from highly interpersonal to highly authoritative, is a matter of many factors. What is clear, however, is that the implicit or explicit choices made along this continuum greatly affect employee productivity and satisfaction.

The "Them" component refers to how the corporate culture deals with the business environment, and in particular, the customer. How committed is the corporation to the customer? How far will the company go to meet its commitment to a customer? Corporate legends, for better or worse, often are strong indicators of the "Them" values. For instance, a disreputable firm might "value" the employee who made a great deal of money by charging a customer more than a reasonable price. More respectable firms celebrate the legends of employees who go the extra mile to fulfill company commitments. Consider, for instance, DuPont's "Adopt a Customer" program in which plant workers are encouraged to visit customers on a monthly basis. Thus the blue-collar worker can develop a sensitivity to customer needs and act as an advocate on the factory floor. Quality is built into the products by workers who are empowered by a vision of their customers' needs (Dumaine, 1990). When employees answer to customers and not faceless bureaucrats, there are bound to be quality differences.

Finally, the "It" theme represents how the corporation feels about what it does. Krueger Incorporated makes high-quality furniture products. When you first enter the corporate headquarters you gaze on a spacious room containing an elegant display of the Krueger products. Guests are encouraged by a pleasant receptionist to sit in the chairs or try out the desks. They are justifiably proud of their products and use every opportunity to display them.

Employees from various branches of one savings and loan formed a committee to select a wardrobe for the tellers that would act as a kind of professional uniform. Why? Simply, they felt that a standard uniform would help communicate to clients that the employees offered a professional service. One committee member even spoke before her colleagues at a regional meeting of financial employees on why a uniform was a "must" for "progressive" savings and loans. She was justifiably proud of the service she offered to clients and, to her, the uniform was an expression of this belief. There are numerous other ways in which corporations may communicate about what they do, but of fundamental importance is the fact that all organizations do communicate about "It."

All organizations have values in these four central areas regardless of whether managers, or even top management, care to recognize the fact. Managers should evaluate the appropriateness of corporate values in each of these areas. Does the corporate culture aid or hinder the achievement of corporate goals? This is, of course, the supreme question. Arrow managers tend to focus on the "It" values, while the priority for Circuit managers is the "We" theme. Dance managers have a bolder and broader charge as they seek to coordinate the themes of the "I-We-Them-It" into workable and consistent behaviors. How do they accomplish this? In a word, communication.

Communicating the Values

The effective manager is, to a large extent, a teacher. There is no more important challenge for managers than to instill corporate values. They must teach employees what is valued by the corporation, why it is valued, and how to transform values into action. This is no simple task. Employees, like students, do not always see the value of what they are doing until after they have done it. They may tire, get discouraged, or even resist. But the farsighted manager overcomes these hindrances while engendering commitment to corporate values and inspiring employees to enact them. Ultimately, the values must move from objective truths to subjective realities; that is, employees must transform corporate rhetoric about values into personal commitments and experiences. This is the supreme task of the manager, and communication is the main tool.

Most organizations construct their culture through an unplanned, haphazard, and trial-and-error process. Effective corporations with healthy cultures contemplate, plan, and manage their corporate values. Every manager creates a kind of subculture in the organization as well. Effective managers consciously construct cultural cues for their employees. Reviewed below are six useful strategies for communicating the values.

First, the successful manager uses the socialization process to communicate the corporate culture. From the moment potential employees enter the organization, they begin to develop a picture of the corporate values (Jablin, 1987). The manner in which they are treated, the way employees talk to one another, the office design, and even the selection process are all indicators of the corporate culture. After being hired, the training procedures, the daily rituals, and practices further reinforce "what this company is all about." Thus the socialization process begins to slowly, yet steadily, build the pieces of the corporate value structure for the new employee.

Through this process, managers can actively encourage the appropriate values. The hiring process itself can render messages to potential employees that the company is serious about hiring the best. Who does the hiring and interviewing can send equally powerful messages. Admiral Hyman Rickover, the founder of the nuclear Navy, was notorious for his rigorous interviews of all cadets who wished to serve on the submarines. In fact, the title of President Jimmy Carter's (1976) book, *Why Not the Best?*, came from a comment by Rickover during one of those interviews. Here was one of the most powerful men in the world interviewing a cadet and asking him if he always did his best. Rickover thus set in motion the standard of excellence he expected from all those in his charge. In fact, his legendary commitment to quality was so great that his programs were usually considered untouchable during defense budget cutting days (Polmar & Allen, 1982).

Research indicates that the initial weeks of employment are a critical period for the manager to exert influence (Clampitt & Downs, in press). Supervisors, to some extent, lose their power to shape the values, beliefs, and behaviors of employees after the first month or so. This makes the training procedures extremely important, for managers are not only teaching specific skills but also the corporate philosophy. Detailed discussions of corporate history and corporate successes and failures help instill corporate values into employees. Some companies, like IBM, go through extensive discussions of corporate values — not just the "whats" but also the "whys" of policy. One IBM employee remarked, "After you're done with their training, you know what they believe, why they believe it and you end up believing it."

Thorough explanations of corporate philosophy or plans also can help embed the value system. These recitations can act as a kind of organizational mantra in which repeating the words weaves a magic incantation (Broms & Gahmberg, 1983). Employees not only need to *think* about values but *feel* them. It is silly to recite over and over again a fact like, "The speed of light is 186,000 miles per second." A fact once spoken is enough. Yet a value once recited is stillborn. We do, in fact, listen to the same music over and over again. It replenishes our strength, focuses our spirit, and energizes us; similar is the effect of "Why not the best?" or "Quality is job one."

Second, effective managers symbolically communicate the organization's values. For example, during executive meetings at Sears there is an empty chair at the conference table with the words, "The Customer," emblazoned on it. Through this simple symbolic device the executives are forced to reckon with the customer's desires. The chair is a visual reminder of the need to satisfy the customer (DeMott, 1984).

One minister believed that church members should volunteer for church responsibilities instead of the usual practice in which various members are "begged" to serve. Not only did he preach the message that "God calls people to serve" from the pulpit, but he also signaled the value through a simple rhetorical device. Instead of a nominating committee that sought volunteers for various church functions, he reversed the spelling to coin the the term "ETANIMON Committee" in which members applied to serve the church. Here, in this deceptively simple act, he reversed the nominating process in both spelling and deed. The pastor also reversed the trend; the church had more applicants than they knew what to do with.

The president of Oryx Energy wanted to shock his company out of its 102-year-old corporate culture. His novel idea was to get a buzzer. He sounded it during executive meetings whenever comments were made that were reminiscent of the former culture. While the device might make even Ivan Pavlov's mouth water, it was a humorous but effective way in which to induce organizational change. Now the buzzer sits unused in the president's office as a symbolic reminder of the new culture (Solomon, August, 1989).

In each of these cases, the symbols reinforced the critical values, acting as continual reminders of what the organization stood for. The creative powers of many managers would be well spent in thinking of such simple and novel methods to symbolize critical corporate values.

Third, the successful manager links values with specific behaviors. Values are, of necessity, abstract concepts. Hence, there are a multitude of different specific behaviors that could spring from one value. Wise managers not only encourage certain behaviors but also link those behaviors to a specific value. Thus the value becomes the focal point which, in turn, encourages other novel behaviors that also express the value. One classic example occurred during the 1984 Olympic trials for the USA basketball team. Leon Wood, a stand-out offensive player at California State University at Fullerton, was a leader in scoring and assists but was not known for his defense. That was bound to change when Mr. Wood met Coach Bobby Knight, who was known for the prowess of his devastating defense at Indiana University. Not one to disappoint, Coach Knight gave Mr. Wood a lot of personalized instruction on how to play defense. At one point, Leon reported that, "Coach Knight came over to me and said, 'Leon, you took a charge, didn't you? That's your first one in camp, isn't it?' I said it was, and so he told me to go to the spot on the floor where I took the charge and sign the court." As requested, Mr. Wood autographed the basketball floor in the Indiana Fieldhouse (Wood shows signs of defensive ability, 1984).

The event must have made a deep and lasting impression on Wood and the other players. Here is an exquisite example of linking the person, Wood, to the value (defense), to a specific action (taking a charge). The genius of the act of Wood autographing the floor is that it created a permanent symbolic representation of the value. There must have been times when Leon was racing down the court that he looked over to that place on the floor and remembered the incident that was indelibly etched in his mind. This memory, no doubt, had the desired effect and encouraged him to play aggressive defense. It must have worked because the team won the Olympic gold medal that year. Employees, like basketball players, need to have experiences that act as reminders of corporate values, and they need to be praised for manifesting them (e.g., Feinstein, 1986). Incidents like this show that the organization takes its values seriously and expects the values to be lived out on a day-to-day basis.

Daily routines or corporate policies can have a similar effect. For instance, Imperial Incorporated, the telemarketing firm mentioned previously, has a "two rings is plenty" policy. Whenever a phone rings at Imperial, someone always answers within two rings. Frankly, it is a refreshing departure from the typical practice. But to focus on the practice itself is to miss the point. Simple in design, but powerful in effect, the policy embodies a central corporate value of serving the customer. An unanswered phone or continually ringing phone can be annoying to customers. Hence, this is one way in which the organization can show respect for the customer. The practice links the corporate value of customer service to a tangible behavior on a daily basis. Customer service is not just a fuzzy idea in the heads of management at Imperial Incorporated but a daily commitment and practice of all employees.

Fourth, the effective manager reconciles the inevitable conflicts between values. There are innumerable practical manifestations of one simple value. Thus practices that are congruent with one value may be incongruent with another one. For instance, a company may simultaneously believe that "All our employees are winners" and "We reward excellence." But if taken to the extreme, these values are philosophically at odds. For if every employee is a winner, then specific employees could not be singled out for awards of excellence. Or, if only the excellent employees are handsomely rewarded, then the vast majority of employees would not feel like "winners." Yet, in practice, the skillful manager unites the values and stresses the balance between the two. For instance, all employees could be paid salaries above the industry norm, a practice that communicates that indeed *all* employees are winners. And still the "best of the best" may be rewarded in other ways like special recognition or even financial compensation. This emphasizes the philosophical alternative that "we reward excellence." In fact, in all likelihood the company could not, in the long run, keep its "winners" unless the corporation recognized excellent performance. In this way, the apparently conflicting values enhance one another.

This discussion may sound something like the incantations of a Zen master, and in many ways that is precisely the role of the manager. The challenge for the manager is to communicate what are seemingly conflicting messages. Managers must seek a balance between the values. They must be sensitive to specific practices that emphasize one value at the expense of another. Taken to the extreme, an employee might believe that "customer service" means providing an excessively costly service to clients. Of course, such practices need to be balanced with the reasonable profit motive. The employee might retort: "I was only trying to serve the customer's needs. After all, that is what our company stands for. Is it wrong to serve the customer?" The effective manager then has a unique opportunity to guide the employee into an understanding of how the corporate values balance one another. Indeed, values that seem to be at odds philosophically with one another may, in practice, actually augment and strengthen one another. The wise manager toils and searches for this synergistic effect and encourages employees to do likewise.

Fifth, effective managers use their financial resources to communicate corporate values. Few messages more clearly and unambiguously communicate what is important to an organization than how money is spent. For example, it is one matter for a company to say that it believes in "customer service"; it is another to alter financial plans in order to do so. L. L. Bean, the legendary mail-order company for the adventurous, had a goal of achieving $1 billion in sales in 1992. But this objective was sacrificed and growth purposely slowed so that the company could focus on customer service. Indeed, in 1988 the company lost the coveted National Quality Award and decided to invest $2 million to improve customer satisfaction (Pereira, 1989).

It is easy to say that a company values employees, but the message is taken to heart when employee compensation is at stake. For instance, Herman Miller Incorporated, an office furniture manufacturer, is one of the fastest growing organizations in the industry. They credit the growth to treating employees fairly and engendering a commitment to corporate goals. One unusual method used to communicate this message is to limit the CEO's salary to 20 times the average income of factory workers. Thus in 1989, including bonuses, the CEO earned only a little over $465,000, which is a far cry from what many CEOs earn (Labich, 1989).

Employee stock ownership plans or ESOPs are another way to link corporate values to compensation. Stock in the company is bought for the employee by the ESOP trust. Employees do not invest their own funds. At many companies, ESOPs become a substitute for a pension plan. When the employee retires or leaves the company, he or she often has the option of taking the ESOP payment in stock or in cash. The ESOP at PepsiCo Incorporated is part of a "SharePower" program meant to build team spirit and send a clear message to all employees that they are important (Solomon, June, 1989). The idea is that workers have incentive to do better since part of their retirement benefit is directly influenced by the performance of their company's stock. Indeed, Corey Rosen, the head of the National Center for Employee Ownership, believes that the key to improved organizational performance lies in using ESOPs to encourage employees to participate in the company. He has found that companies that have ESOPs grow at a rate of 8% to 11% faster than those that do not (McCormick, 1989).

Sometimes the use of financial resources can be used to signal major changes in the culture. For example, when Robert Allen, the CEO of AT&T, bought a competitor, Paradyne Corporation, for $250 million he sent a strong message to employees (Kupfer, 1989). He said, in effect, it is time we break out of this belief that only the best ideas are invented internally. While such sentiments served AT&T well for many years, Allen recognized the need to change. Such practices must be having a positive impact because company stock values continue to steadily improve. How an organization spends its capital may tell employees more about corporate values than any other symbol.

Sixth, prescient managers assist in the evolution of new values. One of the signs of change can be the temporary clash between the stated values and the practiced ones. The conflict can be healthy. Not practicing what one preaches becomes unhealthy if there is not some movement toward greater congruity. For example, it has become fashionable for corporations to espouse the "wellness" value, which is a commitment to healthy living. That concept has a nice sound, it seems "right." Yet, if it rings true, it has to be acted on. Johnson & Johnson did something about it in the late 1970s. They initiated the "Live for Life" program, which involves employees completing a comprehensive questionnaire about health risks. Based on the results, each employee is counseled by a nurse practitioner about appropriate life-style changes. Employees are encouraged to eat right, quit smoking, and exercise in the company-provided gym. In a healthy culture, usually there is a time lag between the proclamation of the value and the full implementation of it. In fact, it was only in October of 1990 that the corporate headquarters became totally smoke-free. The wise manager recognizes the inevitability of the clash between word and deed while searching for specific ways to bridge the chasm.

Anticipating and shaping cultural changes can be beneficial in building employee commitment to new values. One wonders if a smoke-free environment could have been implemented in the late 1970s. Typically, the corporate culture changes slowly, and it takes time to fully embrace the values. But there are benefits in incrementally increasing employee commitment to corporate values. For Johnson & Johnson the result was a savings of $378 per employee in reduced health-care costs. They also formed a new company, Johnson & Johnson Health Management Incorporated, to market their program (Templin, 1990). Indeed, a culture that does not change and continually renew its values can become stagnant and unhealthy.

Finally, effective managers build safety valves into the communication system in order to ensure the values are preserved. A safety valve in a plumbing system is a mechanism that releases excessive water pressure during emergencies and thus prevents damage to the pipes. In the same vein, a safety valve in the communication system is used when the normal channels are clogged and the valves are in danger of rupturing. For example, IBM's "Speak Up" program allows employees to express their sentiments and suggestions to top management. It is a communication channel that exists outside the normal chain of command. At an office of 10,000 people, one top executive responds to 600 such notes a year (Kneale, 1986). This kind of program helps ensure that top management will become aware of any discrepancies between corporate values and behavior.

Successfully functioning "open-door policies" can have the same effect. Employees need to feel they have another court of appeal if their manager has wittingly or unwittingly compromised a corporate value. While a corporation must depend on individual managers to communicate its values, there must be other vehicles as well. The effective manager is not afraid of the safety valves because they help ensure that everyone in the organization is committed to the same values.

Conclusion

As a youngster I remember watching an old black-and-white movie about a World War II naval battle. An American ship was dropping depth charges on a German submarine. Inside the sub the results were devastating. Water was flooding one chamber after another, equipment was failing, and the crew faced what they thought was certain death. To make matters worse, the crew had been instructed to maintain strict silence so that the American ships could not pinpoint their location. Morale was steadily eroding, which prohibited the necessary repairs from being made and the appropriate offensive tactics being enacted. The crew was demoralized, exhausted, and terrified. Then, in a flash of brilliant insight and in direct violation of military procedure, the captain ordered that the German national anthem be played over the speaker system. Because of the silence code, the captain's officers were stunned. At first they refused. Then, with some gentle urging, one weary sailor placed the old scratched record on the record player. At first one by one, then two by two, and finally the whole crew joined in the singing. And with each measure, the strength, the determination, and even the courage of the crew returned as if resurrecting a corpse. They still faced the grim task at hand, but they were emboldened by their anthem, their music. And in the end they triumphed over their peril. Likewise, many managers need to know when morale is more important than procedure, how values can provide meaning and purpose, and why courage triumphs over all. They need to know when to play the music.[1]

Note

1. An interesting sidelight to this story is that the U.S. Army had for years lost international military contests that simulated small-scale skirmishes. In 1987 they won two of the most prestigious contests, and in part they cited the use of rock and roll music in the training session. The songs played included the theme music for the movie *Top Gun* and "Born in the USA" by Bruce Springsteen (Fialka, 1987).

References

Bate, P. (1984). The impact of organizational culture on approaches to organizational problem-solving. *Organization Studies, 5*(1), 43-66.

Broms, H., & Gahmberg, H. (1983). Communication to self in organizations and cultures. *Administrative Science Quarterly, 28,* 482-495.

Bronowski, J. (1978). *The common sense of science.* Cambridge, MA: Harvard University Press.

Carter, J. (1976). *Why not the best?* New York: Bantam.

Clampitt, P. G., Crevcoure, J. M., & Hartel, R. L. (1986). Exploratory research on employee publications. *Journal of Business Communication, 23*(3), 5-17.

Clampitt, P. G., & Downs, C. W. (in press). Employee perceptions of communication/productivity relationship: A field study. *Journal of Business Communication.*

Deal, T. E., & Kennedy, A. A. (1982). *Corporate cultures.* Reading, MA: Addison-Wesley.

DeMott, J. S. (1984, August 20). Sears' sizzling new vitality. *Time,* pp. 82-90.

Dumaine, B. (1990, January 15). Creating a new company culture. *Fortune,* pp. 127-131.

Feinstein, J. (1986). *A season on the brink: A year with Bobby Knight and the Indiana Hoosiers.* New York: MacMillan.

Fialka, J. J. (1987, July 6). U.S. Army units win battle contests for the first time. *Wall Street Journal,* p. 24.

Geyelin, M. (1989, September 7). Fired managers winning more lawsuits. *Wall Street Journal,* p. B1.

Gilder, G. (1981). *Wealth and poverty.* New York: Basic Books.

Jablin, F. M. (1987). Organizational entry, assimilation, and exit. In F. M. Jablin, L. L. Putnam, K. H. Roberts, & L. W. Porter (Eds.), *Handbook of organizational communication* (pp. 679-725). Newbury Park, CA: Sage.

Kneale, D. (1986, April 7). Working at IBM: Intense loyalty in a rigid culture. *Wall Street Journal,* pp. 17.

Kupfer, A. (1989, June 19). Bob Allen rattles the cages at AT&T. *Fortune,* pp. 58-66.

Labich, K. (1989, February 27). Hot company, warm culture. *Fortune,* pp. 74-78.

McCormick, J. (1989, May 30). Taking stock of employee ownership plans. *USA Today,* p. 3B.

McGill, D. C. (1989, August 27). A 'Mickey Mouse' class—For real. *New York Times,* p. 4f.

Mitchell, R. (1989, December). Nurturing those ideas. *Business Week* (special ed.), pp. 106-118.

Nishiyama, K. (1981, May). *Japanese quality control circles.* Paper presented at the 31st Annual Conference of the International Communication Association, Minneapolis, MN.

Pacanowsky, M. E., & O'Donnell-Trujillo, N. (1982). Communication and organizational cultures. *Western Journal of Speech Communication, 46,* 115-130.

Pereira J. (1989, July 31). L. L. Bean scales back expansion goals to ensure pride in its service is valid. *Wall Street Journal,* p. B3.

Polmar, N. & Allen, T. B. (1982). *Rickover: Controversy and genius.* New York: Simon & Schuster.

Simpson, J. A., & Weiner, E. S. C. (1989). *Oxford English Dictionary* (2nd ed.). Oxford: Clarendon.

Smith, K. K., & Simmons, V. M. (1983). A Rumpelstiltskin organization: Metaphors on metaphors in field research. *Administrative Science Quarterly, 28,* 377-392.

Solomon, J. (1989, June 28). Pepsi offers stock options to all, not just honchos. *Wall Street Journal,* p. B1.

Solomon, J. (1989, August 17). Managing: Old culture behavior. *Wall Street Journal,* p. B1.

Straw, W. (1988). Music video in its contexts: Popular music and post-modernism in the 1980s. *Popular Music. 7*(3), 247-266.

Templin, N. (1990, May 21). Johnson & Johnson 'wellness' program for workers shows healthy bottom line. *Wall Street Journal,* p. B1.

Wood shows signs of defensive ability. (1984, August 1). *USA Today,* p. 2C.

4

Information

> Information is not a neutral product of organizational activity, but is a result of an inherently political activity—a political activity often hidden from those engaging in it largely due to presumed neutrality.
>
> Stanley Deetz and Dennis Mumby

> Business isn't complicated. The complications arise when people are cut off from information they need.
>
> John F. Welch Jr., CEO of General Electric
> (quoted in Tichy & Chanon, 1989)

If information had nutritional labels, it would be intriguing to study the dietary habits of managers. There is a virtual smorgasbord of information available to the average manager that is beyond the capacity of any single manager to consume. "A weekday edition of the *New York Times* contains more information than the average person was likely to come across in a lifetime in seventeenth-century England" (Wurman, 1989, p. 32).

How do managers cope with this bountiful harvest? Some gorge themselves and face the inevitable consequences. Others are overwhelmed by the excess. They live off the scraps of others. Many subsist on informational junk food that is easily consumed but of little nutritional value. There are far too many managers who have grown fat on information but are starved for knowledge. The purpose of this chapter is to show how information can provide nourishment when the organization is weaned of bad habits and establishes healthy ones. As surely as a healthy body is a product of wise nutrition, a healthy organization is a product of wise information management.

Myths

A number of commonly believed myths contribute to difficulties in effectively managing information.

Myth 1 — Information is a commodity.

Information can be bought and sold in the marketplace. In this sense information is like a commodity. But there the similarity ends. Information changes form when transmitted; commodities rarely do so. Information is filtered when transmitted; commodities are not. Once sold, the seller no longer possesses the commodity. Not so with information; both the sender and receiver possess the "commodity." In short, information operates on the cognitive plane whereas commodities operate on the physical plane.

So what? Quite simply, problems occur when information is treated as a commodity. Automobiles can be transferred from the manufacturer to the distributor, to the dealer, and finally to the customer without materially changing the car. Information "transferred" through a similar series of linkages would change dramatically. The automobile could even be given back to the manufacturer and still be in basically the same condition. However, if information goes through a similar process, it is likely the original sender of the message would not even recognize the message. The transferral process does not change the essence of a commodity, but it does change the essence of information. In sum, information cannot be "transferred" as such; rather, it is transmitted.

Myth 2 — Information is power.

Arrow managers often live by this credo and there is a grain of truth in it. Certainly those who possess more information *can* be more powerful, and often are, but there is no guarantee. The U.S. government has tremendous information resources but seems powerless in dealing with certain problems like alcoholism, drug abuse, and terrorism. Sometimes ignorance can serve one well. Pleading ignorance of a traffic law in a foreign country can sometimes be more useful than a prestigious law degree. This is not to say that ignorance is preferred over knowledge. Rather, the critical issue is how knowledge and ignorance are managed. Information usually offers greater *potential* for power than ignorance. But the critical concern in business is how the information is used.

A misguided belief that "information is power" naturally leads to difficulties. Those wishing to be powerful rigidly control the dissemination of information. They secretly stockpile information like some rare commodity, hoarding it for some impending famine. Ironically, the result can be a sort of information famine in which employees spend most of their time scavenging for job details, new procedures, and all the staples of corporate life. The focus becomes "who knows what" rather than "how can what they know help achieve organization goals." And in the end, those who are the most powerful may indeed by those who have hoarded the most information. The catch is that the entire system virtually collapses because of a hunger for relevant information. A case in point: the economy of the Soviet Union during the last few decades. Before Gorbachev assumed office, information was protected like the crown jewels. Victor Zaslavsky (1989) eloquently reconstructs the stifling climate:

> The library owned a Xerox machine, but it was guarded like a bank vault. Two trusted comrades – the head of the copying department and the Xerox operator – kept the two different keys to the machine, and both had to be inserted in the appropriate slots for the machine to function. A reader was entitled to ten copies a day. Worse, to copy these ten pages one needed approval of the department head . . . . Everyone knew the extraordinary powers of the copying department bred intrigue and denunciations by the envious. (p. 287)

Such policies naturally restrict the free flow of information that is the wellspring of innovation and the basis for economic growth.

Myth 3 – More information is better.

There is a tendency by some managers, especially Circuit ones, to wait until "all" the information has been gathered and processed before making a decision. Such a posture can lead to unnecessary delays, unwarranted uncertainty, and missed opportunities (O'Reilly, Chatman, & Anderson, 1987). Furthermore, there is a fundamental error in this kind of thinking. Information can never provide a 100% guarantee of what the future holds. Information, regardless of how much, can never provide a complete picture. President Kennedy's father, Joe Kennedy, commented about Wall Street: "I always said that with enough inside information and unlimited credit, you are sure to go broke" (Martin, 1983, p. 24). Indeed it is a mere illusion that information can ever provide certainty. At some point, leaps of faith, inferences, and even hunches must be used.

Sending a proposal to committee for further study or requesting more detailed analysis frequently are not ways to gather better information, but to delay decision making. Walter B. Wriston (1986), former chief executive officer of Citicorp, said: "Our ability to discern what is important and what is not may be impaired if we are inundated by a sea of numbers. Too many numbers may make the decision-making process harder, not easier" (p. 65). There even is evidence from laboratory studies that decision makers seek more information than they can possibly use, even to the point of hindering performance. But the extra information serves to "increase the decision maker's confidence. The net result may be that decision makers arrive at poorer decisions but are more confident in their choices" (O'Reilly, Chatman, & Anderson, 1987, p. 617).

Myth 4—Information is value-free.

Reporters often pride themselves on their objectivity. This is an illusion. Reporters, like managers, have to determine *what* constitutes the news, the story. The choice itself is a screen that reflects the values of the reporter. Why does the fiery crash of an automobile get reported on the evening news but not the successful blood drive at a local business? The guiding force behind the choices are the values of the reporter, which usually are not readily apparent. The values, in turn, influence what is seen, heard, and reported; what is information. So too, with managers. Assumptions underlie all observations. These assumptions or values determine "what counts" and "what does not count" as information. Choices are made about what is important and what is not. All information is value-laden.

Even the scientist is caught in this trap as Abraham Kaplan (1963) notes: "The fact is that no human perception *is* immaculate, certainly no perception of any significance for science. Even if perception itself were immaculate, the perceptual report exposes us to sin, as a necessary consequence of the way in which language works" (pp. 131-132). Managers who believe in "immaculate perception," in essence, assert their own divinity and are destined to an unenviable fate. Such a belief leads to a false sense of security and certainty that precludes looking at a situation from various perspectives. A mousetrap works because the mouse believes that cheese is cheese. Of course, information, like cheese, is not just information. It is always gathered for certain reasons, from different perspectives, and reported in particular contexts, which alters the nature and the meaning of the information. Failing to recognize this can lead to uninformed decisions, premature closures of discussions, the stifling of innovative ideas, and even seductive political traps. In short, information is not divinely conceived; it has all the stains and scars of distinctively human hands.

Myth 5 — Information is knowledge.

Information does not always translate into understanding. Knowledge goes beyond the facts; it connects and explains them. The "facts" often contradict one another. Knowledge seeks to reconcile seemingly disparate findings. Rosalind Franklin studied the DNA molecule at Kings College in London during the 1950s. She was the first person to take clear X-ray-diffraction photographs of the B form of DNA. Yet she is not the one who won the Nobel prize. It was Crick and Watson who won the prize. The photograph was the final piece of the DNA puzzle. Crick and Watson put it all together to form a working model of the DNA molecule (Watson, 1968). Franklin had information, exceedingly important information, but Crick and Watson went further. They transformed information into knowledge. The elegant simplicity of the DNA structure, with all its implications for explaining sexual reproduction, controlling disease, and genetic engineering, unfolded because Watson and Crick knew how to use information. Crick reflected on why others did not discover the DNA structure:

> They missed the alpha helix because of that reflection! You see. And the fact that they didn't put the peptide bond in right. The point is that evidence can be unreliable, and therefore you should use as little of it as you can. And when we confront problems *today,* we're in exactly the same situation. We have three or four bits of data, we don't know which one is reliable, so we say, now if we discard that one and assume it's wrong — even though we have no evidence that it's wrong — then we can look at the *rest* of the data and see if we can make sense of that. And that's what we do *all the time.* I mean, people don't realize that not only can data be wrong in science, it can be *misleading.* There isn't such a thing as a hard fact when you're trying to discover something. It's only afterwards that the facts become hard. (quoted in Judson, 1979, pp. 113-114)

In short, not only is it important to have information but also to know when to discard it.

In a similar vein, part of the task of a manager is to weigh the evidence, to evaluate the information. All information is not equally relevant. Some crucial data may even by missing or unattainable. Assembling information is not enough. Knowledge is not some library file. Plans, theories, and models need to be set forth to organize the information. Hence, the data begins to "make sense," to have meaning. Tests can be conducted, projections made.

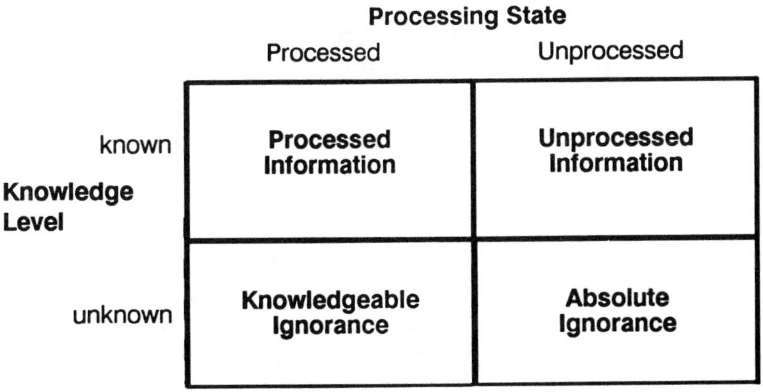

Processing State

Figure 4.1 Information Perspectives

Such are the duties of the manager. It is not enough to have a lot of facts. The wise manager seeks a more encompassing perspective by linking fact to fact, like some kind of conceptual scaffolding. Those who produce information are important, but the prizes usually go to those who can produce knowledge.

Perspective on Information

Effectively managing information involves many perplexities. Managers as well as organizations face two fundamental but related questions: (1) What is available? and (2) Has it been processed? Figure 4.1 illustrates the relationship between these two questions.

Processed Information

The data that has been assimilated, attended to, and duly noted falls in this quadrant. The letter that has just been carefully read or the conversation that has been completed are common examples of processed information. Typically when someone says they have been informed, they mean that they know something they did not know before.

For the manager or organization overloaded with information it may seem that merely processing the information is half the battle. Perhaps. But even at this stage numerous difficulties can occur. Decisions have to be made about who else needs to be informed and when. Furthermore, the information may be too ambiguous to be useful. During a battle simulation conducted at a U.S.

Army training base a scout squad reported encountering "a considerable enemy force." But the battalion commander felt he could not redeploy his troops until he had more specific information. By the time his question was forwarded through the proper channels, the squad was "overrun by enemy forces." Simply processing information is no guarantee that a useful understanding will result. Clearly, the issues of timeliness and ambiguity play a serious role in defining an effective information dissemination system. The consequences of ignoring these two factors can be deadly not only on military but also corporate battlefields.

Unprocessed Information

The reports that go unread, the studies not examined, and the unreturned telephone calls are just a few examples of the unprocessed information quadrant. The information is available but, for whatever reason, is never consumed. Difficulties obviously can ensue. The result can be, and usually is, a poor decision. Of particular concern is that management frequently is held responsible for creating or having information that is not used. During many product liability trials there inevitably is some report unearthed that reveals an internal study that predicted a possible safety problem with a product feature. One of the most tragic examples involved the crash of the *Challenger* space shuttle. The President's investigative committee found a variety of reports that indicated potential problems with O-rings that were believed to be the cause of the crash (McConnell, 1987). Yet, apparently, these reports never reached those who made the critical launch decisions. In other words, there was information available but it was unprocessed by key decision makers.[1]

This kind of difficulty points out the critical process of information filtering that occurs at all levels of the organization, from manager to employees and vice versa. Raw information does not come with identification tags saying, "I'm important" or "I'm believable." There may be clues and signs, but there can be no guarantees. For example, the United States has spent billions of dollars on space exploration but only 10% of that information ever gets analyzed. One result: scientists could have learned about the threat to the ozone layer 10 years earlier if the data from the Nimbus 7 satellite had been fully analyzed (Kneale, 1988). Managers, like scientists, have to use their intuition to determine what is really important. This is what makes information management so difficult. The complete answer does not lie in consuming as much information as possible. Rather, the answer lies in more effective filtering mechanisms.

Knowledgeable Ignorance

Managers who know a lot of facts might be considered intelligent, but those who also know what they don't know are considered wise. The knowledgeable ignorance quadrant represents the known unknowns. The manager or the organization realizes that something is missing. Knowing the right questions, even if the answers are elusive, blazes the trail to enlightenment. Saul Wurman (1989) who "reinvented the guidebook" and restructured the Pacific Bell SMART Yellow Pages said: "My expertise is my ignorance. I ask the obvious questions, the ones everyone else is embarrassed to ask because they are so obvious" (p. 45). As a youngster Albert Einstein asked, "What would it be like to ride on a beam of light?" Later in life he provided the answer: The theory of relativity. Jacob Bronowski (1973) said, "the hardest part is not to answer, but to conceive the question. The genius of men like Newton and Einstein lies in that: they ask transparent, innocent questions which turn out to have catastrophic answers" (p. 247). The ability to question wisely is a powerful intellectual tool that is useful to the scientist as well as the manager.

One of the dilemmas facing managers is that so much of their time is consumed in processing the information already generated that they have very little time to devote to asking the really penetrating questions. An illusion can build up about already having enough information. Walter Wriston (1986), former chief executive at Citicorp, put it this way: "Since we are the prisoners of what we know, often we are unable to even imagine what we don't know" (p. 66). But regardless of the reasons why, the difficult questions still need to be asked. While the answers may not be easily unveiled, at least a more sober view of a situation or decision may be taken, and perhaps a brilliant insight or theory may even emerge.

Absolute Ignorance

The fourth quadrant represents the traditional way in which "ignorance" is understood, the stated of being unaware. Someone who is color-blind is unaware of different colors but would *not* be thought to be ignorant of the concept of color. This is knowledgeable ignorance. Someone who has no concept of color at all would be thought of as absolutely ignorant. A frog placed in a cage surrounded by dead insects will starve to death. The frog's perceptual mechanism is wired to pick up the quick, jerky movements that live insects make. The frog quite literally does not see the dead bugs. Likewise, managers often fail to perceive certain kinds of information and are completely unaware of their ignorance.

There is an old saying that "Fish were the last to discover water." Organizations and managers are in the same boat. Some problems or opportunities are so close that they often go undiscovered. For example, during one communication assessment we found that many of the female employees felt sexism existed in the upper layer of management. In fact, in this company of 150 employees there was only one woman manager. When we brought up the issue the CEO said: "I can't believe this. I thought the girls were happy here." Clearly here was a case of management being absolutely ignorant of the sexist sea in which they swam.

Implications

Three noteworthy implications emerge from this simple perspective on information management.

First, each quadrant suggests a unique set of challenges for the manager. In the Processed Information category, questions of timeliness and ambiguity arise. In the Unprocessed Information quadrant, the issues of how to manage overload and properly filter information arise. The Knowledgeable Ignorance quadrant suggests that managers need to be concerned with how to find the gaps in their understanding. The Absolute Ignorance quadrant challenges managers to effectively deal with uncertainty.

When dealing with information dissemination difficulties one of the first tasks of the manager is to isolate the kind of problem that exists. By determining the quadrant where the difficulties occur, effective solutions can be generated. It is not enough to define the problem as one of information flow. For instance, training employees to write more precise memos (Quadrant 1 problem) will not really impact a problem concerning the improper networking of information (Quadrant 2 problem). Effective remedies can not be given without proper diagnosis (see Table 4.1).

Second, information management must always be viewed from the unique perspective of the individual person or department. One person's "knowledgeable ignorance" may be another's "processed information." The key in this situation is then to find a way to connect the two people. What may be one kind of problem at one level of the organization may be another kind of problem at another level. For instance, one sector of the company may be operating in absolute ignorance of certain information while another department may have the knowledge but does not know who really needs it or how to communicate it.

Third, there are second order concerns implied by this approach to information management. That is, questions are raised about the mix of

Table 4.1 Organizational Concerns with Information

Category	Appropriate Questions
Processed Information	Does the information arrive on time?
	Does the information arrive at the right place?
	Is the information understandable?
	Is the information specific enough?
Unprocessed Information	Has the proper information been transmitted?
	Has too much information been transmitted? Too little?
	Has the information been screened effectively?
	Has nonuseful information been discarded?
	Do employees have access to needed information?
Knowledgeable Ignorance	Have the proper questions been asked?
	Have the "holes" in the information fabric been detected?
	Do we know where to find the answers?
	Can we prioritize our information needs?
Absolute Ignorance	Is there some mechanism built into the system so that certain information is randomly encountered?
	Are new perspectives being sought?
	Are new sources of information being tapped?
	Should consultants be hired to expose the organization to new trends?
Second Order Concerns	In which quadrant do the major organizational concerns lie?
	What is the proper mix of organizational strategies used to cope with the issues above? (i.e. Should the organization be more concerned with absolute ignorance or unprocessed information?)

strategies in coping with information. Where should the organization place its emphasis? Gathering more information? Processing it more effectively? Asking more questions? The central question concerns the design of the entire information management system. While the questions within each quadrant are important, it is also important to determine the general thrust of the system.

Managing information effectively is a truly monumental task. Yet, effective information management lies in supervising the knowledge base as well as the processing mechanisms. To do this, a manager must deal with a number of conflicting forces or tension points. To those issues we now turn.

Tension Points

Management of any kind involves reconciling conflicting forces. Information management is no exception. Some of the more vexing difficulties are reviewed below.

Today Versus Tomorrow

In most cases if information does not arrive on time it is useless. For instance, with a four-month lead time, one university book store manager sent book orders to publishers for various textbooks, only to find out one day before the semester began that one of the books was out of print. The professor was out of luck. Employees often voice this kind of complaint. My data base shows that many employees are not highly satisfied with the timeliness of information (see Figure 4.2). One employee put it this way: "More up-to-date information would help. I hate to get important information through the grapevine."

There are many potential causes of the problem. Sometimes it is just carelessness. More often, other duties assume greater priority than passing along information. Inefficient channels often are used. Some corporations have so many screening devices for messages that this inevitably slows down the process.

Overload Versus Underload

One of the most overwhelming problems facing managers is how to deal with the massive quantities of information that inundate most organizations. The relative ease and low cost with which information can be transmitted through new electronic processes will make the problem even more acute in the future. The consequences of overload can be debilitating: stress, poor decisions, and lower productivity. Underload can be equally problematic and the results often are the same.

Theoretically, communication load "is based on the rate and complexity of communication inputs to an individual" (Farace, Monge, & Russell, 1977, p. 100). A hotel clerk who takes numerous room reservations has a communication load based on a high rate of messages that are low in complexity. The actual load of the clerk may be the same as a manager who deals solely with designing a compensation package, which would involve a low rate but high complexity. Some people can deal more easily with complexity, others with a high volume of fairly routine messages. Or, as Farace, Monge, and

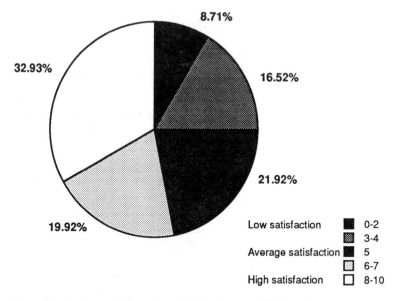

Figure 4.2 Employee Satisfaction with Timelessness of Information

Russell (1977) put it, "One person's overload may well be another's under-load" (p. 101).

This and That

What information should be provided to employees? Should information be open to all or available only on a "need-to-know" basis? There are dangers at either extreme. Organizations have reasonable and legitimate needs to protect certain information, even from their own employees. Trade secrets can be compromised if too many people know. Supposedly, only a handful of people know the formula for Coca-Cola. But inundating employees with information can create overload problems. Processing information takes time which, in turn, means there is less time to spend on the primary tasks. Indeed, one of the values of specialization is that everyone does not need to process all the information. Rather, specialists must become sensitive to the information needs of their colleagues and not burden them with unnecessary information.

A "need-to-know" policy can be stifling and often is a formal excuse to exercise excessive managerial control. Even the concept of "need to know" is somewhat slippery. Clearly, information that is needed to perform job duties lies within those parameters. But even this seems murky at times. For instance, one employee reported that he was not informed that adjustments were made on his paper cutting machine by operators on the previous shift. The result: the employee's hand was almost cut off. The previous operator's explanation: "I didn't think anyone else needed to know." Moreover, the critical assumption behind many "need-to-know" policies is that management is in a position to know what everyone needs to know. Many employees, particularly in the high-tech field, have a greater degree of expertise for their particular jobs than their managers. Hence, the employee is frequently in a better position to judge what information is really needed to do the job. To alleviate this problem, many organizations have developed mechanisms that allow for employees to provide justification for receiving certain information. However, this justification process can raise the cost so greatly, due to the time and effort required, that the information is never requested.

Our research has shown that employees complain most frequently about not being informed of changes, decision making, and the future plans of the organization. Part of the problem is that employees naturally assume that those in management know about changes far in advance. This is not always the case. Another part of the problem is that employees seem to have an insatiable desire for information. In two communication assessments we asked employees to indicate how much information they currently received on a wide range of subjects versus the amount of information they wanted to receive. Remarkably, on every topic area the employees wanted more information. Other researchers have found similar trends (Goldhaber, Yates, Porter, & Lesniak, 1978). Employees are naturally curious about their organization, which to some extent is healthy. But it is important to distinguish between desires and needs. Providing all the information employees desire may prove to be costly and ultimately debilitating to the organization. Therefore, priority must be given to certain types of information. Certainly, information about decision making, job-related matters, and answers to employee inquiries rank high on the list. One survey found that employees were highly interested in the organization's future plans, productivity improvement, and personnel policies (Foehrenback & Rosenberg, 1982). Perhaps this list (see Table 4.2) provides some target areas in selecting information dissemination strategies.

Formal Versus Informal

Every organization has two basic information networks: formal and informal. These networks may complement, conflict, or work independently of one another. Ideally the most important information comes through formal

Table 4.2 What Subjects Are of Most and Least Interest To Employees?

Rank	Subject	% Very Interested/Interested
1	Organizational plans for the future	95.3
2	Productivity improvements	90.3
3	Personnel policies and practices	89.8
4	Job-related information	89.2
5	Job advancement opportunities	87.9
6	Effect of external events on my job	87.8
7	How my job fits into the organization	85.4
8	Operations outside of my department or division	85.1
9	How we're doing versus the competition	83.0
10	Personnel changes and promotions	81.4
11	Organizational community involvement	81.3
12	Organizational stand on current issues	79.5
13	How the organization uses its profits	78.4
14	Advertising/promotional plans	77.2
15	Financial results	76.4
16	Human interest stories about other employees	70.4
17	Personal news (birthdays, anniversaries, etc.)	57.0

* SOURCE: J. Foehrenbach & K. Rosenberg, "How Are We Doing?" *Journal of Communication Management*, *12* (1), 7.
NOTE: ** These findings parallel a follow-up study (Foehrenbach & Goldfarb, 1990). Unfortunately, the complete results are not available.

channels. Sadly, this rarely is the case. Employees often express dissatisfaction with receiving news from the grapevine and, in some organizations, even report that this is the major communication channel. One survey of over 45,000 employees in 40 organizations found the grapevine to be the second most frequent source of information. But the grapevine was ranked last (15th) in terms of the most preferred (see Table 4.3). Supervisors were the most preferred. Moreover, numerous communication assessments have shown that the grapevine is the only information channel from which employees desire to receive less instead of more information.

Why, then, is the grapevine used so frequently? First, it is amazingly fast. One employee said news "spreads like wildfire" in her organization. This is not uncommon. In one communication assessment, airline employees rated the timeliness of five communication channels. The grapevine clearly was the "winner" (see Figure 4.3). Second, informal channels provide outlets when formal channels are clogged. There rarely are information vacuums in organizations. When crises occur or changes are pending, employees usually seek out any information that helps reduce their uncertainty. Moreover, the grapevine may satisfy affiliation needs not met through formal channels.

Table 4.3 Employee Preferences for Source of Information

Rank	% Major Info. Source	Source	Preferred Rank	% Preferred Source
1	59	Immediate Supervisor	1	90
2	42	Grapevine	14	9
3	38	Bulletin Boards	8	38
4	37	Small Group Meetings	2	70
5	33	Employee Handbook	5	46
6	28	Large Group Meetings	4	49
7	29	Company-Wide Employee Publication	10	36
8	22	Orientation Programs	6	45
9	18	Local Employee Publication	7	41
10	17	Annual Business Report To Employees	9	37
11	15	Top Executives	3	62
12	15	Mass Media	13	12
13	14	Upward Communications Programs	11	29
14	13	Audiovisual	11	29

SOURCE: Adapted from: J. Foehrenbach & S. Goldfarb, "Employee Communication in the '90s: Greater Expectations," *Communication World* (May-June, 1990) 7.

Third, the grapevine carries a great deal of information. In one organization, employees reported hearing about "everything" through the grapevine including promotions, salary adjustments, layoffs, and merit raises. This smorgasbord of information provides a virtual feast for the curious employee. Finally, despite the fact that most employees distrust the grapevine, it tends to be fairly accurate. A number of researchers have shown accuracy figures of 80% to 90% for information gleaned from the grapevine (Davis, 1972).

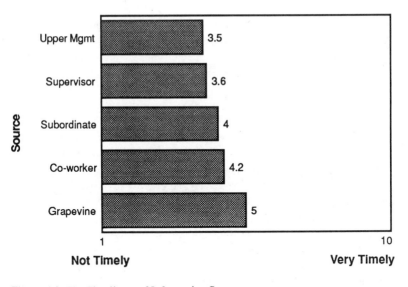

Figure 4.3 The Timeliness of Information Sources

The problem, of course, is that even a small error can have dramatic consequences.

When informal channels are overused, poor quality information can circulate throughout the organization. When this occurs, all the inevitable consequences spring forth: unwarranted anxiety, poor decisions, low morale, perceptions of favoritism, and lower productivity. Moreover, the overuse of informal channels by management may send powerful secondary, albeit unintended, messages to employees like, "We don't have time to communicate with you," which translates into "We don't respect you enough to provide you with formal information." While employees tend to understand the time constraints under which management operates, they may still have a feeling of discontent. Parents sometimes will withhold information from their children, but employees expect to be respectfully treated like adults. There is no more effective way to send this message than through honest, official, and formal communication.

Up Versus Down

The law of gravity does not always seem to apply to information flow in organizations. Information held at the top of the organizational hierarchy does not always filter down. And some information held in the lower echelons of the hierarchy shows an exceptional buoyancy in reaching the top, almost like defying the laws of gravity. But all information is filtered in some way.

Job assignments, directives, and procedures are the typical messages that flow downward through the organization. Employees usually express the most concern over not receiving information about the rationale behind decisions, policies, or directives. Feedback about performance is another classic difficulty. Moreover, in the organizational hierarchy the further a person is removed from the perceived source of information, the more acute the employee concern. Thus employees typically express the least satisfaction, both in terms of quality and quantity, with information from top management. The depth of concern over the general effectiveness of downward communication was reflected in a survey of 611 executives of Fortune 500 companies by Forum Corporation. The results indicate that 82% of the CEOs believed the corporate strategy was clearly understood by those employees who needed to know; yet only 68% of the chief operating officers felt the same way ("CEOs Are," 1989).

Upward communication is plagued by many of the same difficulties. Requests for clarification and suggestions are the typical kinds of messages upwardly communicated. Researchers have recently confirmed what Sir Winston Churchill (1931) long ago noted:

> The temptation to tell a Chief in a great position the things he most likes to hear is one of the commonest explanations of mistaken policy. Thus the outlook of the leader on whose decision fateful events depend is usually far more sanguine than the brutal facts admit. (p. 673)

Sending the good news up is only natural for those who wish to get ahead in the organization. "This tendency is so strong that subordinates who do not trust their superior are willing to suppress unfavorable information even if they know that such information is useful for decision making" (O'Reilly, Chatman, & Anderson, 1987, p. 612). Therefore, managers should be wary of excessively glowing reports.

On the other hand, many managers need to develop greater responsiveness to requests for information from their subordinates. Indeed, a frequent complaint of employees is that their questions go unanswered or that responses are untimely or too vague. One employee for an airline related the following incident:

> About a month ago, I spoke to my supervisor when I heard that one agent and not the whole group was informed about a new procedure. He said he was going to send a letter to all agents. But we are still waiting.

Clearly, if these information needs can be efficiently met, then employee frustration can be decreased and productivity increased.

Fact Versus Theory

The quintessential detective, Sherlock Holmes, said in his first adventure, *A Scandal in Bohemia*, "I have no data yet. It is a capital mistake to theorize before one has data. Insensibly one begins to twist facts to suit theories, instead of theories to suit facts" (Doyle, 1978, p. 13). In contrast, the quintessential physicist, Albert Einstein, felt that if the evidence did not agree with the theory, then the evidence must be faulty. Such a perspective might explain why Einstein slept in peace and confidence the night his general theory of relativity was being experimentally tested (Clark, 1971). But what does a physicist's ruminations or Conan Doyle's imagination have to do with the world of management? In short, a lot.

Managers are faced with an unavoidable tension between the "facts" and the "theory." The facts can contradict the strategic plan (the theory) and vice versa. The market surveys (the facts) showed there was no market for the Xerox machine (Jacobson & Hillkirk, 1986). Yet, in theory, such a device seemed like a sure winner. The theory clearly was right, the "facts" incorrect. But sometimes the theory is faulty. A tenacious belief in the theory despite evidence to the contrary can be disastrous. In theory, the Sargent York tank should have been a good weapon. Even after repeated evidence of holes in the theory, more money was spent on the project. In the end, the tank design was abandoned. The net loss: $1.8 billion. The facts were right, the theory faulty (Biddle, 1986).

One of the great ironies is that often the more money spent on a project, the more credible the idea becomes, regardless of the "evidence." The battle cry becomes, "It must be good, we paid a lot for it," or "We can't be wrong; after all, we spent so much time on it." The implicit but incorrect assumption is that money or time spent translates into theory confirmed. The real reason is that no one wants to admit that a mistake has been made. The same faulty reasoning can explain an overdependence on the evidence. Not only are money, time and effort tied up with our theories but also passions, values, and reputations.

Which should the manager trust? The theory? The facts? There are no easy answers to that question. As a starting point, managers need to keep an objective distance from both the evidence and theories. But that is difficult. Perhaps, the only safe course is to have a clear sense of the nature of theory and proof. Two important notions should be mentioned.

First, evidence is gathered and generated that inherently reflects a bias. There always are more questions, more facts that can be generated than can be possibly answered or utilized. Thus choices are made about what information is and is not important to generate. But what is reported both blinds and enlightens. Sometimes the difficulty is not that the wrong answers have been found but that the wrong questions have been asked. Perhaps the marketing analysts for Xerox asked the wrong questions, the wrong people, or both.

Second, a good theory has a simplicity, an elegance, and even a beauty about it. Scientists have long marveled at the simple elegance of the DNA molecule or even the theory of relativity. Einstein even dismissed certain ideas because they were not "beautiful enough." Likewise, business plans, strategies, and designs that are theoretically sound have a certain elegance and simplicity about them. Steven Jobs commented about the design plan for the Macintosh computer:

> If you read Apple's first brochure, the headline was "Simplicity is the Ultimate Sophistication." What we meant by that was that when you first attack a problem it seems really simple because you don't understand it. Then when you start to really understand it, you come up with these very complicated solutions because it's really hairy. Most people stop there. But a few people keep burning the midnight oil and finally understand the underlying principles of the problem and come up with an elegantly simple solution for it. But very few people go the distance to get there. ("Interview," 1984, p. 60)

The wise manager, of course, goes that distance.

Hard Versus Soft

Information comes in a variety of forms. Corporate decisions are increasingly based on "hard data," or quantitative output. Statistical decision making has become the vogue. While a useful tool, the hard approach has its limitations. Music cannot really be understood or appreciated through statistical analyses. Likewise, a problem cannot be fully understood or an opportunity realized with information gleaned from a spiritless set of statistics. Few people appreciate the rich wealth of information that lies silently at their fingertips, like some obscure composer's score waiting to be discovered. In sum, the wise manager listens to the right brain as well as the left.

One of the most potent ways to understand any phenomena is to examine the metaphors used to describe it. Jonathan Miller (1978) notes that great strides were made in understanding how the human heart works when the dominant metaphor changed from a furnace to a pump. This switch in perspective opened a new realm of explanations, theories, and treatments. Metaphors make reasonable what was heretofore unreasonable; they simplify the complex, provide a structure for the experience of phenomena, and highlight key attributes and obscure others. After all, the human heart looks no more like a pump than a furnace. But there is a price. Different conceptions go unseen. Old visions are eclipsed by the new. Hence, unmasking the dominant metaphor reveals both the strengths and weaknesses of any particular conception and the subtle way in which a metaphor structures information and knowledge.

The organizational environment offers a cornucopia of captivating metaphors (e.g., Morgan, 1986). The military metaphor is one of the more predominant. "Orders" are given and "carried out." If not, the "troops are reprimanded" for "insubordination." This metaphor, a favorite of Arrow managers, naturally underscores the importance of the chain of command and stresses hierarchal relationships between the "ranks." Consequently, messages are "transferred" like "supplies" and information is treated like a commodity. The favorite organizational metaphor of the Circuit manager is the family. Difficulties arise when the "lines" of communication are not "open." Families resolve conflicts by "talking through their differences," and all differences in a family are reconcilable. After all, one cannot be "discharged" from the family like in the army.

The same type of metaphoric analysis can be applied to a whole range of other organizational practices. One telemarketing company had a room in which sales calls were regularly monitored by management. Employees referred to it as the "spy room." The image was completed with certain "spies" on the staff and "a need-to-know" communication policy. Amazingly, when the corporate executives were told about the metaphor they simply laughed and dismissed it as trivial. But such characterizations revealed both the intensity and depth of employees' feelings; they felt deeply mistrusted by management. If taken seriously, this captivating metaphor could have been more useful to management than any detailed analysis of an employee survey.

Hiemstra (1983) has perceptively noted that information technology is heavily laden with metaphoric language. Some regard the technology as "magical," which is indicated in comments like, "It works wonders," "It's so incredible," or "It's amazing; I don't understand how it works." Others see the technology as a "toy" and speak accordingly: "I like to play with it," or "It's like a game." To a large extent how employees approach the new technology will depend on the imagery associated with it. Some people may be willing to play with a "toy," while they believe it is impossible to learn "magic."

This is not to argue that any of these metaphors are wrong or inappropriate. In fact, every organization has operative metaphors. Rather, the point is that the unforeseen consequences of an undetected metaphor can be a narrowing of perspective in which a potentially rich source of information is unheeded or a whole realm of possibilities go unrecognized. We shape our metaphors and, after that, they shape us. For instance, a "family" may not think of firing anyone but it may be the only solution. Likewise, an organization dominated by a military metaphor probably would reprimand a disgruntled employee rather than seek to "foster an employee's growth" as in a family organization. While most managers pay little or no attention to the subtle workings of the imagery, the wise manager recognizes the need for both "hard" and "soft" information.

Strategic Principles

The dilemmas discussed above present a complex challenge to managers. There are no simple solutions. Rather the manager must be guided by a series of fundamental principles.

Principle 1 – The more links in the communication chain, the more likely that information passed along the chain will be distorted.

The child at the end of the line in the game of telephone receives the least accurate and usually the briefest message. Organizations are no different, except the results can be more tragic. Indeed, on a cold January morning, the civilized world was shocked by the fiery disaster that befell the space shuttle *Challenger*. The television pictures recorded in gruesome detail what the mind could not comprehend. In due course, the sorrow and grief gave way to inquiry and investigation. There really was one central but tough question: Was the disaster the price of innovation or carelessness?

There may never be a definitive answer. Perhaps "carelessness" as defined in hindsight is always part of the innovative process. Yet the commission did find flaws – fatal ones. One of the critical findings was that messages sent up the chain of command became severely distorted. In particular, engineers from both Rockwell and Thiokol were deeply alarmed about the impact of ice on the shuttle launch. Consider the following sequence of exchanges:

(1) Rockwell engineers reported to their superiors that they did not have a proper data base on how the shuttle would perform at temperatures below freezing. They concluded that the situation created an "unquantifiable hazard."

(2) Two Rockwell vice presidents reported to NASA that "Rockwell cannot 100% assure that it is safe to fly."

(3) The director of the National Space Transportation System reported to his team that "Rockwell did not ask or insist that we *not* launch." He "felt reasonably confident that the launch should proceed."

(4) NASA's associate administrator, who was in charge of the final decision, stated: "I never thought the ice presented a serious safety problem." (McConnell, 1987)

This sad tale vividly illustrates the fundamental communication principle about what happens to a message as it is passed from person to person. The distortion occurs quite naturally because people have different responsibilities, beliefs, and concerns. Details are omitted. Some are highlighted. Inferences become facts. Even something as permanent as a written memo can be interpreted differently at various levels of an organization. Priorities can shift. Nuances are lost. Indeed, NASA felt so much pressure for a launch that they actively discouraged any messages that might call for a delay. Pace and Boren (1973) sum up the situation aptly: "Messages in serial reproduction, like water in a great river, change through losses, gains, absorptions, and combinations along the route from the headwaters to their final destination" (p. 137).

Principle 2 — The form the information assumes often can be as important as the substance.

Images are powerful communication vehicles. They can summarize or capture a great deal of information easily and quickly. The complex can be made simple. Some information simply cannot be made meaningful without the use of imagery. There are two principle uses of imagery: to personalize information, and to summarize quantitative information.

The Tropicana ad in Figure 4.4 is an excellent example of how imagery can be used to personalize information. There are many ways to state the advertisement's essential message that "Tropicana orange juice is fresh." An explanation of how the juice is extracted from oranges is one alternative. While such an approach may prove enlightening, it fails to arouse the senses. Perhaps, various consumers could testify as to the freshness of Tropicana. Still the emotions are not aroused. The beauty of the straw and orange

Figure 4.4 The Effective use of Imagery

imagery is that everyone can relate to it. Clearly, no one can use a straw to extract juice from an orange. No one, that is, except Tropicana. Through the imagery, consumers can see, feel, and taste the freshness of Tropicana juice.[2] The image is vivid.

Images can be created verbally as well. For example, Teddy Roosevelt's response to his critics, "I have about as much desire to annex more islands as a boa-constrictor has to swallow a porcupine," conveys something more than a simple denial (Morris, 1979, p. 13). It has power and verve. There is no doubt where he stands on this issue. In short, the well-conceived image can often be more captivating than reams of statistical data or a finely honed argument.

The graphic display of quantitative data is another powerful communicator of information. In his marvelous treatise, *The Visual Display of Quantitative Data,* Edward R. Tufte notes:

> Modern data graphics can do much more than simply substitute for small statistical tables. At their best, graphics are instruments for reasoning about quantitative information. Often the most effective way to describe, explore, and summarize a set of numbers—even a very large set—is to look at pictures of those numbers. Furthermore, of all methods for analyzing and communicating statistical information, well-designed data graphics are usually the simplest and at the same time the most powerful. (1983, p. 1)

For instance, three scientists developed one graphic (see Figure 4.5) depicting the results of over 200 experiments assessing the thermal conductivity of copper (Ho, Powell, & Liley, 1974). There is probably no better way to summarize the results of that much research.

The prevalence of microcomputer software makes the use of graphics more feasible than in the past. Yet, as with any powerful tool, graphics as well as imagery can be misused. There is some evidence that shows that using graphics that are not accompanied by precise figures can actually undermine managerial confidence in decision making (Sullivan, 1988). The form can actually obscure the substance. The sword cuts both ways. Information of import can be overlooked and the trivial can appear important. The wise manager recognizes this while still knowing that the form of the information may be as important as the substance. Or as Isadora Duncan, the famous dancer, once said: "If I could tell you what it meant there would be no point in dancing it" (Comstock, 1974, p. 226).

Principle 3—Who sends the information and where it originates may be as important as the substance.

Like it or not, every message has a kind of credibility tag attached to it that determines to a large extent how that message will be treated. Since there are more messages than people, credibility provides an efficient screening mechanism. All messages emanating from a single source can be lumped together for assessment. In essence, credibility acts as a labeling system tagging messages with, "PAY ATTENTION TO ME," "ignore me," or "I May Be True."

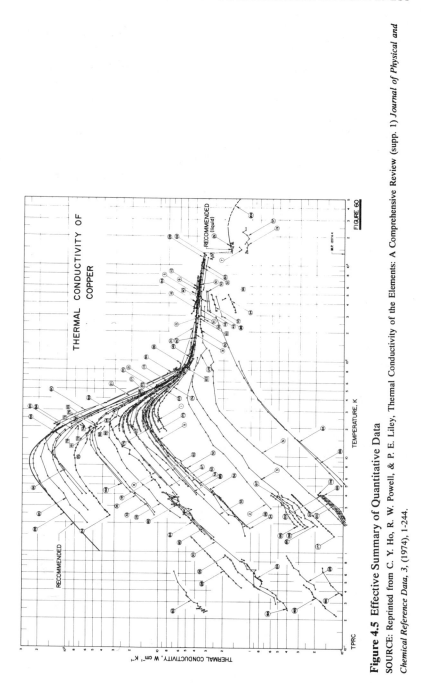

Figure 4.5 Effective Summary of Quantitative Data

SOURCE: Reprinted from C. Y. Ho, R. W. Powell, & P. E. Liley, Thermal Conductivity of the Elements: A Comprehensive Review (supp. 1) *Journal of Physical and Chemical Reference Data, 3,* (1974), 1-244.

For example, Albert Einstein, at the urgings of his colleagues, wrote his famous letter to President Roosevelt encouraging the development of the atomic bomb. Einstein's prestige as a scientist assured that the letter would be considered at the highest levels of government. Others might have presented the same message, but it would not have had the same impact or may have never reached the president. The "Einstein tag" on the message read, "HIGHLY IMPORTANT INFORMATION, READ ME!" Students will dutifully listen as the teacher reflects on the importance of having a professional-looking resume. But when a personnel director for IBM relates the same message, the students do more than nod their heads. Messages cannot be separated from people, for the source forms part of the context.

On the other hand, some messages never get transmitted because of who gathers the information. One of the top salespersons of a large pharmaceutical corporation quit her job in disgust over the practices of her immediate supervisor's boss. During the exit interview, when she was asked why she quit the job, she forthrightly told of her legitimate grievances about the situation. But the information never reached the personnel office or the people who could do something about the problem. The reason: the immediate supervisor conducted the interview and he had to pass the report to the very person at issue. On the exit interview form, under the question about why the employee was leaving, the supervisor wrote "Personal Reasons."

Principle 4 — The way information is organized significantly alters the meaning gleaned from it.

Different relationships are highlighted depending on how the information is organized. For example, the differences between employee performance ratings are underscored in Figure 4.6a. Yet, using the same data, all the employees are seen as above average (see Figure 4.6b). In Figure 4.6c no real pattern seems to emerge from the same data. But displaying the information in the form seen in Figure 4.6d almost begs the viewer to draw a conclusion. The structure of the information acts like the mirrors at carnivals; one stretches the reflection up and down, the other side-to-side. It's the same image but different parts are accentuated, causing the spectator to have dramatically different perceptions.

Principle 5 — The quality of the information decreases as the focus reaches beyond past experiences.

When the maps of one age are compared to those of another, there are always radical differences. When first constructing a map, the information is

A

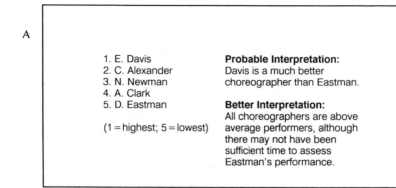

1. E. Davis
2. C. Alexander
3. N. Newman
4. A. Clark
5. D. Eastman

(1 = highest; 5 = lowest)

Probable Interpretation:
Davis is a much better
choreographer than Eastman.

Better Interpretation:
All choreographers are above
average performers, although
there may not have been
sufficient time to assess
Eastman's performance.

B

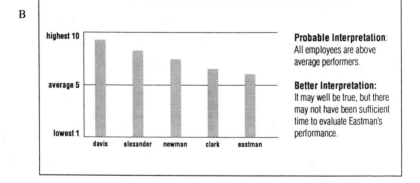

Probable Interpretation:
All employees are above
average performers.

Better Interpretation:
It may well be true, but there
may not have been sufficient
time to evaluate Eastman's
performance.

C

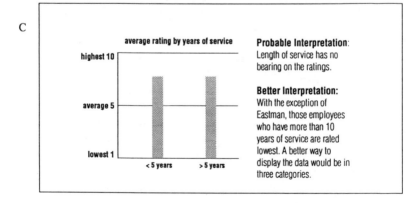

Probable Interpretation:
Length of service has no
bearing on the ratings.

Better Interpretation:
With the exception of
Eastman, those employees
who have more than 10
years of service are rated
lowest. A better way to
display the data would be in
three categories.

Figure 4.6 Organizing the Same Information Differently

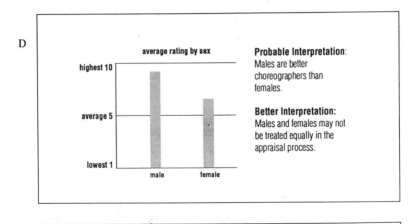

D

average rating by sex

highest 10

average 5

lowest 1

male   female

Probable Interpretation:
Males are better
choreographers than
females.

Better Interpretation:
Males and females may not
be treated equally in the
appraisal process.

E

RAW DATA

name	score	rank	yrs of service	sex	X factor
Davis	9.1	1	2.0	M	?
Alexander	8.7	2	5.5	M	?
Newman	7.3	3	15.5	F	?
Clark	6.8	4	20.5	F	?
Eastman	6.5	5	5.0	F	?

The only way to gain a true
perspective on this
information is to look at it
from a variety of angles.
Even then, there is always
some unkown X factor that
could provide further
clarification.

Figure 4.6 Continued.

sketchy. Inferences and assumptions, right or wrong, are inevitably made.
The result: inaccuracies. Through time, however, as the territories are
explored more thoroughly these inaccuracies are corrected and a more
complete and accurate pictured emerges.

Information generated in organizations is subject to the same constraints.
Budget projections for next year always are more accurate than those five
years hence. Information about potential new markets always will be more
speculative than information about established markets. Innovative practices
will be plagued by significant unknowns. Experts should be more informed
and believable in their realm of expertise than in areas beyond their expertise.
Jane Fonda may be able to tell us about acting, but her information about
foreign policy probably is no better than the average layperson's. In short,
all information is not created equal. It must be analyzed and judged. The

further the information lies in the realm of the "terra incognita" or the unexplored regions, the greater the degree of scrutiny required.

Principle 6 — A variety of factors impact an individual's information load.

Three factors are particularly noteworthy. First, the way messages are channeled influences load. Figure 4.7 shows one communication network or funneling device found in many organizations. In fact, when Jimmy Carter was president, the White House was structured in this way ("How Jimmy's," 1977). The potential for overload in the central position is high, while in the other positions the problem may be an information underload.

Second, the physical setting can alter the load. One employee reported that her biggest improvement in productivity came when her desk was moved away from a hallway where her colleagues used to drop by "to just say hello." As a general rule, the greater possibilities for distractions, the more likely they will occur.

Third, people have unique processing capabilities that are affected by their intelligence, skill level, personality, moods, stress levels, and message characteristics. For instance, one study showed that people tend to focus on less information and fewer alternatives when under stress (Crecine, 1980). Some people naturally seem to desire a lot of information whether they actually need it not. Perhaps this need is born out of a desire to affiliate with others, build self-esteem, or simply escape boredom. The form of the information also plays a role in the load. Information in a standard or familiar format is processed more quickly than that which is new. Thus there is the propensity for employees to cling to older computer software that is decidedly inferior to newer versions.

Useful Tactics

Based on the strategic principles above, there are a wide variety of possible tactics that can be used to meet the challenges of an effective information dissemination system. Some of the more useful ideas are discussed below.

(1) Work on the details.

There are a host of seemingly minor changes that may greatly improve information processing capabilities. One group of top level managers called

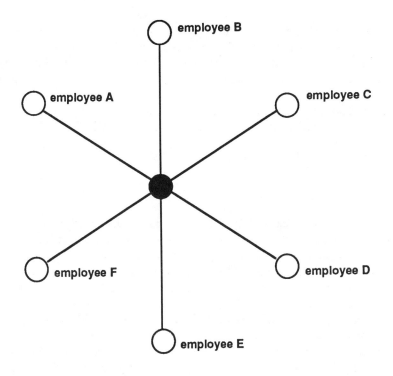

● **Information Overload**

○ **Information Underload**

Figure 4.7 Wheel Communication Network

in a consultant because they felt their meetings were not proceeding effectively. The consultant observed three meetings and made her report. Her
recommendation was simple: paint the meeting room a different color and
get new lighting. She noticed that the managers had complained in all three
meetings about the "feel" of the conference room. What was obvious to the
consultant was not so obvious to the managers. The cost of the changes were
a fraction of the consultant's fee. Amazingly, this minor change had the
desired effect.

One university had a weekly one-page publication that detailed the campus
events for that week. It was distributed in boxes located throughout the

campus. The staff was not satisfied with the readership level. Two simple changes almost doubled readership. First, some of the distribution boxes were strategically relocated. Second, every week the color of the publication was changed. Previously, the information sheet was printed on plain white paper, and students rushing through the halls could not be sure if it was new information or just last week's news. The color change from week to week provided that information in a glance. These are just two examples of how simple changes can have a dramatic effect. The list could go on, but some of the other areas to investigate are seen in Table 4.4.

(2) Realign information priorities.

As has been discussed before, employees and management often have different ideas about what information is most important. In particular, most employees express interest in the organization's future plans, personnel policies, financial goals, innovations, and decision-making processes. Accordingly, within well-defined guidelines regular communication mechanisms can be set up to insure that these information needs are met.

One approach would be to have quarterly or biannual meetings that address some of these issues. For instance, Krueger Incorporated, an office furniture manufacturer, has used one such approach with great success. Every quarter, a half-day meeting is held to review the financial progress of the organization as well as future projections. Top management, middle managers, and a rotating group of employees attend these meetings. At Chevrolet's gear and axle plant in Detroit workers are told about the costs of labor and scraps, as well as profits. "Not even the foremen would have been privy to such information at GM a few years ago. The benefits, to GM's way of thinking, outweigh any harm that might come from revealing competitive information" (Burck, 1981, p. 68). Clearly, special care must be taken in dealing with information like future plans and decision making. Management legitimately needs to have some flexibility to change when the conditions are altered and to protect against leaks of information to competitors. Yet, as these two organizations demonstrate, those concerns can be effectively managed.

(3) Develop special training programs.

One of the ways to reduce communication overload is to increase the ability of employees to process information. In particular, training in speed reading, organizational skills, and time management might prove useful. The proper training of secretaries and receptionists may also prove a useful expenditure in order to improve the efficiency of telephone communication.

Table 4.4 Increasing Efficiency of Information Use

Category	Question
Physical Setting	Can the physical setting be changed to improve information processing capabilities? For example, ergonomically designed chairs have been shown to increase employee productivity.
	Can office noise and distractions be decreased?
	Can the physical layout of the office be changed to increase or decrease certain types of information flow?
Filtering Devices	Can bulletin boards be more clearly organized? Are specific individuals solely responsible for certain boards?
	Can different types of written messages be color coded by priority or urgency level?
	Can simple screening devices be used to eliminate "junk mail"?
Technical Devises	Can software be purchased that speeds up the information flow? Building a data base of typical questions and answers may be a way to free up the time of experts so they do not spend all their time answering routine questions.[3]
	Can videotapes be used as a training devise instead of personal trainers?
	Can audio cassette tapes be used to brief employees while they drive?
	Can the phone system be made more efficient with new features?
User Behavior	Can those who desire information serve their own needs like in a library or supermarket?
	Can simple verbal reminders of meetings be used instead of memos?
	Can regularly requested information be put into a form that is more easily and efficiently disseminated, like in a pamphlet or Question/Answer sheet?

Beyond the traditional methods of training there are managerial assessment centers that emphasize monitoring actual behavior. The "in-basket" exercise is the classic example of the methods used in the assessment center. The trainee is placed at the desk of a recently departed personnel manager with an in-basket full of requests for decisions, information, and ideas. Then

Table 4.5 Questions for Information Analysis

---

* Is the information really needed by everyone one the routing lists?

* Can the number of photocopies be reduced?

* Can the decision making process be streamlined?

* How many people really need to sign off on a purchase before it is made?

* Are reports being generated that are really not needed?

---

the employee is carefully observed for three or four hours as he or she sorts through the basket. Based on a detailed analysis, the observers provide feedback to trainees about their organizational and time management skills. While the process usually proves exhausting and sometimes disheartening to the employee, the long-term results are beneficial.

(4) Conduct a thorough information analysis.

Many information overload problems are not the result of underskilled or poorly motivated workers but rather are the product of the information dissemination system. Only by conducting an in-depth analysis of how information is disseminated throughout the organization can such difficulties be discovered (see Table 4.5). While engineering the turnaround at Citicorp, Lawrence M. Small said: "We have too many people doing too much bureaucratic activity, too many studies, too many reports, too many management information systems, too many staff functions, too many unprofitable relationships" (Boyer, 1986, p. 42). Other corporations may need to take an equally hard look at current administrative practices.

Tracking down the trail of decisions or administrative procedures can be illuminating. For instance, Intel Corporation found that administrative procedures were becoming burdensome. One engineer reported that it took 12 pieces of paper and 95 administrative steps to order a $2.79 mechanical pencil. In response, the corporation conducted a detailed analysis of its own administrative processes. Like a detective,

> the company takes each administrative procedure, examines it methodically, lays it out in meticulous detail, strips off the unnecessary work, and puts it back together in a simpler, more rational manner. A form is dropped here, an authorization there, photocopies eliminated, files thrown out, a superfluous audit removed, and soon hundreds of little steps add up to gigantic stride. (Main, 1981, p. 54)

The breakthroughs come from diligence and attention to detail, rather than from flashes of brilliance, just like most police work. In this manner, Intel reduced the hiring process to 250 steps instead of the previous 364 steps. Expense accounts can now be processed in a matter of days instead of four weeks. Some jobs were even eliminated, and the net result of all their efforts was an estimated savings of $2.5 million a year.

Antiquated procedures and outdated routing lists usually are not the result of any one person's irresponsibility. Rather, the procedures just seem to have an inertia of their own, building up slowly like the sludge at the bottom of a river until the entire organizational processing capabilities become clogged and useless. Rules that at one time made perfect sense are not discarded when the situation changes. Hence, some departments still receive information they no longer desire. More attention is being paid to the rule rather than the reasoning behind the rule. In short, periodic dredgings are required in which procedures and information-flow guidelines are carefully examined in light of new contingencies.

(5) Discover and resolve problematic cycles.

Many overload and underload problems continue to occur because of patterns that feed on each other. Employees point to management as the culprit and vice versa. Managers, like employees, see only one part of the cycle and they propose solutions that perpetuate the difficulty. Only through a broader, more encompassing view can this destructive cycle be halted. Most of the time, the participants are too close and entwined in the situation to see it clearly. Perceptive outside consultants often can provide just the needed insight.

At one branch of a savings and loan, the first-line employees complained about not getting enough information about new procedures. As one teller put it, "I feel this particular office is sort of left out in the cold on many things." At another branch office some 40 miles away, employees did not complain of underload but of overload. They felt they received too much information and it tended to be confusing. In all, six branches complained of overload and four of underload. Thus the managers of these various branches were doing an uneven job of informing their employees. Or so it seemed. Interestingly, information overload was the most significant complaint of every branch manager. Upon deeper examination, the source of the difficulty became clear.

The real source of the problem was at the administrative level. Branch managers were receiving memos from one administrator saying one thing and from another saying something else. Sometimes two administrators would ask for the same information in slightly different forms. In short, the administrators in the head office did not coordinate their messages and requests for information. This trickled down to managers in the form of information overload. One of the ways to cope with the situation was to heavily screen the information, particularly ambiguous directives. Four managers did this. The other way was to provide all the information to the employees and hope they would understand it. Six managers chose this strategy. Yet, both approaches were inadequate. When the administrators were confronted with the situation, they reported that they had never talked to one another about the messages they sent to their managers. They did not know it was a problem. The supreme irony was that the administrators saw each other every day because their offices were within 20 feet of one another.

These problems are all too common. The principle is basic: difficulties at one level of the organization frequently get amplified in a variety of ways at other levels of the organization. At this savings and loan, once the messages were coordinated at the administrative level, both managers and employees had more acceptable communication loads. The important point is to gain a broad perspective and see how the situations interact with one another. Then, breaking the pattern is less difficult. Sometimes drastic solutions like reorganization are required; at other times only a minor modification is necessary.

(6) Develop a communication policy.

One of the challenges of designing an effective information dissemination system is making it flexible enough to deal with novel situations but rigid enough to discourage communication that puts redundant demands on people to provide information. There rarely is a need for the same person to continually answer the same question over and over again. On the other hand, the system should not be so rigid that it restricts truly necessary communications. Developing a communication policy is a way to effectively avoid either of these problems.

Imperial Incorporated, a company that markets nuts and bolts, developed just such a policy that is at once simple and effective. The policy avoids the problems of the Arrow management practices of overly restricting communication while simultaneously sidestepping the tendencies of Circuit managers to open wide the information flood gates. Appendix C contains the details of that policy.

Conclusion

In the past, business schools taught that organizational excellence basically consisted of the effective management of people and task. Today there is a third dimension — managing information. This makes the traditional managerial functions of planning, organizing, leading, and controlling all the more complex and difficult. Yet this may well be the single greatest challenge facing the modern organization. Information may not be tagged with nutritional labels, but wise managers learn to monitor their diets.

Notes

1. This is a decidedly different example from the decision by Ford Motor Company to seek to settle lawsuits associated with the Pinto rather than correct the problem. Ford managers obviously processed the information, but they made a decision, a poor and tragic one.

2. Grinder and Bandler (1976) have suggested that people process information in one of three primary modes: (1) visual, (2) auditory, and (3) kinesthetic. This advertisement appeals to all three modes.

3. This approach was used by a group of heart specialists who constructed a computerized bulletin board, called "St. Silicon's Hospital," that answered common medical questions (Stipp, 1986).

References

Biddle, W. (1986, September). How much bang for the buck? *Discover,* pp. 50-63.

Boyer, E. (1986, February 17). Citicorp: What the new boss is up to. *Fortune,* pp. 40-44.

Bronowski, J. (1973). *The ascent of man.* Boston: Little, Brown.

Burck, C. G. (1981, July 27). What happens when workers manage themselves. *Fortune,* pp. 62-69.

CEOs are out of touch with subordinates. (1989, August 31). *Wall Street Journal,* p. B1.

Churchill, W. S. (1931). *The world crisis.* New York: Scribner.

Clark, R. W. (1971). *Einstein.* New York: Avon.

Comstock, T. (1974). *New dimensions in dance research: Anthology and dance.* New York: Committee on Research in Dance.

Crecine, J. P. (1980). *Human information processing approaches to organization and the study of teams: Possible research directions* (Report No. R-2606-ONR). Santa Monica, CA: Rand Corporation.

Davis, K. (1972). *Human behavior at work.* New York: McGraw-Hill.

Deetz, S., & Mumby, D. K. (1985). Metaphors, information, and power. *Information and Behavior, 1,* 368-369.

Doyle, A. C. (1978). *Sherlock Holmes.* Secaucus, NJ: Castle.

Farace, R., Monge, P., & Russell, H. (1977). *Communicating and organizing.* Reading, MA: Addison-Wesley.

Foehrenbach, J., & Rosenberg, K. (1982). How are we doing? *Journal of Communication Management, 12*(1), 7.

Goldhaber, G., Yates, M., Porter, T., & Lesniak, R. (1978). The ICA communication audit: Recent findings, background, and development. *Human Communication Research, 5*(1), 81-84.

Grinder, J., & Bandler, R. (1976). *The structure of magic II.* Palo Alto, CA: Science & Behavior Books.

Hiemstra, G. (1983). You say you want a revolution? "Information technology" in organizations. In R. N. Bostrom (Ed.), *Communication yearbook 7* (pp. 802-827). Beverly Hills, CA: Sage.

Ho, C. Y., Powell, R. W., & Liley, P. E. (1974). Thermal conductivity of the elements: A comprehensive review. *Journal of Physical and Chemical Reference Data, 3*, 1-244.

How Jimmy's staff operates. (1977, April 25). *Time,* pp. 21-22.

Interview: The Macintosh design team. (1984, February). *Byte,* pp. 58-80.

Jacobson, G., & Hillkirk, J. (1986). *Xerox.* New York: Macmillan.

Judson, H. F. (1979). *The eighth day of creation.* New York: Simon & Schuster.

Kaplan, A. (1963). *The conduct of inquiry: Methodology for behavioral science.* New York: Chandler.

Kneale, D. (1988, January 12). Into the void. *Wall Street Journal,* pp. 1, 13.

Main, J. (1981, June 29). How to battle your own bureaucracy. *Fortune,* pp. 54-58.

Martin, R. G. (1983). *A hero for our time.* New York: Macmillan.

McConnell, M. (1987). *Challenger: A major malfunction.* Garden City, NY: Doubleday.

Miller, J. (1978). *The body in question.* New York: Random House.

Morgan, G. (1986). *Images of organization.* Beverly Hills, CA: Sage.

Morris, E. (1979). *The rise of Theodore Roosevelt.* New York: Coward, McCann & Geoghegan.

O'Reilly, C. A., Chatman, J. A., & Anderson, J. C. (1987). Message flow and decision making. In F. M. Jablin, L. L. Putnam, K. H. Roberts, & L. W. Porter (Eds.), *Handbook of organizational communication* (pp. 600-623). Newbury Park, CA: Sage.

Pace, W., & Boren, R. (1973). *The human transaction.* Glenview, IL: Scott, Foresman.

Stipp, D. (1986, May 22). Doc-in-a-box explains illness on computer. *Wall Street Journal,* p. 27.

Sullivan, J. J. (1988). Financial presentation format and managerial decision making. *Management Communication Quarterly, 2*(2), 194-215.

Tichy, N., & Chanon, R. (1989, September-October). Speed, simplicity, self-confidence: An interview with Jack Welch. *Harvard Business Review, 67*(5), 112-121.

Tufte, E. R. (1983). *The visual display of quantitative information.* Cheshire, CT: Graphic Press.

Watson, J. D. (1968). *The double helix.* New York: New American Library.

Wriston, W. B. (1986). The world according to Walter. *Harvard Business Review, 64*(1), 65-80.

Wurman, R. S. (1989). *Information anxiety.* New York: Doubleday.

Zaslavsky, V. (1989). Mystery in a Soviet library. In G. Wolff (Ed.), *The best American essays 1989* (pp. 279-288). New York: Ticknor & Fields.

5

Communication Channels

The medium is the message.

Marshall McLuhan

Media choice is not the simple, intuitively obvious process it may appear to be at first glance. Appropriate media choice can make the difference between effective and ineffective communication. And media choice mistakes can seriously impede successful communication — in some cases with disastrous consequences.

Trevino, Daft, & Lengel

Who has most influenced the course of history? Unanswerable? Maybe. Of course, the names of Jesus Christ, Muhammad, Buddha, Newton, and Einstein readily come to mind. Even if it were possible to construct such a list, what criteria should be used? And who would be qualified to construct such a list? Michael H. Hart (1978), a physicist and astronomer, took a stab at these intriguing questions. His answer is contained in a fascinating book titled, *The 100: A Ranking of the Most Influential Persons in History.* Disclosing who was ranked first would be like revealing the ending of an Agatha Christie mystery. So I will resist that temptation. Nevertheless, the person ranked seventh on the list would raise some eyebrows. He is a man so unfamiliar to most Westerners that few have even heard the name before. Ranked ahead of Aristotle, Marx, Einstein, Moses, Luther, Hitler, and da Vinci is the inventor of paper, Ts' ai Lun. He was an official in the Chinese imperial court around 105 A.D., and he developed the process for creating paper that we still basically use today. The plentifulness of books, magazines, newspapers is to a large extent due to the existence of Ts' ai Lun's paper process.

Before paper, communication was constrained by space and time. That is, for the most part, communication could only occur when two individuals occupied the same physical space and interacted in synchronous time periods. Paper changed all that, and along with Gutenberg's press (he ranked eighth), profoundly altered the course of history.

Paper is so commonplace that few scholars have thought deeply about its impact on society. In fact, Ts' ai Lun's name is not even mentioned in many encyclopedias, ironically a paper product. Paper was the first in a long line of communication channels that could readily be used by the masses. Telephones, bulletin boards, interoffice mail systems, employee publications, and personal computers are integral parts of the modern business. Just as many Westerners overlook Ts' ai Lun's influence, however, managers often overlook how communication technologies influence their communication.

Since messages must pass through some kind of channel, the messages are necessarily altered by the channel, just as the composition of an electrical wire affects the flow of electricity. Some attributes of the message are accentuated by the channel, while others are deemphasized. For example, written messages typically imbue a sense of finality and formality in communications that may not be intended by the sender.

Communication channels also can radically alter the organization's social structure. Certain channels restrict access to key individuals, while others encourage interactions. For instance, some executives require that all communications be put into writing. Other are more freewheeling and encourage active verbal interchanges in group meetings. In addition, the communication channels impact organizational efficiency and effectiveness. Telephone tag wastes employee time, while electronic mail has the potential to eliminate this futile game. Other new technologies will no doubt radically change the office environment in ways yet to be discovered.

The abiding challenge for the manager is how to effectively manage these communication channels. Hence, thought-provoking questions need to be asked. In what way does the communication channel impact a message? How should a manager decide on what channel to use in communicating with employees? These are the types of questions considered in this chapter.

Myths

As a starting point, the wise manager should recognize the predominant myths about disseminating information that are alive and well in most organizations.

Myth 1: More Communication = Better Communication

There is an old Belgian saying that "Lots is good, but more is better," which typifies many people's feelings about how to effectively inform others. Circuit managers are prone to this way of thinking. Accordingly, photocopies are widely distributed to people who have no interest in the information. Memos are indiscriminately sent to those who have no need or desire to be informed. Paper proliferates, files grow ever larger, but for what purpose? For whose benefit? It may reflect a desire "to keep everyone informed." Or managers may be covering their hindquarters with photocopies. Then no one can say, "How come I wasn't informed?" But there are other alternatives.

Information is not like money, more is not always better. There is an optimum amount of information that any individual can consume. Breaking that threshold is dysfunctional. One study found that during an average year, 130 billion unnecessary photocopies were made in American corporations, which accounts for about two out of every five made or $2.6 billion a year. ("Unneeded Photocopies," 1985) Indeed, one manager told me, only half in jest, that the best way to improve communication in his organization would be to blow up all the photocopy machines. There are less dramatic alternatives. Specifically targeting individuals for communication is more effective. Can individual names or departments be deleted from memo circulation or routing lists? Does everyone have to be informed of all decisions? These are the tough strategic questions that take more work than simply running off copies for everyone. But then effective communication is hard work.

Myth 2: Written Communication = Fulfilled Obligation

Those who assume that more communication is better communication frequently share a belief that once a message is written down the sender has fulfilled his or her obligation to communicate. This myth is the brother of the Arrow manager's belief that information supplied equals information consumed. The error is that just because a message is written down does not insure it will be (a) received, (b) read, and (c) understood in the way intended. Moreover, with many workers having minimal competency in reading and writing, managers may fallaciously assume that the message can be comprehended in the first place.

A manager communicating to colleagues may be able to effectively disseminate information using written communication, but may not be effective at all when communicating with others less learned. Compounding the problem is that written channels are poor vehicles for communicating feedback. The social stigma of not being able to read or even having a limited understanding of certain words precludes employees from asking for clarification. In one case a man recently promoted to a job as shipping and receiving foreman had to shelve special orders until he could discretely ask for help reading the instructions (Mikulecky, 1990). There are estimates that 60 million American adults are functionally illiterate (Casse, 1986). The wise manager is sensitive to these constraints and prudently chooses appropriate channels.

Myth 3: Informing = Persuading

One distraught staff member came to me on a bleak January afternoon and revealed his total frustration with the university faculty. He had sent notices to all the faculty members inviting them to a social function with alumni. Only three faculty members actually attended and those were his personal friends. This failure not only points out the dubious value of some written communications but also revealed this person's hidden assumption that "If I communicate, then others will act."

Persuasion operates at a different level than informing. An employee may understand a supervisor perfectly well but not be in agreement. Hence the employee is informed but not persuaded. Typically the manager labels this a communication problem with laments like, "If only they would listen to my side of the story." But that is not really accurate. It is not a listening or information problem. Rather, it is a persuasion problem.

Persuasion is a process involving multiple communication acts, while informing typically involves a single act. Informing employees that the new parking lot is for executives only may require only one message. Persuading them to abide by the policy may take many acts, and convincing them of the merits of the arrangements may never occur. Indeed, moving others to action, particularly nonroutine action, often takes multiple communication acts in a variety of channels. The more dynamic the channel, the better. This, in fact, explains why the personal friends of the staff member at the university came to the alumni event, for he had communicated in the most dynamic channel of all, face to face.

Myth 4: One Channel = Efficiency

Some managers have a tendency to believe that the use of only one channel is the most efficient way to communicate. For example, informing employees about a corporatewide change in the company newsletter, posting the information on the bulletin board, and mentioning the change in departmental meetings could be seen as a repetitive, inefficient, and wasteful exercise. Granted such a practice is redundant, but it is not necessarily wasteful.

Individuals have channel preferences that may not correspond to the proclivities of message senders. Some people more readily process information through visual channels, others are more attuned to verbal mediums. Therefore, to increase the probability that the message will be received, managers may need to consider using multiple mediums that correspond to the various preferences of the employees.

Myth 5: Channel Proliferation = Increased Informativeness

The number of communication channels available to the average manager has mushroomed over the last 20 years. Video tapes, audio tapes, electronic bulletin boards, personal computers, and videotext are just a few of the new possibilities. Yet, it is erroneous to assume that the increase in the number of communication vehicles means a parallel increase in the degree to which people are informed.

Inose and Pierce (1984), in their book, *Information Technology and Civilization,* observe that, "taking into account population growth, per capita information consumption is increasing very slowly, and information supply grows three times as fast as information consumption" (p. 199-200). Likewise, the proliferation of communication technologies in the workplace creates the illusion of effective information dissemination that vanishes under close scrutiny. Channels do not communicate, people do.

Channel Alternatives

In order to provide greater insight into the alternatives available, the most frequently utilized mediums are briefly discussed below. A comparison of the channels is made in the following section.

Face-to-face

Communicating face-to-face is the richest, yet most restrictive communication channel. The richness is a product of being able to tune into a wide variety of different types of cues like visual, vocal tone, body movements, office decor, language, and even smell. Almost unrestricted access to these signals can allow managers to make subtle distinctions. Moreover, the communicators, not a cameraperson, determine what cues to attend to. A manager can "get the feel" for the person. Three preeminent scholars in the field make this argument:

> A rich medium is perfect for equivocal communications. For example, face-to-face conveys emotion and strength of feeling through facial expressions, gestures, and eye contact. It is as important for a manager to know that participants are satisfied, angry, cooperative, or resistant, as it is to have accurate production data. . . . Memos and other written directives convey a predefined, literal description that can hide important issues and convey a false sense that everyone understands and agrees. (Trevino, Daft, & Lengel, 1990, p. 88)

Hence, face-to-face communication is indispensable in situations where nuance plays a critical role. Complex negotiations, detailed problem analyses, and even initial introductory encounters are situations in which the richness of this channel is fully realized. It is the most dynamic medium available to the manager. No other channel permits communicators to send messages with as much interpersonal warmth, on one hand, and cognitive complexity, on the other.

Yet the channel is one of the most restrictive. The sender and receiver, by definition, must communicate with one another at the same place and time (space-time). It is not always possible for people who need to communicate to do so. It takes energy, effort, and time for people to occupy the same space-time. And these are scarce commodities in the modern organization. Geographical proximity and time synchronicity are the greatest limitations of this channel.

Nevertheless, with all its richness, the face-to-face channel is the one that almost all other mediums seek to emulate. It is the yardstick by which the effectiveness of other mediums is measured. The time-space constraints are the critical barriers all other mediums seek to overcome. In spite of the wonderfully innovative telecommunication technology, the deep faith that most people have in face-to-face communication virtually assures that it always will be a mainstay of organizational life.

Telephone

Probably the most widely used substitute for face-to-face communication is the telephone. With over 400 million phones scattered about the globe, the time is rapidly approaching, at least in the industrialized world, in which almost anyone can instantaneously contact any other individual. Over 95% of all U.S. homes have a phone, and in some cities, like New York, there are more phones than people. The effects of this capability are enormous. Indeed, one scholar has said, "The telephone has changed the behavior of Western Man more than any technology in history" (Ramond, 1974, p. 249). The world is smaller in the sense that geographical distances no longer are barriers to communication. For managers it means that they no longer have to be in physical proximity to issue directives or to keep updated on vital information.

There is a price. The telephone does not effectively transmit visual information. Two consequences are of concern. First, the channel is less rich, so there are difficulties transmitting inherently visual messages like the blueprints of a building or the directions to the local pub. However, one young entrepreneur who owns a limousine company with revenues in excess of $350,000 a year uses the lack of visual cues to his advantage. Since many of his clients and even employees did not take him seriously because of his obvious youth, he started to rely almost exclusively on the phone. The problems disappeared (Robichaux, 1989). Second, senders can never be totally sure if the intended receiver of the message is the only one listening. J. R. Ewing is not the only one to listen in on a "private" conversation. Indeed, a number of people have grown concerned over the speaker boxes attached to so many phones. They feel their privacy has been invaded because they are not always aware of who else may be listening (Zaslow, 1986).

The other major difficulty with the telephone is that users must communicate in a synchronous mode, so a frustrating little game of "telephone tag" can develop. In fact, in an AT&T study of intracompany calls, only 9% ever were completed on the first attempt (Lyman, 1984). The vast majority of telephone calls are not prearranged. According to another study, almost 90% of the business calls last under 10 minutes, and 84% concern only one topic (Reid, 1977). Since the timing of communication is controlled by the caller, it stands to reason that the phone is not the best channel to discuss complex topics or even a wide range of topics when compared to the face-to-face mode. Why? Because the receiver may not be prepared to talk or have the time to do so. Indeed, one survey of 200 vice presidents indicated that unnecessary or unproductive telephone calls account for a needless loss of at least a month out of every executive's year ("Don't Touch," 1989). Yet the phone is useful in coordinating a meeting time or communicating in emergency situations.

Group Meetings

Departmental meetings, training sessions, and group conferences take up a tremendous amount of organizational time and resources. Various studies report from 40% to 70% of the average manager's day is spent in meetings (e.g., Hymowitz, 1988). If a group of 20 managers, earning $50 an hour in wages and benefits, have a one-hour meeting, then the minimum cost to the company is $1,000. But that figure is based on conservative assumptions. There is also the time and energy spent in setting up the meeting and making arrangements for people to get to the conference. Considering all these factors, I believe that group meetings are the most costly communication channel of all.

Yet, it the costs are great, so are the benefits. Face-to-face group meetings afford unique opportunities to coordinate various activities, stimulate commitment, solicit new ideas, motivate high-level performance, and communicate the corporate culture. To a large extent, this channel shares the same richness of the face-to-face encounter. In contrast, more effort needs to be placed on organizing the discussion and avoiding tangential remarks. There is greater peer pressure in small groups that may be a useful motivational tool but may also create "groupthink" in which employees fear sharing opinions contrary to the group norms (Janis, 1982).

Managers frequently complain of unorganized and unnecessary meetings. Rightly so. Meetings, for instance, are not the place to confirm information that could be handled at the participants' leisure or asynchronously. These difficulties can be avoided by carefully considering who should and should not be included in the meeting. Before the meeting, a precisely organized written agenda should be distributed to all participants. Then the agenda should be strictly adhered to within prescribed time limits. If more meetings were handled with just these simple guidelines, there would be far less waste of organizational resources. In fact, I know one manager who started all her meetings by setting an alarm clock for the designated time period. When the alarm went off, she left, and the meeting was adjourned. Therefore, needless conversations were avoided and the agenda was the guiding force. How did the employees feel about the alarm clock? They loved it and some started using it in other meetings.

Formal Presentations

A training program, motivational talk, safety discussion, new product presentation or policy briefing can be a unique communication opportunity. The skill and expertise of one individual gained through years of experience can be shared with many in a relatively brief time frame. The net effect is that the amount of time that the audience members have to spend in learning a task, understanding a subject, or implementing a new procedure can be reduced. Further, entire groups of employees can be collectively motivated and inspired.

Of course, there are constraints. In one poll, public speaking was ranked as the number one fear people experience, even over death. No doubt, for some people these events are one in the same. Additionally, feedback is restricted because the audience is less likely to ask questions than in smaller group settings. The length of a presentation also is limited. As the adage goes: "The mind cannot absorb what the seat cannot endure." The point is that utilizing this medium effectively requires considerable skill and preparation on the part of the speaker. If the speaker is skillful, a formal presentation can be an extremely efficient and effective method to disseminate information.

Memos

The eloquent author, Annie Dillard (1989), insightfully wrote:

> When you write, you lay out a line of words. The line of words is a miner's pick, a woodcarver's gouge, a surgeon's probe. You wield it, and it digs a path you follow. Soon you find yourself deep in new territory. . . . The writing has changed, in your hands, and in a twinkling, from an expression of your notions to an epistemological tool. (p. 3)

Writing memos as well as novels helps us come to know what we really think. Writing is a rigorous discipline that demands a greater precision of thought than speech. Why? Memos by design do not encourage clear and timely feedback. The difficulty occurs when readers fail to understand the memo or, more seriously, fail to recognize that they do not understand. Thus the major responsibility for communication lies with the writer, but many organizations are plagued by writers who lack necessary skills. Their memos lack clarity and brevity (Mitchell, 1985). For example, see Figures 5.1 and 5.2 in which the same memo was drafted with almost half the verbiage (e.g., Yates, 1989).

Training can help. One exemplary study showed that using a "high-impact" memo style, which included starting the objective in the first paragraph, bold type headings, active verbs and simple sentences was more effective than the typical "bureaucratic" style that included abstract language, passive verbs, no personal pronouns, and the purpose statement in the last paragraph. The high-impact style took about 20% less time to read, was more effectively comprehended, and did not need to be reread as often as the bureaucratic style. Surprisingly, the "bureaucratic" writer was seen as more "dynamic and forceful." One explanation offered was that the bureaucratic

TO: All employees of Pas de Deux, International
FROM: Human Resources

Representatives from Pirouette Financial Group will be available on Tuesday, April 24 to
acquaint you with ways that can help you build a secure, comfortable retirement. They will
be discussing investment alternatives and will be happy to sit down with you for a few
minutes to answer any questions you may have about your retirement and financial planning
program.

There is no cost for this service and no appointment is necessary. Feel free to stop in any
time between 10:30 a.m. and 1:30 p.m. in the alcove area for this review.

Total Word Count = 102

Figure 5.1 The Long Form

TO: All employees of Pas de Deux, International
FROM: Human Resources

Come and find out how Pirouette Financial Group can help you build a secure, comfortable
retirement.

    Date: Tuesday, April 24

    Place: Alcove

    Time: 10:30 a.m. to 1:30 p.m.

Representatives will discuss your personal financial concerns about your retirement
planning.

No appointment necessary.

Total Word Count = 53

Figure 5.2 The Short Form

style fits more closely with the organization's culture by allowing the writer
coverage of his "vital assets" (Suchan & Colucci, 1989). Perhaps, this is to
be expected from a study conducted with U.S. naval officers. Thus revising
writing styles in an organization also may involve changing the corporate
culture.

The predominant attribute of an interoffice memo, like all written mediums, is that it provides a permanent record of communication that is useful for documentation purposes. Consequently, a memo imbues a sense of formality. Also, by its very nature, a memo allows the receiver to control the time of consumption, which frees the written medium from the normal space-time constraints of oral channels. Readers have something concrete to refer back to at their leisure. Announcing routine organizational changes, transmitting information between geographically separated divisions, or reporting meeting schedules and agendas are examples of how the positive characteristics of memos can be fully utilized. Yet memos carry a sense of finality about communication that may give senders a false sense of security about their effectiveness.

Traditional Mail

Postal systems date back to the Egyptians in 2000 B.C. The basic function has remained essentially the same, which is to allow parties separated by time and space to communicate with one another (Page, 1988). Historically, the mail system was one of the fastest methods of communication, but with new technologies, it is now among the slowest. Moreover, with the rising costs of physical transport as opposed to electronic impulses, and the labor expense of composing, typing, and copying, the mail system is one of the more expensive communication channels. It has been estimated that the average cost for a letter is $6.63 when labor and material costs are figured in. Of course, some of these costs can be defrayed if a similar letter is sent to many people (Meadow & Tedesco, 1985).

On the other hand, the very expense involved may convey to the receiver the importance of the message. A letter clearly is one of the most formal means of communication. Used in conjunction with word processing equipment, form letters can reach a large number of people who are geographically separated. These advantages of traditional mail often can outweigh difficulties with time lags and expense.

Facsimile Machines

Facsimile or fax machines are rapidly replacing the traditional mail or "snail mail" as it is sometimes called. Indeed, fax accounts for 50% of all the telephone traffic between the United States and Japan (Abelson, 1989). "The process is best described as putting a paper original in a fax machine, dialing a telephone number, and having a copy come out on someone else's fax machine. Paper originals include reports, handwritten notes on fancy letterhead, even drawings and photos" (Jarvis, 1989, p. 65). Most systems have a feature that indicates if the transmission was successfully completed as well as a broadcast feature to send the document to a distribution list. Philip H. Abelson, the editor of *Science,* characterized the benefits:

> Personal experience with fax has made me an enthusiast for it. Often I need quick local delivery of a short document. The mails in Washington, D.C. are erratic. Messenger service costing $5 to $10 is better than mail but usually requires several hours. Fax takes care of the matter for the cost of paper and a local telephone call. The deed is done in a minute or two. (p. 1121)

Fax has been used for a wide variety of purposes, ranging from sending an office lunch order to a deli to verifying signatures when cashing checks. In fact, because of its affordability and widespread use, many expect even small businesses to have a fax number.

It is one of the easiest channels to use and extremely reliable because the mechanism is composed of fewer parts than a photocopier (Staff, 1987). Unlike typical electronic-mail systems, fax can be used to signal levels of formality because information can be handwritten or typed. The capability to transmit handwritten messages is particularly important to the Japanese because the written form of their language is composed of over 1,000 ideographic characters. The traditional Japanese typewriter is extraordinarily cumbersome to use, and keyboard-based communication devices have proved equally problematic (Pierce & Noll, 1990). Moreover, fax can offer other visual cues, including hand drawn sketches, that may prove useful when giving directions, and pictures of objects. "The fax machine has been absolutely magnificent in that regard," according to Paul Cook, CEO of the highly innovative Raychem Corporation. "Our technologists are using it to share sketches and plans, annotate them, and feed them back. The fax machine is much more important than videoconferencing as a tool for technical interaction" (Taylor, 1990, p. 102).

Managers can decide if they want to receive a phone call but not a fax. Senders control the timing, while receivers have to bear the cost of printing up the document as well as tying up the phone lines. This has lead to concerns over "junk fax" in which advertisers fax unsolicited information to organizations. At least one does not have to pay for junk mail. Hence, as a matter of protocol, it is always best to ask before faxing material. While longer documents can be sent via fax, as a practical matter fax is best suited to fairly short memos. Since many fax machines are centrally located, there has been concern over sending confidential documents via fax where any number of people might view it. The speed and simplicity of fax may also pose problems. Memos and reports often are composed one day and revised the next, but the pressure to fax has "destroyed a precious period of communication float" (Solomon, 1988, p. B1). In the fax age, employees often feel that there is no time to dwell on a decision or carefully consider how information is best presented. Moreover, the ease of the process may have the same effect as photocopying and encourage unnecessary communication.

Employee Publications

Another genre of corporate communications is one aimed exclusively at employees and/or their families. The traditional "house organ," employee newsletter, or company magazine is an integral part of most organizations. Indeed, such publications make their way into 75 million American homes at a cost of more than $100 million a year to industry ("Company Publications," 1980). They range from a one-page photocopy to elaborately designed magazines with photographs and graphics. In our research, we found that the typical publication was published on a monthly basis, had an average circulation of 3,000 copies, cost 40¢ a copy, and was mailed to employees' homes. As seen in Table 5.1, the most common published articles are about employee recognition (Clampitt, Crevcoure, & Hartel, 1986).

The challenge in using this channel is to report newsworthy events while avoiding the tendency to take on the characteristics of a high school yearbook. Unfortunately, however, most employee publications are used as a vehicle to recognize employees (Clampitt, Crevcoure, & Hartel 1986). One expert on the subject said, "One of the worst uses of the employee publication is for employee recognition" (D'Aprix, 1982). Why? Because other channels, like face-to-face communication, have proven far better at providing employee recognition. Further, many of these publications are replete with the "Three B's": birthdays, pictures of the company bowling team, and the births of employee babies. This all-too-common blight is compounded by problems of timeliness. When used properly, however, employee publications can help foster better understanding of corporate philosophy, policy, and even company products or services. Feature stories on a new line of products/services and question and answer columns from the president or department heads are just two examples of effective uses of this medium.

Table 5.1 Most Commonly Published Articles In Employee Publications

Rank	Type of Article	Percentage*
1	Employee recognition	93.3
2	Company awards	86.3
3	Personnel changes promotions	78.2
4	Benefit programs	76.3
5	Recognition of departments/divisions	73.9
6	Company policies	69.7
7	Organization's community involvement	68.1
8	Company social functions	65.5
9	Company sponsored sports activities	64.7
10	Organization's future plans	63.9
10	Safety	63.9
12	Promoting goodwill between management & employees	63.0
13	Effect of external events on company	58.0
14	Motivational	54.6
15	Financial results	51.3
16	Personal news (birthdays, anniversaries, etc.)	51.3
17	Questions and answers	42.0

NOTE: Percentage reflects the number of editors that perceived a type of article was "most frequently published." The sample consisted of 135 editors.

Bulletin Boards

Bulletin boards are one of the more traditional mediums of communicating to employees. Work schedules, new job postings, for-sale announcements, and softball schedules are among the items usually posted on the boards. The simplicity of posting, the relatively low expense involved, the ready accessibility, and the speed with which written notices can be posted are among the strengths of this channel. Employees, however, must be in the geographical vicinity of the boards in order to read the messages. All the people who need the information may not be able to peruse the boards on a regular basis. The typical solution is to locate the boards in high-traffic areas. In one organization, however, we found that this actually precluded many employees from reading the information because the push of the crowd made people pass by the boards too quickly. Thus, to be effective in that organization, the messages needed to be low in complexity. Indeed, as a general rule, lengthy and complex information cannot be relayed effectively via the bulletin board.

In order to maximize the effectiveness of a bulletin board system there should be an organizational policy about what can be posted on the boards. Such a policy helps avoid the typical difficulties of cluttered boards with outdated information. A particular individual or office should be in strict control of the board's contents and regularly update the information (Anderson, 1981). Reserving certain colors of paper for particular types of messages is a useful tactic, as is designating sections of the bulletin board for certain types of information.

Publications

If there are difficulties with feedback when using memos, then other publications, like consumer information packages and employee benefit booklets, engender even greater problems. These items simply are not designed to encourage the receivers of the message to ask for clarification. Often the purpose of this kind of publication is to provide a convenient reference source for the readers. In fact, this medium would be a relatively poor communication tool for information that rapidly changes because of the amount of time spent in preparing the publication. On the other hand, when used properly, such publications can be an efficient channel of communication, saving valuable employee time by freeing employees from the boring and tedious task of answering numerous routine questions. This channel is excellent when used to communicate fairly routine information to a large number of people who are widely dispersed in time and place.

Research on corporate annual reports provides a revealing glimpse into the complexities of developing effective publications. First, the editor must cope with the multiple purposes of the document. It must provide relevant financial data, interpret the information, justify current performance, and market the company to potential investors. Harmonizing these objectives is one of the most important task of the editor. Second, the document will be read by individuals in different ways. For instance, potential investors may read the financial "fine print," while certain employees may look merely at the pictures. In fact, one editor felt that many readers treated the annual report as a "news report" and others as "reference book." This editor designed the publication around the assumption that most readers looked at photographs first, the captions second, the president's letter third and so on. This idea is captured in Figure 5.3 and suggests that readership drops off as a function of interest level. Only the most sophisticated readers will consume the footnotes where most of the financial "meat" appears (Chandler, 1987). Editors of annual reports, therefore, must carefully construct their messages in order to be sure that critical information is transmitted before readership or "scannership" levels off.

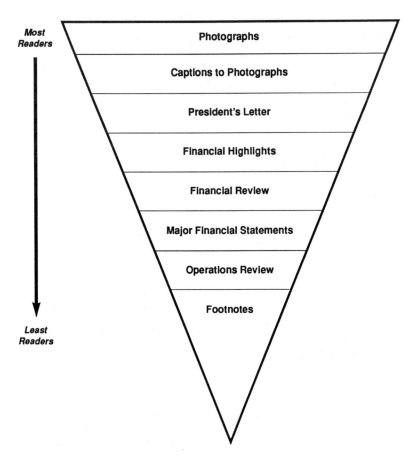

Figure 5.3 Scanning Annual Reports

Likewise, anyone who constructs in-house manuals or publications must be aware of how different audiences are going to use the documentation. This often means that the editor has to become a liaison between various users (Mirel, 1990). For example, during the 1970s, Citibank established a committee to examine consumer-related problems. One of the difficulties noted dealt with the complexity of the promissory note issued to consumers. Without any pressure from the government, they radically revised the written document. Their challenge was to insure that the information was legally binding, while understandable to the public at large. The committee had to act as a liaison between the legal department and the general public in order to create a document that would not suffer from scannership drop-off. In one instance, an immensely detailed paragraph filled with legalese was reduced to one sentence. The results were overwhelmingly positive and included increased market share, a dramatic reduction in the number of lawsuits against consumers for default, and even praise from one of the biggest critics of financial institutions, Senator William Proxmire. He said, "Mr. President, as one who has never been shy of criticizing financial institutions when criticism is deserved, I am just as liberal with praise when I hear of a big bank with a progressive idea" (U.S. Department of Commerce, 1984, p. 6, 7). Therefore, if used properly, this channel can be an effective and lucrative communication tool.

Audio- and Videotapes

Audio- and videotapes can now be mass-produced like corporate brochures and annual reports. The cost of making these tapes has steadily decreased and will no doubt assume a more central role in many organizations. This relatively new channel provides some unique opportunities as well as potential difficulties. Tapes are much like written communication, in that there is the ability to reach large audiences, but with low feedback potential. Unlike a brochure, however, certain parts of the message can be auditorally or visually highlighted. The major drawback, in comparison to written channels, is that tapes are not easily scanned for pertinent information needed by receivers.

One manager with a large paper producer uses cassette tapes as a kind of audio bulletin board that he issues to employees every Monday morning. It works well because his staff is on the road much of the week. In fact, some college professors use audio cassette tapes to critique student papers. This has proved to be an efficient tool to convey a more thorough analysis of the paper than is possible in the traditional written response. Schreiber Foods, Incorporated has developed a monthly video magazine that runs approximately 20 to 30 minutes and is played in lunch rooms throughout the company. Employees also are encouraged to check out copies. Schreiber uses a news interview type of format that not only keeps employees informed but engenders a commitment to the corporate values. A video is a compelling way to tell a motivating story to employees. The Magma Copper Company sent a short videotape to all 4,100 employees during labor negotiations to tell its side of the story (Feinstein, 1989), and British Airways installed "video booths" in two airports so that passengers could tape their comments about service ("Business Travel," 1988). In each of these cases, the video transmits the emotional and contextual components of messages more effectively than most written channels.

Hotlines

In larger organizations one of the great communication challenges is to rapidly disseminate information to a great number of people in a short period of time. Particularly during a crisis of periods of rapid change, such as a rumored or actual takeover, a telephone hotline can help alleviate fears and control rumors. During the Tylenol tampering case, a hotline for consumers was effectively utilized. Over a half a million consumers called, with fewer than 10% asking for a cash refund (Benson, 1988).

Usually hotlines take one of two forms. They may involve a taped message that is updated on a daily basis. Typically, information about corporate changes, stock prices, and even announcements for a blood drive are recorded in a fairly brief message. Then anyone in the company can call up the hotline and get the information. Other hotlines are set up so that callers can anonymously ask questions about the company or even corporate rumors. The questions may be answered on the spot or responses to the most frequent questions recorded within 24 hours.

The cost varies greatly depending on the type and complexity of the system. There is the potential for abuse with trivial calls, but these usually slack off after the system has been in place for a short time. Hotlines are not designed to handle complex messages and work best as a medium to communicate fairly rapidly changing news. As experts put it, "The essence of hotlines is speed, simplicity, and honest reporting with a minimum of interpretation or editorializing" (Anderson, 1981, p. 165). Sometimes managers resent employees calling the hotline instead of asking "the boss," and there is a slight danger employees can become overly dependent on the channel. In sum, a hotline can be a useful "safety valve" for employees, but should not, and indeed really cannot, replace the communication responsibilities of the supervisor.

Electronic Mail

Electronic mail, or E-mail, is an asynchronous method of electronically transmitting text from one computer terminal to another. An employee can instantaneously send a message to another employee's "mail box," and it will be read at the receiver's leisure. Most systems have a broadcast feature that allows the sender to "zap" the message to any of a number of different distribution lists. Some systems even are designed so that the message sender can determine if the electronic message has been read or not. This is a capability that is not available with most written documents. E-mail is used by at least 4 million workers as the method of interoffice communication (Rothfeder, 1989). The major advantages are speed, lower costs, and increased access to other employees (Azzi, 1989). For example, administrators of one Fortune 500 company reported that 60% of the messages they received from E-mail would not have been sent via other channels (Kiesler, 1986). In another study at British Columbia Telephone Company, employees felt that the E-mail system decreased telephone tag by 83% (Francas & Larimer, 1983). In yet another study, managers felt that E-mail "could replace 4% of business trips, 9% of face-to-face contacts, nearly 20% of telephone contacts, and up to 60% of mail contacts" (Picot, Klingenberg, & Kränzle, 1982, p. 687).

E-mail systems are probably best at communicating brief, noncomplex, but time-sensitive information. It is hard to imagine much persuasion or negotiation going on through an E-mail system. In order to work, there needs to be a critical mass of users who are separated geographically but have easy access to their own computers. Even sharing a terminal with one other user has been shown to decrease commitment to E-mail. Most importantly, employees must be persuaded of the utility of E-mail (Steinfield, 1986). For example, after utilizing E-mail for six months, one manager remarked:

> I thought it would be great because Mr. A would *have* to respond to all my memos. But sometimes days and weeks go by before he even downloads them on to his terminal and by then everything is out of date. Or, I'll see him in the hall and I won't know if he's even seen a memo I sent last week. These things are great but you have to turn them on.

Some networks provide slick devices to get around a few of these difficulties but, in the final analysis, the effectiveness of this channel comes down to the skills and commitment of the people using it.

Computer Conferencing

Related to E-mail is the synchronous or asynchronous use of the computer to conference with small groups of fellow employees. Andrew Finn (1985) of AT&T Communications says, "while most forms of group discussion become unwieldy if more than 8-10 people are included, CC can handle 10-30 people with little difficulty, and there is no reason why more participants could not be accommodated" (pp. 12-13). In one system I worked with, however, keeping track of 12 different participants proved to be as exasperating as following 132 plot lines in a movie. Nevertheless, a computer conference proves to be an excellent place to share new ideas or brainstorm. Participants can "scroll" back through the conversation and even get a hard copy of everyone's comments, which may allow even greater creativity. Many systems allow anonymous monitoring and commenting. Some participants are more candid, but others feel inhibited because they never know who is really listening (Phillips, 1983).

In general, computer conferencing has a "democratizing" effect on the organization since "all messages have an equal chance because they all look alike" (Zuboff, 1984, p. 371). Messages do not contain the usual cues that denote status. For example, one study indicated that 40% of the users did not know the sex of the senders and 32% had no idea of the sender's position in the hierarchy (Sproull & Kiesler, 1986). Indeed, some employees who feel physically unattractive report being more confident and participative in a computer conference than they do face-to-face. More attention is paid to the ideas and less to who is communicating. Thus an employee can engage in a battle of wits and not of power.

Two scholars, Mary Culnan and Lynne Markus (1987), have perceptively noted that such technology creates another communication opportunity never before possible:

> Many electronic messaging systems allow a sender to address a communication to a "communication space" (sometimes called a "file," a "conference," or a "bulletin board") that can be read by any interested or authorized person. This feature allows individuals to "meet" other like-minded people, whom they might not otherwise have come to know because of differences in geographic location or position in the organizational structure. (p. 432)

"Rapport" is one such system developed by Bell Labs, which even allows voice and video links over the computer file (Wright, 1990). One of the main benefits of computer conferences, however, arises from the lack of certain visual and auditory cues. Less person-centered information has to be processed by the group. Some studies have found that computer conferences are up to 55% faster than typical meetings. When Phelps Dodge Mining Company conducted its first planning meeting electronically, the process took 12 hours instead of the normal couple of days. One of the reasons is that a lot of people can "talk" at once without being considered rude (Bartimo, 1990).

But being message-centered instead of person-centered in an organization can become problematic. In one organization, the computer conferencing system led to such internal revolts and lack of concern with power-status issues that top management felt threatened and dismantled the entire system (Zuboff, 1984). Walter Wriston (1990) has eloquently commented on the situation: "The most basic fact about the world we live and work in is this: information is a virus that carries freedom" (p. 83). Since these systems, by nature, lack important contextual cues, there is a need to carefully consider the social impact on the organization. For instance, the corporate culture cannot be effectively communicated via this technology — it takes a more dynamic channel (O'Connell, 1988). Calvin Pava (1983) of Harvard Business School sums up the challenge best:

> Use of advanced telecommunications means less face-to-face contact, upon which goodwill, complementary objectives, and matching styles of getting work done depend. Without these social-psychological prerequisites, it is very difficult for parties to coordinate their efforts, especially highly complex nonroutine work. (p. 135)

Voice Mail

The next evolutionary step beyond the answering machine is voice mail. These systems use touchtone phones as the input device. A computer then digitizes the caller's voice and deposits the message in an individual's voice mail box. Although anyone can call and leave a message, the employee is the only one who can get access to the messages via a special code number. Hence, there is greater privacy and confidentiality possible than with a fax. It only takes about 15 to 20 minutes to train employees how to use the system ("Voice Messaging System," 1983). There is a broadcast feature that allows a caller to send a voice message to a distribution list with a touch of a button. While this is certainly a time saver, it also can create some unusual problems, such as the employee who inadvertently sent a voice love note to his entire department (Lewyn, 1989). While systems are somewhat costly, the benefits are equally great. For example, Travelers Insurance Company has used a voice mail system for years and has seen a 30% increase in staff productivity (Seal, 1989). Why?

- 60% of the phone calls placed before voice mail required no response (e.g., Siragusa, 1986).
- 70% of those calls never reached the person intended.
- 90% of the phone messages taken by secretaries contained errors.

Indeed, with an estimated cost of $13 to successfully complete a traditional telephone call, it is no wonder that the investment is recouped (Wessel, 1984). Schneider Communications boasts of an almost paper-free organization because of voice mail which, again, cuts expenses.

Most voice mail systems are used as a replacement for short memos and phone calls that require no response (Wessel, 1984). Some employees have even started sending voice messages to themselves to remind them of a great idea when they get back to the office (Siragusa, 1986). Voice messaging is particularly useful for employees who are on the road, like salespeople. One large trucking firm, Schneider National Carriers, Incorporated uses voice mail to keep in contact with truckers all across the nation. Thus there is 24-hour access to employees, secretaries are not burdened with taking messages, and even family members can keep in touch. One problem is that these systems will not work on rotary dial phones, which may be the only option for a trucker in a rural area. Another problem with voice mail is the lack of ability to easily scan through messages. Although some systems have features to control these inconveniences, many employees still report that they may have to listen to 20 or 30 minutes of messages in order to figure out which ones really are important. Thus voice messaging is most effective when communicating fairly short and unambiguous messages. Voice mail, like E-mail, needs a critical mass of users in order to be effective, which means that users must regularly check their voice mail box. Communicating to a "machine" in a clear and brief way is difficult for some employees, but clearly it is a skill that will need to be mastered in the modern organization.

Teleconference

The teleconference is the telephone equivalent of the group meeting. Small or large groups can simultaneously communicate in a single conversation via the phone line. The channel provides, in some cases, an economical alternative to travel for managers who need to participate in a discussion with people who are geographically separated. Sometimes preliminary selection interviews are conducted with applicants via teleconferences. Schneider Communications holds a teleconference every Friday morning with up to 100 employees in five different locations to keep everyone informed of upcoming events. This channel is best suited to meet informational needs of the participants, but is not very effective for negotiations (Williams, 1987).

Despite the widespread availability of teleconferencing, it has not replaced travel because of some obvious limitations, such as the lack of a visual component. A more subtle limitation is that secondary conversations are discouraged in this medium. During face-to-face group meetings involving more than four or five people, there are usually other conversations occurring simultaneously in smaller groups of two or three. Since a single phone line transmits the communication in a teleconference, secondary conversations often are avoided, which may mean some valuable information is not shared (see Figure 5.4). Or, if they do occur, time is taken away from the primary discussion. Participants may get background on some topic that is of little concern to them. Either way, the net effect can be detrimental. On the other hand, the tacit elimination of some secondary conversations may actually speed up the process and make participants focus more on the task than is possible in a traditional meeting (Williams, 1987). In short, a teleconference offers an efficient alternative to many face-to-face group conferences, but it does not totally simulate one.

Video Conference

The video conference completes the circle of channels by providing a telecommunication alternative to face-to-face and group communication mediums. A video conference transmits audio and video images to employees, often via a satellite hookup. Systems vary widely. Some are one-way mediums like the traditional use of television, while others are interactive, allowing parties at various sites to simultaneously communicate with each other. For instance, Federal Express used a video conference to explain to its 30,000 workers the new Zapmail delivery service. Obviously, all those employees could not be brought to one meeting place in order to explain the service. Even at a cost of $1.3 million, the price per employee was more reasonable than other alternatives (Reilly, 1985). Hotel chains like the Hilton, Marriott, Hyatt, and Holiday Inn are investing thousands of dollars in video conferencing networks to be rented by other businesses. Some companies, such as Apple Computer, are even purchasing their own television studios to produce programs for employees. Apple feels the investment of $1.5 million is a wise use of funds to help communicate and train its 10,000 employees. (Rebello, 1989).

Video conferences have been shown to be effective for a wide variety of tasks, ranging from training sessions and sales meetings to conducting promotion reviews and selection interviews. A district attorney's office even found that they could gather more useful information from victims located at various police precincts via a videophone (Guyon, 1989). Indeed, participants often perceive little difference between a video conference and a face-to-face meeting, but this is a dangerous assumption that ignores subtle

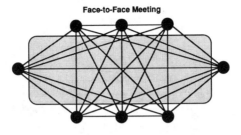

Face-to-Face Meeting

In the typical face-to-face meeting, participants can break into smaller groups for discussion without interrupting the primary conversation because all the communication lines are available.

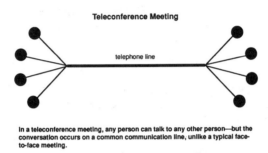

Teleconference Meeting

telephone line

In a teleconference meeting, any person can talk to any other person—but the conversation occurs on a common communication line, unlike a typical face-to-face meeting.

Figure 5.4 Comparison of Meeting Types

channel effects. For instance, researchers have seen that video conferences typically are shorter, more topic focused, and contain fewer social conversations than traditional conferences. Moreover, video conferences often include employees who normally would not attend certain meetings because of travel costs (Fulk & Dutton, 1984). All of these factors can have a major impact on the flow of communication in organizations, ranging from stifling employee creativity to spreading out the power base.

One expert further counsels:

> Video teleconferencing is a growing medium where, in a sense, *you* become the visual aid. And just as you are not born with the ability to communicate brilliantly, so you are not born knowing how best to utilize video communicating. You must learn to make the medium work for you rather than the other way around. (Frank, 1989, p. 142)

It is easy to see how some video conferences could become more matters of personal style and visual appeal than true rational exchanges. Television often tests one's ability at verbal ping-pong rather than the mental rigor of deep thought. In spite of these concerns, video conferencing will no doubt prove to be more commonplace in the future. Then a more thorough evaluation of the medium can be completed. It is clear, however, that even the video conference will never completely replace the traditional face-to-face conversation.

Channel Comparisons

The following twelve dimensions are useful in evaluating the communication mediums:

(1) Feedback potential: How quickly can the receiver respond to the message?

(2) Complexity capacity: Can this channel effectively process complex messages?

(3) Breadth potential: How many different messages can be disseminated through this channel?

(4) Confidentiality: Can the communicators be reasonably sure their messages are received only by those intended?

(5) Encoding ease: Can the sender easily and quickly use this channel?

(6) Decoding ease: Can the receiver easily and quickly decode messages in this channel?

(7) Time-space constraint: Do senders and receivers need to occupy the same time-space?

(8) Cost: How much does it cost to use this channel?

(9) Interpersonal warmth: Does the channel have the potential to communicate interpersonal warmth?

(10) Formality: Does the channel imbue a sense of formality?

(11) "Scanability": Does the channel permit the message(s) to be easily browsed or scanned to find relevant passages?

(12) Time of consumption: Does the sender or receiver exercise the most control over when the message is consumed?

With the exception of the final category, all the other dimensions can be classified on a high to low scale. There are a handful of studies that have comprehensively compared the various channels available to the manager (e.g., Picot, Klingenberg, & Kränzle, 1982). Nevertheless, some basic trends emerge from the research and theoretical work of other scholars. Based on the literature and organizational experiences, in Table 5.2 I have estimated how each channel appears to rate. Therefore, one can determine the suitability of each channel for a given organizational situation.

Table 5.2 Channel Ratings

Channel	Feedback Potential	Complexity Capacity	Breadth Potential	Confidentiality	Encoding Ease	Decoding Ease	Time-Space Constraint	Cost	Personal Warmth	Formality	Scanability	Consumption Time
Face-to-face	1	1	1	1	1	1	1	2	1	4	4	S/R
Telephone	1	4	2	2	1	1	3	3	2	4	4	S/R
Group meetings	2	2	2	4	2	2	1	1	2	3	4	S/R
Formal presentations	4	2	2	4	3	2	1	1	3	3	5	Sender
Memos	4	4	2	3	4	3	5	3	5	2	1	Receiver
Postal mail	5	3	3	2	4	3	5	3	4	1	1	Receiver
Fax	3	4	2	4	3	3	5	3	3	3	1	Receiver
Publications	5	4	2	5	5	3	5	2	4	1	1	Receiver
Bulletin boards	4	5	1	5	3	2	2	4	5	3	1	Receiver
Audio/videotapes	4	4	3	5	4	2	3	2	3	3	5	Receiver
Hotlines	2	5	2	2	3	1	4	2	3	3	4	Receiver
E-Mail	3	4	1	2	3	2	4	2	4	3	4	Receiver
Computer conference	1	2	2	4	3	2	3	2	3	3	4	S/R
Voice mail	2	4	2	1	2	1	5	3	2	4	4	Receiver
Tele-conference	2	3	2	5	2	2	2	2	3	3	5	S/R
Video-conference	3	3	2	4	3	2	2	1	2	3	5	S/R

NOTE: Ratings are on a 1-5 scale where 1 = high and 5 = low. Consumption time refers to who controls the reception of communication. S/R means the sender and receiver share control.

Selecting the Appropriate Channels

With this bewildering array of options it is tempting to just spin the wheel and select a channel. In fact, that is what most managers do. *The major criterion used by most employees in selecting a channel is personal convenience.* As a channel's ease of use increases, so does the likelihood of use. Little consideration is given to how the message is filtered by the channel or even the secondary messages of the channel. There is evidence, however, that effective executives are sensitive to the impact of the medium and select the appropriate channel for their messages (Lengel & Daft, 1988). How do they do it?

One approach is based on a simple model of communication. Selecting the appropriate channel is akin to hitting a row of cherries on a Las Vegas slot machine. The objective should be to align four elements:

- the needs of the sender
- the attributes of the message
- the attributes of the channel
- the needs of the receiver

Unlike a one-armed bandit, the alignment of these four communication variables should be a product of skill and insight rather than chance. The odds of "winning" can be markedly increased by carefully considering five fundamental questions.

(1) Are the needs of the sender compatible with the attributes of the intended message?

All messages have attributes that characterize their content. Messages can vary along numerous dimensions, including level of complexity, length, personal warmth, formality, and degree of ambiguity. Senders of messages also have a wide variety of intentions in communicating messages, including motivating, informing, persuading, and soliciting ideas or opinions.

Ideally, the needs of the sender should harmonize with the type of message sent. Such is not always the case. A manager seeking to motivate others is hindered in doing so by using an overly complex message. Or take the case of the supervisor who wanted to solicit the opinions of his staff on a proposal, but scheduled the meeting at the end of the day and provided "background" for three quarters of the meeting. In both instances, the attributes of the message are not congruent with the intentions of the sender and, consequently, the communication effort is less successful than possible.

(2) Are the messages sent compatible with the channels utilized?

William F. Buckley Jr., when running for mayor of New York City, was asked to explain his economic plan for the city on a television talk show. He refused. He believed his plan was too complex to be explained in a cursory fashion within the time constraints of that television show. Some might call this arrogance. But his position makes perfect sense when viewed from the perspective of the channel limitations. Simply, the message he had to convey could not be effectively communicated in this channel.

Likewise, managers must realize that every channel has limitations that filter out parts of the message. Channels that are nondynamic, such as memos or bulletin boards, are not effective in communicating extremely complex messages. On the other hand, bulletin boards can be useful and efficient when communicating a fairly simple message, like the company softball schedule. Hence, to effectively communicate, managers must be alert to the dynamic interplay of the message and channel attributes.

(3) Are the sender's needs compatible with the type of channels utilized?

Suggestion boxes have been used for years in countless organizations. Most businesses, however, have found them of limited utility. Part of the reason is that many new ideas or suggestions are not readily captured on paper. Further, if one is motivated by personal recognition, the suggestion box is not an effective tool. Indeed, employees often are told that suggestions should be made anonymously, which even further removes the incentive. One employee artfully described his feelings in a picture that nicely captures the essence of the problems with suggestion boxes (see Figure 5.5). This employee's motivations are not really compatible with the channel. Ideas are personal, warm, and alive. They are a source of joy for employees. Impersonal media strip away these very elements from the message. The result is inevitable: innovative ideas never surface in such channels.

The broader picture is this: Since communication channels have certain attributes, senders must be sure that their intentions are congruent with the dynamics of the channel. Therefore, if the sender seeks to imbue a sense of formality, then more formal channels, like written memos, should be used. If the sender seeks to relay a confidential message, then voice mail is better

Figure 5.5 The "Suggestion Box"

than fax. If an executive wants to stimulate creativity but is afraid that status differences inhibit a free exchange of ideas, then computer conferencing might be best. If the CEO wants to instill an emotional commitment to corporate values, then a visual channel, such as a formal presentation, video conference, or videotape, would be the channel of choice. In sum, formal intentions require formal mediums, dynamic intentions require dynamic mediums, and so on. This is the pattern of success.

(4) Are the messages compatible with the receivers' needs?

This is the classic question asked by market researchers, advertising executives, and television programmers. In short, do people like what I have to sell or say? If not, change it. If viewers don't buy brussel sprouts with a commercial about nutritional value, then change the advertisement to include a sexy health spa. If viewers will not watch "highbrow" opera, then give them a "lowbrow" sitcom. Appeal to the lowest common denominator. Unfortunately, even communication consultants fall into this trap.

This obvious overstatement is the danger to avoid when seeking to adapt a message to an audience. Managers need not get into the tail-wagging-the-dog syndrome. Yet there is a need to be sensitive to how a given message will impact listeners. Messages can be adjusted without destroying the integrity of the idea. Sometimes managers must communicate difficult news, and one of their prime responsibilities should be how to share the information in a sensitive manner. Sugar-coating and brutal honesty, both can be avoided. Somewhere in the vortex between the sender's intentions and the receiver's sentiments is the ground of ethical responsibility.

(5) Are the channels utilized compatible with the receivers' needs?

We conducted an analysis of how information was distributed at the University of Wisconsin — Green Bay. Most of the students are commuters, and a higher percentage of the students hold outside jobs than at most universities. Time is of the essence to these students. The research showed that bulletin boards were heavily relied on and seen as a credible medium by those sending messages. The data also revealed that many students felt inadequately informed about campus events.

When the question above was posed by the researchers, it was apparent why students felt uninformed. Students needed channels that presented information in an easily consumable format. Bulletin boards could not do this because the students did not have time to read them, given the unique dynamics of the campus. The solution: widely distribute information through a channel that was transportable and that students could easily read at their leisure. Hence, boxes with a weekly schedule of activities were placed at the entrances and exits of the campus. The results have been quite positive.

The implication is that in order to be effective, the channels used must be uniquely suited to the needs of the receiver. Perhaps the receiver prefers more dynamic verbal channels while the sender, like former President Jimmy Carter, prefers written channels. Such personal preferences should be considered. Receivers may not even be aware of their underlying needs. For example, voice mail would be particularly useful for employees who need to communicate across time zones. An employee who needs to see a diagram as soon as possible would be best served by a fax machine. In sum, effective communicators adapt both their messages and channels to their audience.[1] (See Table 5.3.)

The five questions reviewed above provide a glimpse of the complexities involved in effectively communicating. The salient issue is one of compatibilities between senders, messages, channels, and receivers. Suppose that for each of these four variables there were five possible alternatives, like a column of a slot machine. Senders could have one of five possible purposes for communicating a message. Likewise one could chose among five possible channels: bulletin boards, memos, group meeting, telephone, or face-to-face meetings. There are many more, but if we limited each variable to only

Table 5.3 Sample Situations of Media Choice

Situation 1

A midsize construction firm wants to announce a new employee benefit program.

Poor Choice: Memo   **Better Choice:** Small group meetings

Rationale: The memo does not offer the feedback potential necessary to explain what may be seen as arcane information. Moreover, with these kinds of employees there is a possibility of literacy problems. A group meeting will allow for an oral explanation and will mean that participants can easily ask questions about any of the complex materials.

Situation 2

A manager wishes to confirm a meeting time with 10 employees.

Poor Choice: Phone   **Better Choice:** Voice mail or E-mail

Rationale: For a simple message like this, there is no need to use a rich and synchronous media when a lean and asynchronous one will do the job.

Situation 3

Garner support in midsize insurance company for a program that encourages employees from different departments to work on the same project teams.

Poor Choice: E-mail, voice mail   **Better Choice:** Face-to-face, telephone

Rationale: Persuasive situations demand that the sender be able to quickly adapt the message to receiver in order to counter objections. This is not a feature of either E-mail or V-mail. Face-to-face communication offers the sender the greatest flexibility. The phone is the next best alternative.

Situation 4

A group of engineers, who are geographically dispersed, want to exchange design ideas with one another.

Poor Choice: Teleconference   **Better Choice:** Fax, computer conference

Rationale: A teleconference is apt to overly accentuate the status and personality differences between the engineers. Fax or computer conferencing would allow the quality of the ideas to be the central focus of interaction. Moreover, quick feedback is still possible in these media.

Situation 5

Describe a straightforward, but somewhat detailed and updated version of a voice mail system to 1,000 employees who are geographically dispersed.

Poor Choice: Newsletter   **Better Choice:** Videotape

Rationale: As long as employees already are persuaded of the system's merit, you can probably use asynchronous media. But a videotape more easily conveys messages that require demonstration.

---

five, then there would be 625 different combinations. Such is the range of choice for a communicator. The odds of correctly aligning each variable are exceedingly small. But, unlike a casino, a prudent manager can effectively manage this complexity by pondering the questions reviewed above.

Conclusion

John R. Pierce (1983), who had a distinguished career at Bell Laboratories, said of musical composition:

> Indeed, the kind of sound that is available influences the kind of music that peoples and composers produce. Piano music is different from harpsichord music in more than the sound of the individual notes. The music of Liszt, Chopin, and Debussy exploits the unique capabilities of the piano. So do Beethoven's and Mozart's piano sonatas and concertos. But Mozart's piano was different from ours, less loud and with less dynamic range. Later music would suffer if played on it. (p. 2)

Likewise, the point of this chapter has been that the communication channel alters the message, sometimes overtly but more often subtly. There is no one best communication medium, as there is no one best musical instrument. Rather, a communicator, like a composer, seeks to choose the proper instrument to precisely communicate a particular theme. To wisely select the proper instrument requires a complete knowledge of the possibilities and the complexities of the entire process. Then the message becomes something more than notes on a piece of Ts' ai Lun's paper.

Note

1. Of course, axiomatically, if the sender's needs were compatible with the message attributes and the message attributes were compatible with the channel attributes, then the sender's needs would match up with the channel attributes. But that is in an ideal world. More realistically, a sender has to make tradeoffs. Hence, the question must be raised about the degree of congruency between the sender and the channel. Then the sender can decide on the appropriate message and channel, as the attributes of each variable modify one another in a dynamic interactive kind of dance.

References

Abelson, P. H. (1989, March 3). Fax. *Science,* pp. 1121.

Anderson, W. G. (1981). Bulletin boards, exhibits, hotlines. In C. Reuss & D. Silvis (Eds.), *Inside organizational communication* (pp. 157-168). New York: Longman.

Azzi, J. (1989). The ease of E-mail. *Mail, 1*(2), 53-54.

Bartimo, J. (1990, June 11) At these shouting matches, no one says a word. *Business Week,* p. 78.

Benson, J. A. (1988). Crisis revisited: An analysis of strategies used by Tylenol in the second tampering episode. *Central States Speech Journal, 39*(1), 49-66.

Business travel. (1988, September 12). *USA Today,* p. 6B.

Casse, D. (1986, September 2). Reading and writing as an entitlement. *Wall Street Journal,* p. A15.

Chandler, R. C. (1987). *Organizational communication to corporate constituents: The role of the company annual report.* Unpublished doctoral dissertation, University of Kansas, Lawrence.

Clampitt, P. G., Crevcoure, J. M., & Hartel, R. L. (1986). Exploratory research on employee publications. *Journal of Business Communication, 23*(3), 5-17.

Company publications. (1980, December). *CPA Journal,* pp. 91-94.

Culnan, M. J., & Markus, M. L. (1987). Information technologies. In F. M. Jablin, L. L. Putnam, K. H. Roberts, & L. W. Porter (Eds.), *Handbook of organizational communication* (pp. 420-443). Newbury Park, CA: Sage.

D'Aprix, R. (1982). *Communicating for productivity.* New York: Harper & Row.

Dillard, A. (1989). *The writing life.* New York: Harper & Row.

Don't touch that phone. (1989, July 25). *Wall Street Journal,* p. A1.

Feinstein, S. (1989, July 11). Magma Copper Co. *Wall Street Journal,* p. A1.

Finn, T. A. (1985, May). *A comparison of organizational uses of voice and electronic (text) messaging systems.* (TaP Working Paper #85-06). Piscataway, NJ: AT&T Communications.

Francas, M., & Larimer, E. C. (1983). *Impact of an enhanced electronic messaging system.* Unpublished paper.

Frank, M. O. (1989). *How to run a successful meeting in half the time.* New York: Simon & Schuster.

Fulk, J., & Dutton, W. (1984, January). *Organizational communications via videoconferencing: Emerging perceptions of electronic meetings.* Unpublished paper.

Guyon, J. (1989, January 16). Fiber optics may help make airplanes safer. *Wall Street Journal,* p. B1.

Hart, M. H. (1978). *The 100: A ranking of the most influential persons in history.* New York: A & W Visual Library.

Hymowitz, C. (1988, June 21). Survival guide to the office meeting. *Wall Street Journal,* p. 33.

Inose, H., & Pierce, J. R. (1984). *Information technology and civilization.* New York: W. H. Freeman.

Janis, I. (1982). *Groupthink: Psychological studies of policy decisions.* Boston: Houghton Mifflin.

Jarvis, P. (1989, February). Using fax technology to contact the world. *The Office,* pp. 65-66.

Kiesler, S. (1986). Thinking ahead. *Harvard Business Review, 64*(1), 46-60.

Lengel, R. H., & Daft, R. L. (1988). The selection of communication media as an executive skill. *Academy of Management Executive, 2*(3), 225-232.

Lewyn, M. (1989, July 17). Voice mail is booming. *USA Today,* p. 6B.

Lyman, G. C., III. (1984). Voice messaging comes of age. *Speech Technology, 2*(3), 11-15.

Meadow, C. T., & Tedesco, A. S. (1985). *Telecommunications for management.* New York: McGraw-Hill.

Mikulecky, L. (1990). Basic skill impediments to communication between management and hourly employees. *Management Communication Quarterly, 3*(4), 452-473.

Mirel, B. (1990). Expanding the activities of in-house manual writers. *Management Communication Quarterly, 3*(4), 496-526.

Mitchell, C. F. (1985, October 4). Firms seek cure for dull memos; find windy writers hard to curb. *Wall Street Journal,* p. 21.

O'Connell, S. E. (1988). Human communication in the high tech office. In G. M. Goldhaber & G. A. Barnett (Eds.), *Handbook of organizational communication* (pp. 473-482). Norwood, NJ: Ablex.

Page, J. (1988, September). One in 500 million: Tracking a letter across the country. *Smithsonian,* pp. 96-107.

Pava, C. (1983). *Managing new office technology: An organizational strategy.* New York: Free Press.

Phillips, A. F. (1983). Computer conferences: Success or failure? In R. N. Bostrom (Ed.), *Communication yearbook 7* (pp. 837-856). Beverly Hills, CA: Sage.

Picot, A., Klingenberg, H., & Kränzle, H. (1982). Office technology: A report on attitudes and channel selection from field studies in Germany. In M. Burgoon (Ed.), *Communication yearbook 6* (pp. 674-692). Beverly Hills, CA: Sage.

Pierce, J. R. (1983). *The science of musical sound.* New York: Scientific American Library.

Pierce, J. R., & Noll, M. (1990). *Signals: The science of telecommunications.* New York: Scientific American Library.

Ramond, C. (1974). *The art of using science in marketing.* New York: Harper & Row.

Rebello, K. (1989, September 11). Apple polishes business tv. *USA Today,* p. 2B.

Reid, A. A. L. (1977). Comparing telephone with face-to-face contact. In I. Pool (Ed.), *Social impact of the telephone* (pp. 386-414). Cambridge: MIT Press.

Reilly, J. (1985, May 6). Cost, reluctance hinder growth of video conferences. *USA Today,* p. 5B.

Robichaux, M. (1989, June 9). Teens in business discover credibility is hard to earn. *Wall Street Journal,* pp. B1-B2.

Rothfeder, J. (1989, May 8). Neither rain, nor sleet, nor computer glitches . . . *Business Week,* pp. 135-139.

Seal, M. (1989, March). The facts about voice mail. *Vis a Vis,* pp. 40-46.

Siragusa, G. (1986, April). Voice mail takes off. *Administrative Management,* pp. 43-48.

Solomon, J. (1988, October 27). Business communication in the fax age. *Wall Street Journal,* p. B1.

Sproull, L., & Kiesler, S. (1986). Reducing social context cues: The case of electronic mail. *Management Science, 32,* 1492-1512.

Staff. (1987, December). Study shows reliability valued most. *Business Fax,* p. 1.

Steinfield, C. W. (1986). Computer-mediated communication in an organizational setting: Explaining task-related and socioemotional uses. In M. L. McLaughlin (Ed.), *Communication yearbook 9* (pp. 777-804). Beverly Hills, CA: Sage.

Suchan, J., & Colucci, R. (1989). Analysis of communication efficiency between high-impact and bureaucratic written communication. *Management Communication Quarterly, 2*(4), 454-484.

Taylor, W. (1990, March-April). The business of innovation: An interview with Paul Cook. *Harvard Business Review, 90*(2), 96-106.

Trevino, L. K., Daft, R. L., & Lengel, R. H. (1990). Understanding manager's media choices: A symbolic interactionist perspective. In J. Fulk & C. Steinfield (Eds.), *Organizations and communication technology* (pp. 71-94). Newbury Park, CA: Sage.

Unneeded photocopies cost firms $2.6 billion a year. (1985, May 10). *Wall Street Journal,* p. 40.

U. S. Department of Commerce. (1984). *How plain English works for business.* Washington, DC: Government Printing Office.

Voice messaging system improves productivity of marketing staff. (1983, June). *Communications News,* pp. 22-25.

Wessel, S. (1984, October). Tapping the potential of voice messaging. *Communication Age,* pp. 11-13.

Williams, F. (1987). *Technology and communication behavior.* Belmont, CA: Wadsworth.

Wright, K. (1990, March). The road to the global village. *Scientific American, 262*(3), 83-95.

Wriston, W. B. (1990, January-February). The state of American management. *Harvard Business Review, 68*(1), 78-83.

Yates, J. (1989). Emergence of the memo as a managerial genre. *Management Communication Quarterly, 2*(4), 485-510.

Zaslow, J. (1986, April 23). Speaker-phones stir urge to reach out and bop someone. *Wall Street Journal,* pp. 1, 28.

Zuboff, S. (1984). *In the age of the smart machine.* New York: Basic Books.

6

Performance Feedback

Feedback is one of the fundamental facts of life and ideas of science, yet only in the last fifty years have we recognized its all-pervasive presence. The idea is simple: a feedback mechanism registers the actual state of a system, compares it to the desired state, then uses the comparison to correct the state of the system. Feedback is goal-oriented. . . . Movement is the essence of feedback. It implies purpose and progress. Like a walker on a high wire, it continually achieves balance in order to achieve something beyond balance. It can never rest.

Horace Freeland Judson

What if there were no feedback? What if feedback not only rested but took a "Rip Van Winkle" sojourn? Cells would multiply uncontrollably. The economy would fly out of kilter. Democracy would collapse. Without feedback, the world as we know it would not exist; the high-wire walker would fall. No system can survive without feedback.

Yet employees in organizations throughout the world feel that is just what they are expected to do. In every organization in which we have conducted an analysis of the communication system, feedback about performance has surfaced as a problem area (see Appendix B). Over 53% of the employees expressed below-average satisfaction with feedback. An astonishing 12% of the employees surveyed indicated they had little or no satisfaction with the feedback system. In countless interviews employees have made comments like this: "Performance evaluations don't really exist here. If they do, I don't know what they look like. It's like pulling teeth." In short, there is probably no more pervasive and perplexing difficulty in the modern organization than how to effectively give feedback to employees about their performance.

The cynic might ask, "So what? Does performance feedback actually make any difference?" Indeed, I mentioned to one vice president that employees felt they did not get adequate feedback. He responded, "They get their paychecks every two weeks, don't they?" Researchers have a more sanguine view. Performance feedback has a high correlation with job satisfaction (Downs & Hazen, 1977). In another study, employees indicated that performance feedback had a greater impact on their performance than every other communication variable, including the communication climate, coworker communication, and even supervisor-subordinate relationships (Clampitt & Downs, in press). In sum, employees like to know how they are doing.

Why? There is not one simple reason. For some, feedback is a reward or motivation, while to others it is useful information to correct behavior or a way to build self-esteem. Feedback systems that are designed simply to let people "know how they are doing" may be doomed for failure. Employees do not want information only, they want recognition as well. At Oxford Industries, a nonunion clothing manufacturer, modern computer technology can monitor how long it takes an employee to sew a pocket on a pair of pants and bases pay on how closely employees match standards (Miller, 1985). While this system provides accurate and timely feedback, it still may not satisfy other noninformational desires for feedback. In fact, many employees who are at the mercy of these so-called "electronic watchdogs" complain of stress and report numerous health problems. While feedback about performance clearly is one of the most important communication tasks of the manager, it is equally clear that the design and implementation of the feedback system has a major impact on its effectiveness.

The Fundamentals

Effectiveness in football, dance, or management ultimately comes down to a complete mastery of the fundamentals. For the design of an effective feedback system, the following seven principles provide a solid basis.

(1) Everyone, whether they acknowledge it or not, has standards of performance.

In every task, duty, and decision, employees assess their own level of effectiveness. If deemed satisfactory, they seek to maintain it. If they fall short, they make changes. For example, Mike Schmidt, the Philadelphia Phillies' perennial all-star third baseman, retired in the middle of the 1989 baseball season, without any pressure from the owners. He felt he was not living up to his personal performance standards. He could have continued earning millions for several more years. On the other hand, employees who send memos chock-full of spelling errors have unambiguously communicated what is acceptable to them. Performance standards are a nonoptional part of the human experience; they guide our behavior, determine our aspirations, and ultimately define our essence.

(2) The ultimate goal of an effective feedback system is the mutual identification of, performance of, and commitment to the standards.

Employees and managers do not always share the same standards. In particular, new employees, because of their different backgrounds, training, and experiences, often have quite different standards than their managers. Indeed, researchers have shown that initial employee training is the single most critical time in which managers can impart their standards, values, and expectations (Clampitt & Downs, in press). After that period of time, employees tend to be more influenced by their coworkers and other organizational factors. As seen in Figure 6.1, if proper selection procedures have been utilized, employees will share, to some extent, the performance standards of their managers. The training process should result in a more complete sharing of expectations, therefore increasing the degree of overlap. As situations change, the manager matures, and the employee develops, the standards may be altered. Yet, the objective is constant: to close the gap between the standards of the employee and the manager.

The employee must not only know the standards but be committed to them and also perform as expected. The effective feedback system involves the mind, the will, and the heart. A teacher, for instance, may set a standard of professionalism in writing that includes not having any spelling errors on reports. The teacher may announce this at the beginning of the term. But such exhortations are useless unless the students actually turn in papers of this quality. Clearly the teacher can encourage proper writing by actually lowering the grades of students who fail to meet the standards. The long-term goal, however, is for the students to recognize the importance of correct spelling and be committed to this level of professionalism. The aim is not merely knowledge, but performance and commitment. It is one step to know what is right, it is another to turn knowledge into action, and yet another to transform action into resolve.

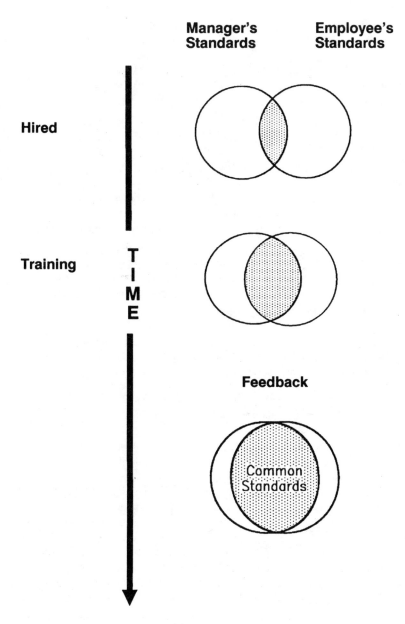

Figure 6.1 Feedback Process

(3) Performance standards are necessary to maintain corporate integrity and develop employee potential.

Ultimately the integrity of a corporation's products or services is inextricably bound to the organization's viability. One of the reasons for the preponderance of Japanese products in the United States is that the performance standards for the Japanese products have, in the recent past, been more rigorous than those for American products. Lee Iacocca admitted as much in rallying Chrysler to its incredible turnaround. When organizations have lower standards of reliability, performance, and service than their competition, the result is as inevitable as it is fatal. Indeed, the United States automobile industry was in serious trouble. Corporations and managers need have no apologies for high performance standards.

Moreover, employees also are benefactors of high performance standards. Those who are challenged to achieve their potential are more satisfied and productive. "Self-actualization," the term Abraham Maslow (1970) made famous in his theory of the hierarchy of human needs, places this assertion on firm theoretical ground. The famous philosopher and poet, Jacob Bronowski (1973), beautifully expressed it:

> The most powerful drive in the ascent of man is his pleasure in his own skill. He loves to do what he does well, and having done it well, he loves to do it better. You see it in his science. You see it in the magnificence with which he carves and builds, the loving care, the gaiety, the effrontery. The monuments are supposed to commemorate kings and religions, heroes, dogmas, but in the end the man they commemorate is the builder. (p. 116)

Most people would like to fulfill their potential. Companies should not frustrate this desire but seek to utilize it by offering challenging tasks and high standards. To sustain performance in this demanding atmosphere, employees' efforts and accomplishments must be acknowledged, supported, and rewarded. When standards are low in one department, productivity in other divisions suffers and may eventually threaten the job security of all employees. Ideally when standards are universally high, everyone reaps the financial benefits of high productivity.

(4) Everyone "receives" feedback about their performance.

Frequently employees complain about that they "don't get any feedback." But this is misleading. Even if employees do not receive explicit feedback, they will make inferences about the acceptability of their work. From the organizational context employees extract messages and come to conclusions like: "No news is good news," "I must be doing okay, I haven't heard any complaints," or, "If the boss doesn't like it, he can tell me about it." When employees receive no explicit feedback, they infer it and continue to perform at levels they deem acceptable to themselves. Or to put it another way, a manager cannot not give performance feedback. Of course to use words like "receive" and "give" is somewhat misleading because no explicit message is sent or actually received. But context and inference are powerful instruments of communication. Indeed, in many cases this is the only method used to "communicate" about performance.

(5) Few employees receive useful feedback about their performance.

The difficulty with this inferential method of feedback is that employees *can* and *do* make inaccurate speculations. For example, one insurance claims adjuster had never received any explicit feedback in his short nine-month tenure. He had an exceedingly pleasant manner but was disturbingly sloppy in his work habits. The manager had already decided to fire him after the mandatory nine-month trial period. Top management knew of the decision. The other employees knew. Everybody knew but the employee. And he quite literally went on his merry way, doing his job in perfect peace and in complete ignorance of his impending fate. In due course, when the man was fired, he justifiably expressed complete bewilderment. Predictably, he filed a lawsuit, which was later settled out of court for a considerable sum of money. This is a case where an employee made a terribly inaccurate inference based on an information vacuum. The manager's lack of courage in confronting the situation is regrettable but all too typical.

Less dramatic — though more frequent — many managers sugarcoat their feedback (e.g., Cusella, 1987). They overemphasize the positive and downplay the negative. Employees may assume the best, in which case true problems go undetected and uncorrected. On the other hand, employees may assume the worse, in which case anxiety and undue stress are the likely results. Either way, employee performance suffers. In the end, both the employee and the company lose.

(6) Both positive and negative deviations from the standards should be specifically noted.

While the precise techniques that should be employed are discussed in detail later, the fundamental process is really quite simple. Managers who have, as a first step, informed employees of the standards, should use the standards as a springboard for both praise and criticism. If the employees exceed the standards, they should be praised. If their performance is substandard, they should likewise be informed. Initially, even if they just meet the standards, they should be told.

The benefits are many. First, employees will realize that management takes the standards seriously. This is why it is important, at least for new employees, to specifically note when they achieve even the minimal standards. Also, some standards are, of necessity, ambiguous, and employees may not even be aware of what they are doing right. Second, precise feedback acts as a motivator. In one study, employees were asked to recall a specific incident that caused their productivity to increase. Over 65% of the employees mentioned some kind of feedback from management, like a written note of praise from the company president or an extra bonus for effectively completing a challenging task (Clampitt & Downs, in press). Finally, when employees are given feedback they are more likely to develop a commitment to the standards. Ultimately, the goal of any feedback system is to have employees internalize the standards instead of depending on external commentary by others. After repeated performance at a certain level, aided by appropriate feedback, employees begin to develop a set of personal expectations. Actions then spring from a well of resolve and determination. This is why true professionals in any field, whether sports, dance, or management, consistently strive for excellence. To paraphrase an old jingle: "They expect more of themselves, and they get it."

(7) Standards of performance should be regularly and systematically reevaluated.

The competitive environment changes, technology changes and, consequently, expectations change. Thus it is natural to regularly reconsider the usefulness of current performance standards. Are the present standards sufficient to meet corporate goals? To be competitive? Have the employees suggested any new standards? These are the kinds of questions that must continually be asked to ensure the viability of the standards. For instance, only a few years ago it took up to two months to process an insurance claim. Now most companies can do it in several days. A new standard has been forced on the industry because of both competitive pressures and technical improvements. Firms that cannot meet those industry standards will eventually perish. This is not to say that standards always are in a state of flux. Employees need to know what is expected. Somewhere between frozen rigidity and chaos lies a semipermanent middle ground that provides both flexibility and reasonable certainty.

Implementing a Successful Feedback System

The principles discussed above provide a useful background, but they can not ensure a successful feedback system. Success is a product of both sound principles and effective actions. There are countless systems and methods for providing employees with feedback. No doubt more will be developed in the future. Ultimately, however, the success of any system hinges on four basic questions.

(1) Do employees know their job responsibilities?
(2) Do employees know the standards of evaluation?
(3) Is the informal feedback system effective?
(4) Is the formal feedback system effective?

There cannot be a weak link in the chain. The answer to each of these questions must be affirmative in order for the feedback system to work. If there is weakness at any point, the entire system collapses.

(1) Do employees know their job responsibilities?

Organizations that are more dynamic and in a constant state of flux tend to experience the most difficulties in this area. For instance, an employee at a large newspaper said: "I would like my position more defined. Where exactly do I fit in this organization? What is my importance?" These are the kinds of comments that indicate problems with the job description link in the feedback system. Our research in over 30 companies revealed that 16.6% of the employees felt unsatisfied with information about their job requirements. Clearly, if employees do not know their job responsibilities, they are probably not doing their job. The reasons for this are many. A manager may have assumed the employee already knew. Employees may have never read their job descriptions. Situations may have changed so much that the written job descriptions are outdated. The employee may get conflicting messages about the actual job duties from coworkers and the supervisor.

A variety of tactics have been used to inform employees of their job duties. For instance, the appraisal interview has often been used by managers to "compare notes" with their employees on job duties. Another highly touted suggestion was to have written job descriptions for every employee. But because job duties are always evolving, this approach often falls into disfavor. Here is a classic example of confusing the end-product with purpose. It is not really the end-product that is important, it is the process of writing out the duties that leads to the achievement of the purpose. The secret of the initial success of written job descriptions was that managers and employees were forced to think and communicate about job duties. Indeed, this is the fundamental principle regardless of the method.

(2) Do employees know the standards by which they are being evaluated?

The evidence indicates that this is an area of great concern for employees. Our research suggests that 43% of the employees were unsatisfied with information about how they were being judged. For example, one manager at a bank said: "I know my job, my manager knows I know my job, but I haven't a clue in this world how he evaluates me." More specifically, an employee may know her job is to troubleshoot for an engineering division but may be completely unaware of how her performance will be judged. Is it the number of problems she solves that counts? Does the complexity of the problem matter? What about the elegance of the solution? These are questions about standards of evaluation, not about job duties. Employees need to see the yardstick.

Why such problems exist is less easily determined. Sometimes managers never sit down to discuss, even in general terms, how employees will be evaluated. Managers may even feel some comfort in the ambiguity, which allows them greater flexibility in evaluating. Or, they may think that it is too difficult to specify criteria.

Some criteria can be easily quantified. A bank teller can be told that one performance criteria is the number of IRA accounts sold. In almost every job, there are at least a few quantifiable criteria. Surely managers should discuss these with employees. But there are also qualitative aspects of every job that are equally important. Bank tellers must be concerned with effective customer relations. Some overly enthusiastic behavioral psychologist might argue that even this can be quantified. A few businesses, for instance, insist that the employee smile at the customer at least six times while conducting a transaction and conclude with a canned, "Have a nice day." These dictates may work for robots, but they quickly wear thin with employees and clients. Thus, I do not share in the behaviorists' mad rush to quantify everything that can be counted. Harry Levinson (1970) has perceptively commented, "The greater the emphasis on measurement and quantification, the more likely the subtle, nonmeasurable elements of the task will be sacrificed. Quality of performance frequently, therefore, loses out to quantification" (p. 99).

How then can these qualitative criteria be communicated while maintaining employee accountability? There is no easy answer. Discussions need to take place with employees so that they can begin to get the feel for the more subtle criteria. Sometimes it is only through daily feedback and coaching that an employee develops an understanding of the more qualitative criteria. It happens over time. There is an added benefit of using some qualitative criteria. Employees often will think of novel ways to fulfill the criteria. There are countless ways to maintain effective customer relations, and as employees learn what is meant by the criteria they may discover new approaches. Moreover, employees will develop greater commitment to their own novel ideas as opposed to a manager's edicts. In the end, these employees are far more effective than the "six-smiles-a-client" automaton.

In 1989 David T. Kearns, the CEO and chairman of Xerox, was named *Financial World*'s "Man of the Year" for engineering the turnaround of the company. One of the critical parts of his initiative involved developing benchmarks for evaluating performance in 240 areas, ranging from billing systems to public relations. Accordingly, he sent his managers all over the country searching for better yardsticks by which to measure performance. For instance, the company went to American Express to learn about billing and to Ford for standards of factory floor layout. These measures, along with a new corporate strategy, worked and eventually resulted in quality improvements and competitive advantages (Siwolop, 1989). Many companies would reap equivalent benefits by copying such an aggressive campaign.

(3) Is the informal feedback system effective?

In the long run, the day-to-day "pat on the back" or reprimand may have a greater impact on employee performance than any other communication event. Regrettably, most employees are not satisfied with the daily feedback they receive:

- Specific positive reinforcement is their (management's) worst problem. Can't seem to praise anyone. You'd think it was costing them money. (Airline reservation clerk)
- You feel good when someone says you have done good, but thanks are not given around here. (Newspaper employee)
- (I need) more feedback on how well I am performing at other times besides the annual job development review. (Television station employee)

The problem is pervasive in organizations across the spectrum, from service-oriented companies to manufacturing firms. Indeed, over 40% of the employees in our study felt dissatisfied with the extent to which their efforts were recognized by the organization.

Reasons for the Problem

There are two primary reasons for this problem. First, many managers simply do not take the time to give regular feedback. The difficulty is compounded by the inherently different perspectives of employees and managers. For example, assume that a manager of a 20-person department decides to spend three minutes every week giving honest feedback to each employee. From the manager's viewpoint, a substantial commitment is being made: an hour a week. On the other hand, three minutes a week is a mere commercial break to the employee. Thus managers almost always overestimate, at least from the employees' perspective, the amount of daily feedback they communicate. Second, many managers simply do not notice employee performance unless there are difficulties. *Managers get more credit for problems solved than problems avoided.* No wonder they are quick to comment when employees fail but slow to praise a job well done. Employees want to be recognized, and they bemoan the "I only hear when things go wrong" managerial philosophy.

Managers must learn to separate the urgent from the important. If the job of managers is to solve problems, it is equally part of their job to train employees. Daily feedback, positive and negative, is an important part of the training process. It helps employees learn the performance standards, especially the qualitative ones, as well as reinforces the importance of the standards. By encouraging performance of the standards, daily feedback can rally employee commitment to the standards and provide that much-sought tonic of personal recognition. For instance, the relations between management and labor became so unsettling at Preston Trucking that they instituted the "Four-to-One Rule." Managers were required to give four messages of praise for every message of criticism. One can imagine the truckers' initial reaction, but over time tensions not only eased but became collegial. In fact, in 1988 employees submitted over 4,000 ideas to the suggestion program with an average value of $300 each (Farnham, 1989).

The Message

Given the imperative to provide daily feedback, it is important to consider precisely what should be communicated. In particular, there are three distinct types of information that can be communicated on a daily basis.

First, the most obvious areas for feedback revolve around agreed-upon standards. Therefore, both positive and negative deviations from the standards should be specifically noted. If a teller is required to sell 12 IRA accounts over the year, and after three months has not sold one, then this should be brought to the employee's attention. On the other hand, if the teller has already sold six, then likewise, the employee should be praised.

Second, uncommunicated performance standards can be discussed on a daily basis. Some standards, by their nature, are difficult to articulate ahead of time. It is impossible to specify every standard. Who could anticipate, for instance, that an employee needs to be told about some specific grooming habits or proper modes of address? There are countless other examples, all of which only can be dealt with on a case-by-case basis, ever widening the circle of congruence.

Third, there also are attributes of success that take the form of character qualities that can and should be discussed on a regular basis. Thoughtfulness, attentiveness, flexibility, discretion, sensitivity, thoroughness, and diligence are just a few examples. Any opportunity to reinforce these values should be seized by the manager. The traditional view of motivating employees is built around praising/criticizing, as in rewarding or punishing specific performance behaviors. But people are more than rats. These behavioral techniques encourage the repetition of the same behavior. Because situations change and novel contingencies arise, the same behaviors may actually become dysfunctional. There is a better way.

Specifically, the manager should praise *both* the behavior and the implicit character quality. The employee who turns in an insightful proposal and has anticipated numerous potential objections could be praised for an "excellent report." Such a comment might encourage future reports of this type. But more could be said: "The insights of your report are remarkable. It shows a quality of *thoroughness* that we value in this organization." Not only is the specific behavior reinforced, but, more importantly, the quality of thoroughness. The key is to link the specific behavior to the character quality. Then employees are encouraged not only to repeat this behavior but to find other novel situations in which to exhibit this quality. The charm of a character quality, like "thoroughness," lies in its ambiguity. It can be applied in numerous and varied situations that even the wisest manager could not anticipate (see Figure 6.2). Such an approach brings to bear the naturally motivating creative instincts in people. It has the indelible mark of the human touch.

The Method

How praise and criticism are given is as important as the message itself. Many people react more to style than substance. The wise manager is attentive to both.

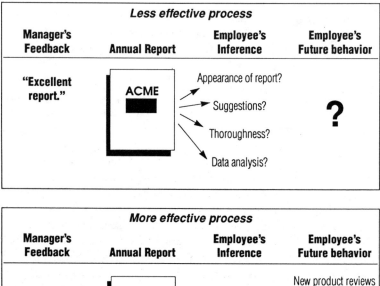

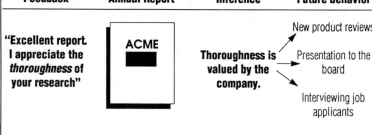

Figure 6.2 Linking Praise to Attributes

The need for praise seems almost insatiable. People love it. Of course, if the praise is insincere or dishonest, employees will resent it. Great statesmen, like great managers, seem to have special insights into the unique characteristics of those with whom they work closely. They have an extraordinary grasp of the essential and fundamental qualities of the person. One of the greatest leaders of all time, Winston Churchill (1931), writes of Lloyd George:

The new Prime Minister possessed two characteristics which were in harmony with this period of convulsion. First, a power of living in the present, without taking short views. Every day for him was filled with the hope and the impulse of a fresh beginning. He surveyed the problems of each morning with an eye unobstructed by preconceived opinions, past utterances, or previous disappointment and defeats. In times of peace such a mood is not always admirable, nor often successful for long. But in the intense crisis when the world was a kaleidoscope, when every month all the values and relations were changed by some prodigious event and its measureless reactions, this inexhaustible mental agility, guided by the main purpose of Victory, was a rare advantage. His intuition fitted the crisis better than the logical reasoning of more rigid minds. (pp. 688-689)

This is the kind of praise the wise manager gives. It is based on keen observation and shows deep thought into the person's uniqueness. Employees will perceive this type of praise as sincere and be motivated by the manager's thoughtfulness. It is not some blanket "warm fuzzy" cast on any passerby. In short, it demonstrates insight into an individual's character.

This is not enough, however. Otherwise, all biographers would be great statesmen. There also must be the knowledge and willingness to transform insight into action. In addition to Churchill's extraordinary discernment into Lloyd George's qualities, he also demonstrated an amazing perceptiveness of situations in which the Prime Minister would be most effective. Herein lies the essence of effective management.

The most frequent problem with management's effort to praise employees lies in the level of specificity (Larson, 1986). Typically, praise runs along these lines: "Good job"; "Way to go"; or "At-a-boy." While abstractness is useful in some circumstances, it is not in this case. Moreover, this kind of praise tends to be more evaluative than descriptive. Researchers have found that descriptive praise is more effective (Downs, Johnson & Barge, 1984). For example, the typical manager tends to say, "You really are effective with customers." A more useful and descriptive comment might be, "You really have an ability to communicate effectively with customers. The way you smile and ask pertinent questions shows your sensitivity to their needs." These remarks show that the manager pays precise attention to the employee's performance. Moreover, the manager links the behaviors to the character quality of "sensitivity," while personally recognizing the employee—one life touching another.

Criticism needs to be handled with equal finesse. "Giving criticism must satisfy multiple goals—stating a problem clearly while at the same time remaining attentive to the relational implications" (Tracy, VanDusen, & Robinson, 1987, p. 46). Certainly it should be done in private, with an emphasis on behavioral corrections rather than so-called "personality defects" (Arvey & Ivancevich, 1980). There is a distinction between person- ality traits, which are most often treated as nonchangeable aspects of an individual, and character qualities, which anyone can develop. Indeed, criticism of a specific behavioral problem could be couched in terms of acquiring a certain character quality. Students may be encouraged to spell correctly and use grammar properly by exhorting them to become more professional and show an attentiveness to detail. Thus specific writing skills are related to two qualities useful in a wide variety of settings.

There is probably no situation more delicate than criticizing someone. Buck Rogers (1986), who served as vice president of marketing at IBM for ten years, remarked:

> I think that at one time I was perceived as an easygoing type of manager with a superior staff of people. That's because I always praised in public and criticized in private. I never thought it necessary to let others know that someone in my department didn't do his job properly. . . . I entered each of these private conversations with the assumption that both of us wanted to accomplish the same thing: perform our job with the highest degree of excellence possible. And, with a minimum of bruised feelings, correct our mistakes and get on with the job. (pp. 40-41)

Clearly, the proper motivation and setting is the place to start. Note that Rogers links his criticism to a larger positive context. This is one of the keys to effective criticism. Another is that the feedback should be maximally informative and minimally evaluative (Downs, Smeyak, & Martin, 1980). People react differently to criticism. Employees who are confident and have a high need for achievement react more positively. They may even actively seek negative feedback in order to improve their performance. Employees with lower self-esteem and achievement needs may become disheartened and discouraged (McFarlin & Blascovich, 1981). Clearly, the wise manager adapts to these different contingencies.

While at a conference in Philadelphia, I noticed a building a few blocks from my hotel that was being torn down to make way for a new structure. A massive crane with a huge wrecking ball pounded into the building and slowly ripped apart the structure. For five days this enormous crush of iron on brick went on, and still, the small 10-story structure was only partially demolished. What a contrast to the instantaneous destruction of much larger buildings by the careful placement of dynamite charges at strategic points. In a matter of seconds, even a 50-story building can be toppled. Unfortunately many managers, like this massive wrecking ball, thrash into their employees with salvo after salvo of criticism. The source of irritation is never really removed and the new structure cannot be built. There is a need for managers who can discern those strategic points and quickly remove the offending behaviors, so as to erect in the same spot a new and gleaming building of character.

(4) Is the formal feedback system effective?

Much ink has been spilled over the issue of performance appraisals. Business journals, periodicals, and books are filled with discussions on how to more effectively conduct the performance review. And with good reason; there is probably no greater area of employee dissatisfaction. In fact, in a survey of 300 public and private agencies, Lopez (1968) found that 75% maintained performance evaluation plans, but fewer than half said that the plans were achieving their stated objectives. This disgruntled employee expresses the sentiments of many:

> My immediate supervisor felt it was her duty to give me my evaluation as required once a year. It was handed to me with, "I'll discuss it later." What I asked her, "Why not now?", she said, "I don't have time." This was my year's work, and it was no big deal! *It was to me.*

Other complaints abound. Unfair rating scales, lack of objectivity, and lack of specific examples are just a few of the ones frequently mentioned (e.g., Laird & Clampitt, 1985). But this is not to say employees want to avoid the formal appraisal. Employees want this kind of feedback. In spite of problems, one survey found that 90% of the employees reacted favorably to the idea of a formal evaluation (Mayfield, 1960). In short, the manager who seeks an effective feedback system faces a formidable challenge.

Reasons

There are a variety of reasons for the problem but three are particularly noteworthy.

First, many managers react negatively to the feedback process because it is used to accomplish multiple goals that sometimes are incompatible. (See Table 6.1.) One airline we investigated used the appraisal form for individual feedback to employees, promotion, and salary determination. Many of the managers felt the variety of goals encouraged distortions such as inflated ratings and the lack of negative comments. Some managers did not want to hurt employees' long-term promotion opportunities, so they made vague general comments. Others were less virtuous. One manager took a Machiavellian approach. He gave a troublesome employee high marks so

Table 6.1 Potential Objectives of Appraisal Systems

Objective	Concern
Salary Increase	Salary decisions are rarely based solely on performance. Factors like market conditions, length of service, and corporate economic outlook enter into the decision.
Promotion Potential	An employee may perform one job with a high degree of competence, but be unsuitable for greater responsibility.
"Grade" Past Performance	At times a "grade" may not motivate employees and fail to uncover important reasons for performance levels.
Motivate	Many managers leave out the "bad news" when trying to motivate employees.
Improve Performance	Sometimes managers are so "problem-oriented" they fail to effectively and specifically praise employees.

as to promote him out of his department. That is, of course, one way to get rid of a problem — give it to some one else.

Since the objectives of the airline's appraisal system were unclear, many managers voiced frustration:

> The uses are very nebulous. I don't know who sees the form or what is done with them. We are told one thing and another happens. The first year, they told us our workbooks were for our private use, so everyone was very candid. Then the department head collected them and put them in his files. It leaves great uncertainty as to how it is to be used.

This is the price of imprudence: The entire system falls into disrepute. And the basic purpose, indeed the entire rationale, for the feedback process falls by the wayside.

Second, many managers feel compelled to inflate ratings. It might be called the "Lake Wobegon Phenomenon," where "everyone is good looking and all the employees are above-average." Part of the problem lies in the natural competition between different departments. Many managers feel that other department managers rate their employees highly, and if they do not do the same, then their employees will be penalized in the long run. Another part of the problem lies in the meanings attached to the numbers or categories typically used in appraisal forms. In one study we asked a group of managers from the same company to respond to a series of precise questions about what they meant when they used terms like "above-average," "average," and "below-average" on their appraisal forms. Many discrepancies were found. One of the more striking was the meaning of the word "average." Over 60% of the managers believed it meant, "the employee completed all jobs satisfactorily," while 37% felt it meant, "performance was uneven, some above average and some below" (Laird & Clampitt, 1985). Clearly such discrepancies can lead to uneven evaluations.

Third, many managers resist the appraisal process because they feel that they are "playing God." Douglas McGregor (1972) puts it eloquently:

> Managers are uncomfortable when they are put in the position of "playing God." The respect we hold for the inherent value of the individual leaves us distressed when we must take responsibility for judging the personal warmth of a fellow man. Yet the conventional approach to performance appraisal forces us not only to make such judgments and to see them acted upon but also to communicate them to those we have judged. Small wonder we resist! (p. 6)

Understandably, managers try to avoid situations involving the deity-to-sinner kind of relationship. Yet, in many cases, this fear of "playing God" masks a deeper problem of an inability or unwillingness to face conflict.

Regardless of the actual reason for the reticence, managers are destined to "provide" some kind of feedback. The key, then, is to provide useful information. Furthermore, providing objectively based judgments need not imply a divine verdict of a person's worth. The alternatives are worse. Harold Mayfield (1960) puts the matter in perspective:

> Is there one of us who has not kicked himself for some inglorious episode in our human relationships? This risk I believe to be one of the prices we must pay for any attempt at serious communications. Against it, we must weigh the cost of silence. It, too, leaves scars. (p. 30)

The Message

For many managers, performance appraisal is a perfunctory and sometimes dreaded task. Indeed, Figure 6.2 is an example of the all too common approach to this critical communication event. Part of the problem is that training is either nonexistent or lax (Moscinski, 1979). Yet, the wise manager makes virtue out of necessity by effectively managing the message as well as the process. The manager's message should be shaped by five guidelines.

Dialogue		Commentary
MANAGER:	Hi, Chris. Welcome. Please sit down.	
EMPLOYEE:	Thank you.	
MANAGER:	As you know, this is the regularly scheduled performance appraisal that I conduct with each employee. The purpose of this talk is to review your performance during the past year. Actually, there should be few surprises because I've tried to keep you informed throughout the year. You've read over my report, I assume, so I want to spend our time discussing some critical areas and answer any of your questions.	*The manager does an effective job of orienting the employee. Could discuss how the information in the interview will be used.*
EMPLOYEE:	Fine, that sounds good because I do have some questions.	
MANAGER:	I'd like to start with the positive areas. Let me just list your greatest strengths:	*The manager has clearly thought about the strengths of the employee.*
	1. You seem to be able to handle the cash drawer without assistance or errors.	
	2. You have the ability to explain savings services effectively to customers.	*The manager could discuss specific communication abilities that are valued by a company that stresses "customer service."*
	3. Your general attitude toward the job is quite positive.	*The manager could isolate a quality, like enthusiasm, that is essential for the job and provide examples of how Chris exhibited this quality.*
	In general, I'm impressed by your abilities after being here only nine months.	
EMPLOYEE:	Well thanks — I've really tried hard. I enjoy working here and that really helps. My coworkers are really a joy to work with — they make it easy.	*Employee reveals that coworkers are a source of motivation.*

Figure 6.3 Sample Appraisal Interview

MANAGER:	Now I'd like to explore with you three areas of improvement. First, I've rated you average in organizational abilities. At times, you seem unorganized.	*The manager does not bring up specific evidence or the harm done by poor organization.*
EMPLOYEE:	Well, I just try to do so much — sometimes I don't take time to keep things organized. I mean, I try to keep my papers straight and stuff — but my priority is on customer service.	*The employee sees no relationship between organization and customer service.*
MANAGER:	Oh, but I still think some improvement is needed here.	*The manager should show some link between organization, working well with coworkers, and effective customer service.*
EMPLOYEE:	I've always had this problem and frankly, it seems more important to serve customer needs.	*The employee fails to take responsibility for the problem.*
MANAGER:	The second area that I'd like to see improvement in is cross-selling. We set a goal of cross-selling seven NOW accounts. You actually sold five NOW accounts. I'd like to see that up to par next year. You know this is a high priority in the business.	*The manager ignores the employee's denial and fails to offer useful suggestions. The manager does provide specific evidence to back up evaluation #2.*
EMPLOYEE:	I know I've kind of failed in that area, but sometimes it's so hard — I feel kind of awkward mentioning it — I just try to be friendly. I don't want to offend the customer. I feel like I really do service the customer effectively.	*The employee attributes the problem to the goal, not to self.*
MANAGER:	Well, you do, but I'd still like to see more cross-selling. The third area is bringing in new customers. We set a goal of 10 new customers — I have only five new customers credited to your efforts this year.	*The manager misses the opportunity to link the sale of NOW accounts to customer service.*
EMPLOYEE:	You know that goal is practically impossible — all my friends are already customers, and I just don't know what to do.	*The employee attributes the problem to the goal, not to self.*
MANAGER:	I understand — this isn't really criticism. Overall, you're doing a fine job — I want to emphasize that! For only being here nine months, I'm impressed. Really!	*The manager soft-pedals the criticism.*
EMPLOYEE:	So you think I'm doing a good job!	*The employee seeks out a positive evaluation.*

Figure 6.3 Continued.

Dialogue	Commentary
MANAGER: Yes, basically yes. You are making progress — I'm pleased. Do you have any questions?	*The manager obliges.*
EMPLOYEE: No, it's basically what I expected — I mean you always tell me I'm doing a good job. Thanks.	
MANAGER: Well, there are some areas of improvement.	*The manager is halfheartedly fulfilling an obligation but is not trying to change Chris's behavior. The employee feels good and sees no need to change. The manager feels relieved because it's over.*
EMPLOYEE: Yes, I know, but basically, I'm doing a good job. I mean I like my job and the people I work with. Is that all?	
MANAGER: Yes, I guess so, except I need you to sign this form.	

Figure 6.3 Continued.

First, communicate the exact purpose for the interview. As is well documented above, numerous problems arise when the purpose of the interview is not precisely understood by employees and management. It can become a sham. A written policy that is widely available throughout the organization that details the purposes of the process is a useful starting point. All managers in the organization should have a similar view of the purpose of the formal feedback system. At the outset of the interview, every employee should be reminded of the appraisal's purpose as well as how the information will be used. This helps new employees determine what type of information is appropriate to share. Even though this may become a bit repetitive over the years, it helps ensure that employees are continually focused on one objective.

Second, communicate the importance of the interview. Setting a specific time and place for the interview sends a powerful secondary message that the interaction has great significance. Interruptions like phone calls should be avoided. Even the written documentation used can communicate the serious nature of the encounter.

Third, be specific and descriptive when making evaluations. This means providing evidence to back up the ratings or assessments. Every manager must be able to confidently answer this question: Can I prove my assessment? The problem usually does not occur on the negative items but, surprisingly, with the positive issues. Instead of saying: "You did a great job designing the advertising campaign this year," the manager could say: "Your ad campaign was quite successful. Our market share increased after it was implemented. I was particularly impressed by our creative use of dialogue in the campaign." These kinds of remarks are more readily accepted by employees and provide insight into the manager's yardstick.

Fourth, avoid commenting on personality characteristics. Employees are naturally defensive if they feel their personality is what is really being evaluated. Yet, if managers deeply ponder the matter, they will often see that the problems lie in some basic behaviors. Someone, for instance, might remark: "You are a very stubborn individual." The wise manager comments on a specific behavior: "During meetings you need to listen more carefully to others' ideas and suggestions. You could look at people while they talk and even try to restate their opinion rather than your objections." Even linking the behaviors to a character quality might prove useful: "I personally appreciate the way you stand by your convictions. This is admirable but this could be balanced with a greater sensitivity to others. It is important to be a person of conviction, but it is equally important to know when to use this quality." The employee still might bristle at those comments, but in the long run change is more likely.

Fifth, capitalize on employee motivations. Effective managers not only are sensitive to the natural motivators of their employees, but know how to link the motivators to critical objectives. Indeed, there is abundant evidence from scholars that feedback without employee commitment to improve does not increase performance (e.g., Pinder, 1984). In Figure 6.3, the manager fails to pick up on the fact that the employee is highly motivated to provide quality service to the customer. The manager could have linked "customer service" to the problem areas of "organization" and "selling NOW accounts." For example, the manager might have said: "I'm impressed by your commitment to quality customer service. But by being organized you can better service the customer. For instance, you will be able to find vital information more quickly, which will translate into speedier service for the customers. . . ." Such linkages are difficult to execute but the dividends may be great.

Methods

The process may be as important as the message. Five guidelines are noteworthy.

First, decide on a useful method to achieve the purpose. Essay evaluations, rating scales, observation periods, ranking methods, and critical incident techniques are just a few of the options (Oberg, 1972). Deciding on which approach depends on the specific objectives of the system (see Table 6.2). If the purpose is basically to encourage employee growth, then written essays about employee performance would prove useful. If there is a highly competitive situation within the unit, like a sales force, then perhaps ranking employees is the best approach. Rating scales are the most widely used approach. A scale of from five to nine categories tends to produce the most consistent ratings. Regardless of the method used, training is the key to insuring that practice harmonizes with purpose.

In some cases, managers do not have a say in the evaluation methods. They are told by the company what forms to use. This makes it all the more important to know the limitations and advantages of the various options. The wise manager then can supplement the mandatory system with other "home-grown" measures.

Second, utilize "task-inherent" feedback. Sometimes the most useful feedback comes from the task itself, not the supervisor. For example, commission salespeople are inherently aware of their level of sales. In this case, a supervisor may not need to comment on the discrepancy between goal and performance level. Rather, the supervisor's role becomes that of a coach and counselor. Indeed, when an employee has developed a commitment to certain

Table 6.2 Appraisal Techniques

Method	Strengths	Weaknesses
Rating Scale	Allows comparison between employees without forcing distinctions. Easy to use.	Disagreement over meanings of the numbers.
Essay	Allows the appraiser the flexibility to uniquely characterize each employee.	Difficulties in comparing employees. Variances between raters in level of specificity.
Rank Order Employees	Creates clear distinctions between employees. Often used for salary purposes.	Forces unfair or artificial comparisons between employees.
Critical Incidents	Focuses on employee behavior. Avoids appraisals of employee personality. Provides specific evidence.	Takes time to record every incident., May cause manager to delay daily feedback. May encourage an overemphasis on the peaks and valleys of performance, rather than typical performance.
Management by Objectives	Increases employee motivation and understanding of standards.	Takes a great deal of time and effort. May be difficult to compare employees.

standards, task-inherent feedback may be more important to the employee than feedback from a supervisor. Employees are more likely to accept feedback from those who have directly experienced their work and whom they therefore deem credible. This may include clients, coworkers, and even top management (Cusella, 1987). The wise course for a supervisor might be to create mechanisms for employees so that they receive feedback about their performance from the task itself. For example, a group of tellers could observe a videotaped focus group about the bank's service reputation. Such methods subtly augment the appraisal process.

Third, assign employees specific preparations. Many organizations provide appraisal forms for both the manager and the subordinate that are parallel in format. The manager rates the employee's performance in designated areas, and the employee rates his or her own performance on a similar form. These documents are to be completed before the actual appraisal interview and may even include task-inherent measures. This step reinforces the importance of the process, while ensuring that employees come to the meeting fully prepared. The two documents can serve as a stimulus for focused discussion on the employee's performance. No topics are skirted out of fear or anxiety. All issues are more objectively addressed. Using these forms, the interview can proceed after a thorough discussion of the employee's job responsibilities.

Fourth, carefully consider how the appraisal process is influenced by interpersonal needs. Generally, managers try to avoid giving negative feedback unless severe problems have been recognized. Moreover, because managers do not wish to appear judgmental, they frequently distort their feedback in a positive direction (Fisher, 1979). For example, note how the manager in Figure 6.3 says, "This isn't really criticism. . . . Overall you are doing a fine job." On the other hand, employees seek to maintain a positive self-esteem and typically see negative information as more positive than it actually is (Ilgen, Fisher, & Taylor, 1979). They often attribute problems to factors beyond their control. Compounding the matter is that poor performers actively try to short-circuit criticism by seeking out positive comments (Larson, 1989). Note, for example, how in Figure 6.3 the employee implies that there is simply not enough time to be organized; in other words, it is not the employee's fault.

Poor performers may even build the excuses into their inquiries or ask leading questions about their performance (Larson, 1989). For example, in Figure 6.3, the employee's final remarks end with a question that almost begs the manager for confirmation of an overly glowing assessment. Therefore, the manager and employee, by virtue of their predispositions, cocreate a process in which each party inevitably draws seemingly reasonable but decidedly warped impressions. Employees "may hold positively inflated views of their organizational performance" (Cusella, 1987, p. 653). But managers frequently have an equally skewed view and feel that employees have a clear understanding of the areas of improvement when, in fact, they do not. Certainly, this is what happens in the situation depicted in Figure 6.3 with the result that the employee's performance never improves. Wise managers are aware of these powerful forces at work in the appraisal interview. They seek to control the process so that employees have an unclouded view of their performance, while carefully avoiding needless damage to self-esteem. The former CEO of three companies including Uniroyal Goodrich Tire Company, Charles Ames (1989), summarizes the manager's responsibility best:

> There is nothing kind about glossing over weaknesses that could be corrected if the individual were aware of them. Nor is there anything kind about deluding

someone into thinking that he or she is doing well or has greater opportunities than is actually the case. Failure to be completely honest can easily hurt someone's chances of becoming an effective contributor. And it may even jeopardize the person's career. No manager has the right to do that. And if that manager can't get up the nerve or confidence to talk straight about this, that manager shouldn't remain a manager — because that person isn't. (p. 138)

Fifth, use past performance as a bridge to the future. While part of the appraisal process should be dedicated to an evaluation of the past, there also is a need to seek change for the future. New contingencies brought on by the inevitable changes in the organization and the competitive environment can be discussed as a focal point for new standards and goals. After all, the focus of the entire feedback process is the relationship between actions and goals — in a word, performance. Goal setting can be addressed at the latter part of the interview. In the end, the employee, regardless of the course of the appraisal, should be offered the most basic of all human needs — hope.

Final Thoughts

In the long run, the effective feedback system seeks to improve employee performance so as to increase organizational performance. Whatever method is chosen to accomplish this end, this goal must be central in the manager's mind. Harold Mayfield (1960) puts it: "Stripped of all jargon [the performance appraisal] is simply an attempt to think clearly about each person's performance and future prospects against a background of this total work situation" (p. 27). It takes effort, thought, and dedication to accomplish, but the rewards to managers, employees, and the organization are manyfold.

We conducted one communication assessment in which the company scored considerably below the average on every feedback question. Upon arriving at the company to present the results, we walked past an isolated cluster of brown, brittle, and dying shrubbery in front of the company's office. At the time, I thought what a perfect symbol for this company's management philosophy! The company watered and cared for those bushes about as well as they gave feedback to their employees. The employees had no job descriptions, they had no idea how they were being evaluated, they never were praised, and appraisal reviews had not been conducted in years. The results were predictable: low job satisfaction, poor motivation, uneven performance, and a host of other communication difficulties. Most companies are not in such severe shape. Many have neglected certain critical areas. But every company could pay much closer attention to its feedback system. As any horticulturist knows, this can be done only day by day and with the utmost of care.

References

Ames, B. C. (1989). Straight talk from the new CEO. *Harvard Business Review, 67*(6), 132-138.

Arvey, R. D., & Ivancevich, J. M. (1980). Punishment in organizations: A review, propositions, and research suggestions. *Academy of Management Review, 5,* 123-132.

Bronowski, J. (1973). *The ascent of man.* Boston: Little, Brown.

Churchill, W. S. (1931). *The world crisis.* New York: Scribner.

Clampitt, P. G., & Downs, C. W. (in press). Employee perceptions of communication/productivity relationship: A field study. *Journal of Business Communication.*

Cusella, L. P. (1987). Feedback, motivation, and performance. In F. Jablin, L. Putnam, K. Roberts, & L. Porter (Eds.), *Handbook of organizational communication* (pp. 624-678). Newbury Park, CA: Sage.

Downs, C. W., & Hazen, M. (1977). A factor analytic study of communication satisfaction. *Journal of Business Communication, 14,* 65-74.

Downs, C. W., Johnson, K. M., & Barge, J. K. (1984). Communication feedback and task performance in organizations: A review of the literature. In H. Greenbaum, R. Falcione, & S. Hellweg (Eds.), *Organization communication abstracts* (pp. 13-47). Beverly Hills, CA: Sage.

Downs, C. W., Smeyak, G. P., & Martin, E. (1980). *Professional interviewing.* New York: Harper & Row.

Farnham, A. (1989, December 4). The trust gap. *Fortune,* pp. 56-78.

Fisher, C. D. (1979). Transmission of positive and negative feedback to subordinates: A laboratory investigation. *Journal of Applied Psychology, 64,* 533-540.

Ilgen, D. R., Fisher, C. D., & Taylor, M. S. (1979). Consequences of individual feedback on behavior in organizations. *Journal of Applied Psychology, 64,* 349-371.

Judson, H. F. (1980). *The search for solutions.* New York: Holt, Rinehart & Winston.

Laird, A., & Clampitt, P. G. (1985). Effective performance appraisal: Viewpoints from managers. *Journal of Business Communication, 22*(3), 49-57.

Larson, J. R., Jr. (1986). Supervisors' performance feedback to subordinates: The effect of performance valence and outcome dependence. *Organizational Behavior and Human Decision Processes, 37,* 391-408.

Larson, J. R., Jr. (1989). The dynamic interplay between employees' feedback-seeking strategies and supervisors' delivery of performance feedback. *Academy of Management Review, 14*(3), 408-422.

Levinson, H. (1970). Management by whose objectives? *Harvard Business Review, 48*(4), 125-134.

Lopez, F. M. (1968). *Evaluating employee performance.* Chicago: Public Personnel Association.

Maslow, A. H. (1970). *Motivation and personality.* New York: Harper & Row.

Mayfield, H. (1960). In defense of performance appraisal. *Harvard Business Review, 57,* 80-85.

McFarlin, D. B., & Blascovich, J. (1981). Effects of self-esteem and performance feedback on future affective preferences and cognitive expectations. *Journal of Personality and Social Psychology, 40*(3), 521-531.

McGregor, D. (1972). An uneasy look at performance appraisal. *Harvard Business Review, 50*(5), 133-138.

Miller, M. W. (1985, June 3). Productivity spies. *Wall Street Journal,* pp. 1, 15.

Moscinski, P. (1979). *The appraisal system in American business and industry.* Unpublished master's thesis, University of Kansas.

Oberg, W. (1972). Make performance appraisal relevant. *Harvard Business Review, 50*(1), 61-67.

Pinder, C. C. (1984). *Work motivation.* Glenview, IL: Scott, Foresman.

Rodgers, F. G. (1986). *The IBM way.* New York: Harper & Row.

Siwolop, S. (1989, December 12). Man of the year. *Financial World,* pp. 57-59.

Tracy, K., VanDusen, D., & Robinson, S. (1987). "Good" and "bad" criticism: A descriptive analysis. *Journal of Communication, 37*(2), 46-59.

7

Communicating Change

> There is nothing more difficult to carry out, nor more doubtful of success, nor more dangerous to handle, than to initiate a new order of things. For the reformer has enemies in all those who profit from the old order, and only lukewarm defenders in all those who would profit from the new order, this lukewarmness arising partly from the incredibility of anything new until they have had actual experience of it.
>
> Machiavelli

> Failure is never fatal, but failure to change might be.
>
> John Wooden

Change is an inevitable and sometimes brutal fact of corporate life. Technological progress, market fluctuations, hostile takeovers, and new governmental regulations make change a certainty. The sudden impact of a political crisis, a recent competitive challenge, an innovation, or a shift in consumer demand can quickly force radical changes on management. Internal forces like personnel developments, reorganizations, budgetary restraints or technical innovations also ensure that change, for better or worse, will be the lifelong companion of the manager. In fact, managing and communicating change may be the greatest challenge facing today's managers.

Change is, of course, ubiquitous. Some changes are welcomed, others abhorred. Some are induced out of necessity, others inspired out of vision or prescience. Every change in every organization is a distinctly unique event. Hence, communicating those changes requires a thorough knowledge of the particular change to be implemented as well as a special sensitivity to the culture of the organization. There is no one simple recipe that can ensure success. Situations are too complex and variable for that. There are, however, some basic principles that have proven successful in a number of organizations. These ideas are the focus of this chapter.

Approaches to Change

All organizations either explicitly or implicitly have an orientation to change that defines for employees who can suggest, institute, and act on a new idea. Three typical patterns emerge: (1) management orientation, (2) employee orientation, and (3) integrative.

Management Orientation

The most traditional approach is for top management to assess the need for change and dictate that the change be carried out through the chain of command. This is the approach taken by the Arrow manager. The assumption is that those in leadership positions are in a better position to *recognize* the need for change, to know *what* needs to be changed, and even *how* the change should be implemented. There are variations on this general theme, but such is the archetype.

Some corporations out of necessity adopt this approach because of a turbulent business environment or rapidly changing conditions. The court-ordered reorganization of AT&T and Bell telephone companies certainly is one such example. Mr. Zane Barnes, the CEO of Southwestern-Bell, remarked that after deregulation, top management identified 2,000 different major changes that were needed to comply with the court order. Not only was rapid change needed, but phone service, telephone hookups, and other services had to continue to be maintained at the high level of service that customers had come to expect. According to Barnes, "It was like trying to take apart and reassemble a 747, while in flight" (personal communication). If leadership from the top had not been exerted, then chaos would have been the likely result. In this case, as in many others, the top-down strategy was the only reasonable alternative.

Change may also be instigated at the top when a CEO or a manager has a bright new vision of where the organization can be in the future. Former Secretary of State Henry Kissinger (1982) has perceptively written on statesmanship:

> A nation and its leaders must choose between moral certainty coupled with
> exorbitant risk, and the willingness to act on unprovable assumptions to deal

with challenges when they are manageable. I favor the latter course. . . . The statesman's duty is to bridge the gap between his nation's experience and his vision. If he gets too far ahead of his people, he will lose his mandate; if he confines himself to the conventional he will lose control over events. The qualities that distinguish a great statesman are prescience and courage, not analytical intelligence. He must have a conception of the future and the courage to move toward it while it is still shrouded to most of his compatriots. (p. 169)

Likewise, some prescient managers see beyond the sights of the colleagues and predict with astonishing regularity the future trends while leading the company in that direction. A. P. Giannini of Bank of America was such a man. As the corporate founder, he was one of the first to introduce advertising by banks, bank cards, and a host of other ideas. By leading the way, visionaries ensure that the organization has a stake in the future. Without courageous leadership, a company can only adopt the innovations of others, when it usually proves more costly and difficult to capture the market share. Or the opportunity is simply lost. There is a price for complacency.

An overly zealous management orientation can, however, be problematic. Stifling the innovative spirit of employees is one possible result. If the operating principle appears to be, "The only good ideas come from the top," then opportunities can be squandered with amazing ease. Moreover, employee satisfaction and productivity may decline. And even "visionary leadership" can go awry. Coca-Cola is not the only company to have a new product (New Coke) hailed as a bold new innovative change, only to have difficulties in the marketplace. Visions do not always translate into reality; they may be mere delusions.

Employee Orientation

The heart of this approach is *intrapreneurship* (Pinchot, 1985). That is, ideas for changes and innovations percolate up through the organizational hierarchy. Employees are encouraged to have input into changes and methods of implementation. The underlying premise of this approach is that employees are in the best position to suggest changes. The basic operating principle is that those who participate in making the decisions for a change are more likely to wholeheartedly accept and implement the change. Therefore, resistance to change is minimized. This is the approach favored by Circuit managers.

Lucrative opportunities may be lost when employees' ideas are ignored. A kind of collective blindness can occur in which management views a situation in a similar way. Ralph Lauren tried for years to sell his superiors and colleagues on his unique fashion concept. He failed. He then struck out on his own, and is now one of the most successful retailers in the world. Not only has he created the distinctive "Polo" look, but he has also branched out into home furnishings (Trachtenberg, 1988). The voice of a solitary prophet in the wilderness may be more trustworthy that the chants and choruses of the multitudes.

A variation of this approach involves seeking employee approval of managerial ideas. One rather unusual example of this approach occurred at Multimate International Corporation in 1985. The company of 250 workers makes word-processing programs for personal computers. Management contemplated developing products that would compete head-on with IBM. Corporate President Wilton H. Jones said, "We didn't feel we could commit them (the employees) to something this large without their permission." The novel solution: have employees vote on whether they wished to take on Big Blue. The result: 92% of the employees voted "Yes, go for it!" Even more astonishing was that 42% said they would take a pay cut in order to pursue the endeavor (Lewyn, 1985). Mandating change from above without employee approval, especially when it involved employee time and money, might have been met with some fairly stern resistance. This was a useful strategy for a company of this size and at this stage of development. The idea of a formal vote, regardless of the actual outcome, was a stroke of genius, for it sent a strong and powerful message to employees that their feelings actually mattered. Moreover, it demonstrated in a tangible way that the corporation honestly believed change was something all employees participated in and was not the sole province of a select few. Since this incident, the company has been purchased by the Ashton-Tate Corporation, and the Multimate software has undergone numerous revisions. Now there are over one million users of the product.

Integrative Approach

The critiques of the two previous approaches suggests a third and more appropriate choice for managing change. The central focus is not on *who* champions the change but on the *who, what, when, and where:* the situation. In the integrative approach the manager has to determine if the situation warrants either the management orientation, employee orientation, or some combination. There is no one best strategy for coping with change, just as there is no one best form of transportation. It all depends on who is traveling with you, what you intend to do, when you plan to leave, and where you intend to go. A car is best for a trip to the grocery store, but a plane would surely prove more useful on a transatlantic journey. Likewise, the wise manager needs to chose the appropriate vehicle for change.

Many effective and useful changes can be initiated at the grass roots of the organization. Benefits such as greater understanding and commitment to change naturally flow from this approach. All changes cannot, however, be initiated at this level of the organization. The very element that makes grass roots innovation so uniquely enlightening also acts as a conceptual blinder. That is, the grass roots vantage point is excellent for suggesting changes at the grass roots level, but it often precludes a clear understanding of changes needed at other levels of the organization. For example, the supervisor of the printing shop may have excellent suggestions about how to improve the efficiency and effectiveness of that department. However, the supervisor's boss, who is in charge of the printing, purchasing, and maintenance departments, may need to ask a more fundamental question: Can the corporation as a whole function more effectively by having material printed by an outside vendor? Almost by definition, this is a change that the print shop supervisor cannot recommend. On the other hand, the manager has a broader company-wide perspective from which to view the situation. Indeed, in one study, Paul, Robertson, and Herzberg (1969) make precisely this point. They found that when personnel specialists were asked to suggest changes in their own jobs, the specialists typically came up with fewer than 30 minor changes. Yet their managers came up with a list of over 100 ideas involving substantial change to enhance the personnel job.

Labeling this approach "integrative" is not incidental. A management and employee orientation are needed in an organization. The successful business uses a strategy in which the natural strengths of each approach are realized, while the unique weaknesses of each are masked. This is not to imply that in some haphazard way employees are given orders one moment and asked for participation the next. Rather, the point is to integrate the two approaches in a logical and meaningful way, just as our left eye compensates for the distortions of the right eye. Employees need to understand why certain changes are appropriately and necessarily made at different levels of the organization. There is an added bonus: binocular vision, which produces depth perception—and almost every organization could benefit from a deeper and clearer vision.

Misconceptions

The manager who wishes to embrace the integrative approach must begin by taking an inventory of the hidden barriers to success. Most often the barriers take the form of untenable assumptions. Hence, the discussion below centers around the major misconceptions that make communicating change problematical.

(1) Change is unnatural.

The inertia of tradition is a strong and powerful force in most organizations. And it should be. Tradition can help a company maintain high standards of performance. Tradition exploits the benefits of knowledge gained through repetition, just as basketball players practice for hour after hour on their free-throw shot. But to carry this logic to extreme and argue that change is unnatural can be devastating. The historic declines of the American steel and automotive industries in the 1970s are cases in point. American corporations used to dominate these markets but necessary changes never were made. Traditions, while important, can become debilitating.

In an effective organization there is a kind of healthy tension between the traditions of the past and the beckoning of the future. A violin string that is too taut will break. A string that is too loose is equally useless. Either way, the results are the same. Even Issac Stern could not make a poorly tuned violin sing. Likewise, too great a tension between the past and future can quite literally pull apart a corporation.

Apple Computer had just such a dilemma during the mid-1980s. The traditional Apple ii product line was ignored by the more "progressive" personnel developing the Macintosh line. This happened in spite of the Apple ii line being responsible for most of the corporate profits. Ultimately, the turning point occurred when John Sculley, the president, eased Apple's cofounder, Steven Jobs, out of the company. In an odd irony, the very progressiveness and ingenuity that created Apple Computer Company was the stumbling block to the future success of the corporation (Uttal, 1985). Change needs to occur with some semblance of respect for the traditions of the past. But, as numerous historians have noted, the past is, at best, an imperfect guide for the future (Tuchman, 1982).

(2) Change is always disruptive.

In an article designated as a "Harvard Business Review Classic," Paul R. Lawrence (1969) writes:

> When we stop to think about it, we know that many changes occur in our factories without a bit of resistance. We know that people who are working closely with one another continually swap ideas about short cuts and minor

changes in procedure that are adopted so easily that we seldom notice them or even think of them as change. The point is that because these people work so closely with one another, they intuitively understand and take account of the existing social arrangements for work and so feel no threat to themselves in such everyday changes. (p. 9)

The thrust of his message is that all changes are not necessarily resisted. In fact, they are a normal everyday occurrence that need not disrupt the workplace.

The integrative approach to managing change stresses that change is something that is to be expected and dealt with in a professional manner. An organizational climate can be fostered that encourages innovations in light of corporate goals. Indeed specific changes make perfect sense in light of the direction and vision of the corporation. Football teams regularly trade or dismiss players in an effort to get into the Super Bowl. This is not unusual. It is expected. The only time trades are questioned is when the changes do not seem to further the team's goals. This is not a reaction to change per se but to the wisdom of a specific incident. In fact, the challenge for the coach is to communicate how changes in personnel make sense in light of the overall strategy.

(3) Change always is progressive.

In direct contrast to the previous myth is a belief that is equally problematic. There are those who hail every new approach, buy all the new corporate toys, and are constantly in search of the next trend. These people can be quite refreshing; they like to live on the edge. To these individuals "newness" is more important than merit, and the act of changing is more fulfilling than the feeling of accomplishment. In the end, though, the results are always uneven. That which is new is not always the best. The serious manager must take a more sober approach.

When American airplane manufacturers passed up the opportunity to produce the supersonic transport, which could fly between Europe and the United States in under two hours, there were critics who said it was a poor decision. Some even said America was losing its innovative spirit. Yet passing up one idea does not indicate a fear of change. Perhaps it is a mark of prudence and thoughtful analysis. Indeed, the Europeans did go ahead and produce the SST. The results now have proven the wisdom of the American airplane manufacturers. Even into the mid-1980s the costs of development were yet to be recovered.

(4) Change always is stressful.

There are many tests designed for measuring individual stress levels. One such test is based on the number of changes a person experiences over a certain period of time. More points are generated for the greater the degree of change and conversely fewer points for lesser changes. For example, more points are assigned for getting married than changing physicians. Respondents gauge their personal degree of stress by totaling the points.

The only problem with this kind of test is that it fails to take into account the meanings people associate with the changes. Getting married may be stressful but hopefully the benefits are many. The meanings associated with marriage may be companionship, camaraderie, and stability, which are great stress reducers. On the other hand, changing doctors could be deeply stressful because it may mean that the former physician was inept in diagnosing an illness. The uncertainty of that situation could wreck havoc with body and soul.

Three important observations can be made. First, change need not be stressful; it can be seen as a natural part of the job. Second, there are positive changes as well as negative ones that have a different effect on the psyche. People cry tears of joy and sadness — they do not mean the same thing. One chemist even showed that there is a chemical difference between the two types of tears. Third, the critical factor is the personal meanings an individual attaches to the change. Does the change offer hope? Is it beneficial? Is it exciting? These are the salient questions.

(5) Change indicates that previous practices have been in error.

As a former debater, I can still remember my first encounter with what was to me the esoteric concept of a "comparative advantage case." The classic approach to debate is to establish that there is a problem and then suggest a solution. The controversy occurs around whether there is, in fact, a problem and whether the solution meets the need. For example, the case could be made that deficit spending causes a multitude of problems and that raising taxes would solve the dilemma. In contrast, a comparative advantage case does not argue about the problem but suggests that there is a better way to accomplish the designated goals. It would be like arguing that some changes in the tax structure could reduce the federal deficit. It appears that suggesting a change, by necessity, indicts the previous practices or tacitly acknowledges a problem. But this need not be the case. The argument simply becomes that the previous system worked well before but now the situation has changed and enhancements are needed. This is a subtle but important distinction.

In much the same way, many employees believe that changes are initiated because they made errors, were incompetent, or simply made poor decisions. If these same employees have enjoyed any kind of success under previous circumstances, they may even resent the changes. Reasoning much like a novice debater, they assume that a change obviously indicates that there was a problem with past practices. A wise manager understands this but is aware of the importance of timely change. Thus the manager must communicate a difficult message composed of two seemingly conflicting parts:

(a) *Part one:* Previous practices were successful because they were appropriate at that time.

(b) *Part two:* Changes are needed to meet the challenges of new and perhaps novel circumstances.

If these two ideas can be communicated successfully, then the change can be instituted without needless employee resentment or resistance.

(6) Real change can be born only out of crisis.

Sometimes a crisis is the only vehicle through which managers are forced to reckon with the facts, make choices, and set priorities. Lee Iacocca's rescue and dramatic turnaround of Chrysler is one such case. In this situation, real change was, of necessity, born out of crisis. In fact, one survey of 22,000 manufacturing employees found that 63% felt a crisis had to flair up before anything was done about a problem ("Our Bosses," 1989). Yet to contend that change can occur *only* under crisis conditions is to extend the argument too far. There are leaders, in certain circumstances, with enough vision, courage, and savvy to persuade others of the importance of change before the impending doom of a crisis.

For example, John G. Smale, the CEO of Procter & Gamble, recognized that the company's traditional product lines, including Pampers diapers and Crest toothpaste, were reaching maturity. Hence, during the early 1980s he decided to acquire health product companies. In fact, P&G acquired more than twice the number of companies in the 1980s than it had during the 1960s and 1970s combined. The result: profits rose 18% to $1.21 billion for fiscal 1989. While P&G experienced some tough times during the 1970s, there was not any immediate crisis that forced such changes (Swasy, 1989). But providing direction amid turmoil is the crux of leadership. For managers there is a valuable lesson: Wisdom and foresight can triumph. The benefits of initiating change before the onset of crises far outweigh the costs. Crises always involve innocent victims. Crises are not always effectively managed. And crises can bring disaster. This is what the wise manager avoids by initiating change before a crisis erupts.

A Perspective on Change

All changes are not of equal magnitude. In fact, a useful way to describe change is on a continuum from routine to nonroutine because unique communication strategies are employed depending on the degree of change. On the routine extreme would be changes that occur on a regular basis. For instance, financial institutions frequently change interest rates and airlines are typically involved in a variety of different promotions. On the other end of the continuum are changes such as major reorganizations, new product lines, or a redeployment of resources. Other instances of nonroutine change would include IBM's decision to enter the personal computer market or the reorganization of AT&T.

Some communication strategies that are useful for routine changes may prove less effective with nonroutine changes and vice versa. Therefore, the discussion that follows is divided into these two categories.

Routine Change

With astonishing regularity, employees make comments such as the following:

- I need more information on what is being marketed and how it is going to work. I don't like to look stupid to customers!
- Policy changes boggle me and I have to ask questions all the time.
- Changes in procedures are not really communicated here. We find out through the grapevine.
- I need more information on government reports and current changes in legislation. Changes aren't communicated in time. It makes you look foolish if you don't know the changes.

Notice the impact of this kind of negligence: bewilderment, frustration, embarrassment, low morale, and poor customer service.

These are not isolated instances. Employees voice the same sentiments in organizations ranging from financial institutions to engineering firms. Almost 20% of the employees in our data bank expressed no satisfaction to

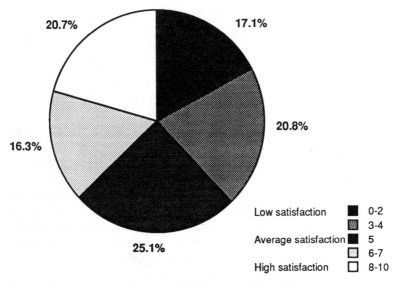

Figure 7.1 Employee Satisfaction with Information About Changes

extremely low satisfaction with information about changes (see Figure 7.1). The point is abundantly clear: many employees simply are not satisfied with the amount and/or quality of the information they receive about fairly routine changes.

How can the situation be rectified? Actually this is one of the few communication problems that is fairly easy to solve. First, the precise informational needs of employees must be identified. That is, in what areas do employees need more information to effectively do their jobs? Communication assessments or roundtable discussions with employees are effective tools in identifying these needs. Second, communication vehicles must be set up to provide this type of information. Perhaps all that is needed is a weekly companywide memorandum announcing changes or a strategically erected bulletin board. Some larger companies use videotapes that are produced in-house. There are various alternatives, but the key is to fit the channels to the employees' needs. Furthermore, a cogent communication policy greatly helps in dealing with the more complex dynamics of some information problems. Finally, after the mechanisms for communicating changes have been identified, the system must be used accordingly. In the end, it comes down to people fulfilling their communication obligations.

Nonroutine Change

A more difficult challenge is how to communicate nonroutine change. There has been a great deal written on organizational development, which involves reworking the entire organizational climate or changing managerial style (e.g., Blake & Mouton, 1976). My purpose here is not to rehash those theories or even to discuss organizational development. Rather, the objective is to develop a more general approach that is useful for the manager who has to deal with the day-to-day problems of instituting an organizational change. Installing new technology in the workplace, like facilitating the switch from typewriters to word-processing equipment, is one instance.

Elisabeth Kubler-Ross (1969) wrote the keenly perceptive and monumental work, *On Death and Dying*. This modern classic presents a theory about the psychological stages that terminally ill patients go through in learning to cope with their impending death:

Stage 1 — Denial and Isolation
Stage 2 — Anger
Stage 3 — Bargaining
Stage 4 — Depression
Stage 5 — Acceptance

The heart of her approach is to ease the natural pain, stress, and trauma of the situation by using communication strategies that are compatible with the patient's stage in the coping process. Such efforts require a deep sensitivity to the patient's unique psychological makeup. There are no pat answers, only some general principles to follow. Moreover, Kubler-Ross makes the important point that, to a large extent, how well a patient handles the situation depends on how effectively the doctors, nurses, and family members communicate.

When faced with major changes, many employees will go through similar, though less severe, stages of reactions. The manager's skill in guiding employees through this process greatly impacts the smoothness of the transition. If a manager can be sensitive enough to the verbal and nonverbal cues so as to discern the stage of employee reaction, then communicative adaptations can be made in order to enhance the acceptance of the change.

A common first reaction to impending change is characterized by these kinds of comments: "Oh no, not here," or, "It can't happen like that, not with my job." In the denial stage it is important for the manager to clearly and calmly communicate the particulars of the change while providing as much factual material as necessary. An employee may react emotionally, but the manager should realize that it is a normal reaction and should allow the denial to take its natural course. An unduly negative reaction may indicate that the announcement of the change did not take place at the right time and place or that it was done in an insensitive fashion. A common problem at this stage is that upon encountering initial emotional reactions, managers may back off or sugarcoat the change, and thus not fully inform the employees. The other tendency is to try to browbeat or ridicule employees into acceptance. This does not demonstrate much sensitivity and may lead to resentment. Moreover, it rarely helps managers achieve their objective. If these tendencies are avoided, then employees, in due course, experience a partial acceptance.

Stage 2 involves a kind of anger over the "whys" of the change: "Why did this happen to me — at this time?" Little incidents can set off major emotional outbursts. Employee behavior may seem inexplicable. The worst response is for the manager to take the anger personally and exacerbate the difficulties. Another common reaction is that the manager and employee play a game of "mutual pretense." The game is one in which each party tacitly acknowledges, "I know that you know, but I won't talk about it to upset you, and you won't talk about it to upset me." The net result: an implicit conspiracy of silence with resentment simmering underneath the veneer of civility. Then the problem is compounded by interpersonal conflicts. The best response is for the manager to acknowledge the anger, gently guide the employees' attention to the real source of anger, and help them work through it. Then it should subside.

Bargaining is the third stage, and employees may attempt to make various exchanges to forestall the impending change. Creativity abounds when faced with an unpleasant alternative. Deal making with various people is attempted, as employees seek to alter the course of events. Many times deals are attempted outside the normal chain-of-command structure, in essence, behind the manager's back. But making deals at this stage only prolongs the matter and puts off the inevitable. Resolution and perseverance are the manager's tools at this point.

Stage 4 is characterized by depression. It is the phase in which employees begin to accept the inevitable. Just allowing the employees to voice their concerns or feelings at this point can be helpful. At other times sensitive silence or a gentle touch may be most effective. Sharing a sadness with someone who can empathize can be amazingly therapeutic. An insensitive, "Hey, it's not that bad," can have the opposite impact.

The final stage is acceptance, where employees honestly and wholeheartedly endorse the change. It is important for the manager to show respect for the employees and not chide them for their initial reactions. They still are a bit fragile at this point. Even seemingly innocent verbal jousting may be deeply but secretly wounding. The critical point is to preserve employee dignity.

All of this may sound like a fairly drawn-out process. But these reactions can take place in the span of hours or extend over several months. Doubters, like the Arrow manager, may even question if an employee really goes through those reactions. The following example should clear up those doubts.

From Ink and Paper to Computer Monitors and Floppy Disks

As changes go, switching from typewriters to word-processing units may not seem all that major. In this case it was. Moreover, it became an incredible source of tension in the office, affecting morale and productivity. To be frank, the supervisor did not handle the situation very well. In part, an unawareness of the stages of reaction to nonroutine change was at the crux of the matter. Extensive interviews with all the parties involved revealed the following scenario.

Day 1	The office supervisor announces to the office secretaries that new word-processing equipment has been acquired and they will have to make room in their work day to go for two days of training. It is left up to the secretaries to work out their schedules to attend the sessions.
Days 2-10	No activity.
Day 11	The supervisor asks employees when they have scheduled their training time. Employees' response: "We haven't had time to set it up yet." Supervisor's response: "You have a week to set up your training."
Analysis	**Employees are clearly denying that any change is needed and seek to avoid anything or any person that would dispel the myth. It is the game of "mutual pretense" described above. The supervisor's response seems appropriate because it gives employees maximum flexibility and avoids conflict. But it fails to deal with the reasons for the denial. Moreover, all the aspects of the change have not been fully explained. The abruptness of the supervisor's comments on Day 11 creates added tension.**
Day 18	The office supervisor again asks when the training sessions are scheduled. The same response: "We didn't have time to schedule it." Reasons are given about the value of learning about the new equip-

ment. A nasty little skirmish ensues that is highlighted by threats and counterthreats. Another deadline is set.

Analysis   **The anger stage is clearly in full swing. Providing a rationale for the training is a little late at this stage and should have been done earlier. Furthermore, the supervisor still has not explained how the word-processing equipment will actually be used on the job. She assumes the secretaries know it is the wave of the future. The threats only exacerbate the situation into an interpersonal conflict.**

Day 20   Again the employees refuse to go to training, which the supervisor has now scheduled for them. One threat has been actualized: a meeting is scheduled with the employees, supervisor, and the supervisor's boss, the department head.

Day 21   A meeting is held with "reconciliation" as the goal. The secretaries offer excuses like, "I know I'll work faster on the typewriter." Some compromises and exchanges are offered. One secretary says she will take the receptionist duties performed by the supervisor if she doesn't have to go to training. The department head expresses "understanding" and gently explains the need to do the training. New training times are set up.

Analysis   **A textbook example of the negotiation stage. The department head makes an error by not being firm enough.**

Day 24   The employees do not show up for their scheduled training.

Day 25   The supervisor is furious and refers the entire matter to the vice president. The supervisor wants them fired. They "can't" be fired because of union hassles.

Analysis   **Almost a reversion back to the anger stage. The secretaries have dug their heels in. Leniency and understanding did not pay off.**

Day 26   The vice president lays down the law in a somewhat sensitive manner. Training is scheduled the next day.

Days 27-28   All employees reluctantly participate in the training session.

Days 29-36   Supervisor does not speak to employees. Even after training, employees rarely use the equipment. They speak in hushed tones to one another. There is a somber atmosphere.

Analysis   **The depression stage has set in. The supervisor may have done the wise thing given the current situation. But the silence results**

more from bitterness than from sensitivity to the emotional state of the employees.

Days 37-50	Equipment gradually gets more use with gentle prodding by the supervisor. Relationships slowly return to normal. An uneasy calm pervades the office.
Analysis	**Acceptance, finally! Maybe not wholehearted acceptance, but acceptance nevertheless.**
6 months later	Daily use of the word-processing equipment.
1 year later	One secretary says, "This is a super machine to work on. I only wish I had learned sooner."
2 years later	Employees lobby supervisor for a more technologically advanced version of the word-processing equipment.

This example shows how closely the acceptance of a change can parallel the stages discussed above. If the supervisor had a knowledge of the employees' likely stages of reaction, she could have felt more in control of the change process. There was a need not only to plan for the change itself, but to plan how to communicate the change. The change could have been instituted more smoothly and effectively had the supervisor met the communicative needs of her employees at each reaction stage. Clearly, there are different messages that need to be communicated at each stage of reaction (see Table 7.1). If that is not enough of a challenge, there is also the very real possibility that all the employees were not at the same stage at the same time.

Strategically Communicating Change

The well-known military historian, B. H. Liddell Hart (1967), writes that, "In strategy, the longest way round is often the shortest way home" (p. 5). Communication strategies are no different. Planning a strategic communication process takes both time and effort; it is the "long way round." But it is also the smoothest, simplest, and most effective way to implement change. Typically, changes are communicated in a haphazard way, a catch-as-catch-can philosophy, the "short way." There is a better way, the principles of which are discussed below.

Table 7.1 Communicating Change at Reaction Stages

Stage	Identifying Actions	Appropriate Actions	Inappropriate Reponse
Denial	• Not showing up for meetings • Overly busy with routine tasks • Less socializing • Procrastinating	• Discern actual points of resistance • Discuss positives & negatives of change • Legitimize concerns • Discuss rationale of the change (sell)	• Ignore the resistance • Ridicule the person's denial
Anger	• Being irritable • Contemplating sabotage • Being confrontive • Appearing "short-fused"	• Stay calm & professional • Clarify the details of the change • Show understanding of the anger while firmly emphasizing need for change. • Allow some ventilation	• Escalate into a relationship conflict • Threats • Blame others for the change • Take anger personally • Ignore anger
Bargaining	• Trying to make deals • Trading favors • Promise making	• Be flexible, with regard to inconsequential items • Be firm, with regard to the basic position • Focus on long-term benefits	• Reject suggestions briskly • Give in to employee demands • Give impression of agreement
Depression	• Being untalkative • Seeming apathetic • Missing work • Appearing listless • Looking somber	• Show concern • Give them "space" • Encourage discussions with others who have fully accepted change	• Pressure for full acceptance • Jest about feelings • Overly happy or giddy
Acceptance	• Change is fully implemented • Return to normal atmosphere	• Encourage auxiliary suggestions • Resume "normal" communication • Praise	• "I told you so" • Joke about previous reactions

(1) Determine how the organization has communicated past changes.

The historical communication patterns set the context of interpretation for employees. In fact, one researcher has shown that employee reactions to change can be traced back to an organization's founding conditions. The corporation's origin somehow deeply imprints employees, even those subsequently hired (Boeker, 1989). Sir Winston Churchill stated, "The longer you look back, the farther you can look forward. This is not a philosophical or political argument — any oculist can tell you it is true" (Manchester, 1983, p. 12).

One president of a small manufacturing firm related the following story. He was concerned about the rough financial times his company would soon be experiencing. Some cost-saving measures would have to be implemented, but layoffs were not even discussed. The president considered himself a moral and straightforward person. Therefore, he felt he had an ethical obligation to inform his employees of the news. In due course, he called a meeting of all employees to discuss some of the difficulties ahead as well as the requisite changes involved. In good faith, he mentioned that there were no plans for layoffs and employees would be dealt with "as fairly as possible under the circumstances." So far, so good. Or so it seemed.

Within a few days the entire plant was buzzing with rumors about an impending plant closure and wage reductions. In fact, there was not a bit of truth in either rumor. The president was completely bewildered. He felt he had told the employees the truth and was honest about the situation. How could such vicious rumors spring from such noble intentions? Weeks of meetings took place in order to quell fears. Still, for months, morale and productivity suffered.

Upon deeper probing and with a year's worth of hindsight, it became abundantly clear why employees came away from the meeting with precisely the opposite message that the well-intentioned president had so sincerely sought to communicate. Employees had never before had a companywide meeting to discuss any issue, much less this kind of anxiety-producing news. Hence, they legitimately, although incorrectly, reasoned that "things must be really bad" if the president had been "forced" to call a meeting of this type. There was the feeling that management "must not be telling us all they know." Like a virus in an unhealthy body, rumors and inaccurate inferences naturally flourish under such conditions. Had meetings like this been held on a regular basis, the possibility of such an interpretation would have been minimized. The context of the situation spoke louder than the actual message. The president was bewildered because he had focused on the inner message — his actual words — and had no understanding of the context in which employees interpreted the words. Both the employees and the president erroneously focused on only one part of the actual communication event. Pure intentions do not always guarantee perceptions of integrity.

The moral of the story is that when instituting a change, managers must carefully consider the context in which employees interpret the message. The context may prove more powerful than the message itself. This incident also provides vivid proof of how important it is to continually update employees on corporate news. Furthermore, it may mean that in order to institute a change with full employee support, management may need to apologize for past errors in failing to communicate effectively. A successful future can only be built on the firm foundation of the past. Rosabeth Moss Kanter (1983) thoughtfully states,

> The architecture of change thus requires an *awareness of foundations* — the bases in "prehistory," perhaps below the surface, that make continued construction possible. And if the foundations will not support the weight of what is about to be built, then they must be shored up before any other actions can take place. (p. 283)

In short, the context of interpretation is etched as much by action as by words.

(2) Know what needs to be changed.

This may seem ludicrously self-evident. However, many change efforts have gone awry for lack of this knowledge. Most managers underestimate what really needs to be changed. There are a host of other minor changes that need to be in place to support a major change. These may include realigning incentives, measuring performance, adjusting informal processes, and altering attitudes. Through the realignment of the details, a supportive infrastructure for the major change is developed. One of the critical difficulties in the word-processing case reviewed above was that the supervisor never really identified precisely what needed to be changed. The secretaries later admitted that they were scared of the technology and afraid they would never be able to master it with the level of proficiency they had on the typewriter. This fear was never directly addressed by anybody involved in the incident. An important attitude change was needed that had never been properly identified.

Many technological changes involve not only hardware and software alterations, but also another kind of "software" change — the human kind. Interpersonal relationships in the organizations can facilitate or hinder even the most carefully thought out change efforts. These issues need to be clearly identified so that appropriate strategies can be developed to smooth the transitions. For instance, implementing a new electronic bulletin board system seems like a major technical and training challenge. But, many an electronic bulletin board system lies around unused because employees could not be weaned off their more time-consuming habits of "dropping by the office." Thus, the social component—the human "software"—impedes the use of technically sophisticated and useful hardware.

(3) Recognize that the meaning of the change is far more important than the change itself.

Perception is an extraordinarily powerful force in the affairs of a corporation. Regrettably, it often is overlooked by management. Some people readily accept the change to a computerized environment; others are horrified. The key, regardless of the specific type of change—from electronic bulletin boards to new medical plans—is to assess how employees perceive the change. What does it mean to them on a personal basis? How will the change affect their job duties? These are the really important questions when determining a strategy for communicating change.

Changes in an office environment often are met with mixed reactions. Some employees welcome the change because it means getting upwind of smokers. Others are resistant because it means disruptions of long-time interpersonal relationships. Employee reactions cannot be predicted on the basis of the change itself; rather, what is important is the perceived impact of the proposed change on their individual circumstances. Effective managers realize this and try to understand employee perceptions in order to overcome possible resistance points. They encourage employees to look beyond their own individual interpretations and share in a larger vision.

Some organizations, like Honda, institutionalize change to such an extent that it becomes a natural part of the culture. In fact, a Honda executive remarks: "There's a hunger for change here, and we've become conditioned to the challenge it creates. So many people here need this kind of excitement—it's part of the Honda culture" (Shook, 1988, p. 199). Perceptions of change are shaped by the incremental nature of the alterations. The net result is that major changes evolve through minor but continual changes. Therefore, change at Honda is instituted with considerably less resistance than is generally associated with nonroutine change. Honda realigns employee perceptions of change by placing them in the context of other small adjustments. This may be one reason why Honda grew by 200% from 1980 to 1988 (Prahalad & Hamel, 1990). The mistake that organizations sometimes make is that change is instituted all at once, when it could be instituted incrementally and with less employee resistance.

(4) Develop a unifying vision of the change that energizes and motivates employees.

When Stanley C. Gault became the CEO of Rubbermaid he took the company from modest success to "superstar" status. He did it by becoming the "No. 1 quality controller." He constantly talked to consumers about Rubbermaid's products and was known to order the redesign of a product based on one customer's complaint. He said, "On quality I'm a sonofabitch." He has a reputation for becoming absolutely "livid" about poor quality workmanship. Yet, as one observer puts it, "Ultimately it's Gault's infectious pride in Rubbermaid's products, rather than his wrath that motivates his troops. When it comes to encouraging quality, passion at the top counts as much as engineering precision at the bottom" (O'Reilly, 1990, p. 43). In order for employees to buy into change, they must see a vision of the future, even if it is a bit of a clouded one. They must know the global goals, the possibilities, and hopes implicit in the change. In short, they must be collectively inspired by the change.

How? Leaders energize by creating a few simple rallying points. In an insightful article, David Nadler and Michael L. Tushman (1989) suggest:

> Successful long-term changes are characterized by a careful self-discipline that limits the number of themes an organization gives its employees. As a general rule, managers of a change can only initiate and sustain approximately three key themes during any particular period of time. The challenge in this area is to create enough themes to get people truly energized, while limiting the total number of themes. The toughest part is having to decide not to initiate a new program — which by itself has great merit — because of the risk of diluting the other themes. (pp. 199-200)

This is exactly what Gault did at Rubbermaid. He gave employees a vision, in part through his well-known antics, but, more importantly, by preaching a value that everyone in the organization could relate to — quality. Clearly sermons alone will not do. Every major change has many subsidiary changes associated with it. But all these minor changes need to be put in the energizing context of a few encompassing themes.

(5) Recognize that change cannot be perfectly planned.

There always are unknowns when venturing into a new endeavor. That is part of the fun. These natural "holes" in the plan can be beneficial. Employees can be encouraged to "discover and fill in the holes" with their ideas and approaches, thereby gaining greater commitment to the change. Furthermore, the "holes" allow for flexible adaptations to uncertainties.

The questions and unknowns in the change strategy need to be fully acknowledged to employees. If done properly there is no need to fear that some will feel the change has not been adequately thought out. Rather, they may feel a sense of participation. Even Mendeleyev, who developed the periodic table used by scientists throughout the world, included gaps for "missing" or undiscovered elements. In time, with discoveries, the gaps gradually were filled in with new elements. The "holes" did not tarnish the brilliance of his original idea. Likewise, an honest reckoning with the necessary ambiguities of a change need not obscure the basic correctness of a new course. There need be no punishment for knowledgeable ignorance.

(6) Provide as much information to employees as is reasonably and prudently possible.

There are no information vacuums in times of change. If information is not provided or there is the appearance of "hiding something," then rumors naturally are spawned. The best way to control the grapevine is to provide consistent, frequent, and reliable information. Management must aggressively communicate vital information. Rumor control centers, hotlines, special bulletins, and ad hoc committees are among the alternatives that could be considered.

In an exemplary piece of scholarly research, Katherine Miller and Peter Monge (1985) examined the impact of information on employee anxiety about an impending change. All the employees (180) of a state department of education were about to move from a traditional office arrangement to a new building that used open landscaping. Some implications of the change included new working arrangements and different social relationships. In short, the change was a major one. In order to conduct this field experiment, a variety of different types of messages about the move were prepared for six groups of employees. One group, the control group, received no information about the impending change, another, only positive information, and still another, only negative information. The results showed that providing *any* information — whether it is good news or bad — is better than silence.

In particular, managers need to carefully consider five questions when providing information to employees:

- Is the change perceived as advantageous over the past practices?
- Are the benefits of the change readily observable?
- If the change does not pan out, can the plan be modified?

- Is the change congruent with the culture and needs of employees?
- Is the change seen as being noncomplex and manageable?

To the extent that managers can inform employees about these themes, they will speed the process of employee acceptance. Indeed, scholars of the "diffusion of innovation" have discovered five factors that hasten the adoption rate of innovative products (Rogers, 1983). These factors correspond precisely to the questions above.

(7) Choose the appropriate communication channels.

Chapter 5 contains a detailed discussion on how to select the appropriate communication channels. Nothing could be more important than choosing the appropriate channel when a change is contemplated. Two general guidelines deserve special emphasis.

First, the more nonroutine the change is, the more important it is to use dynamic channels (see Figure 7.2). This allows management to be as flexible as possible in adapting to employee concerns. For example, a group meeting is better than a memo because feedback can be more easily and fully addressed. When change is instituted in a large corporation, the same principle applies. A group meeting, of course, could not be held with all employees, but still a more dynamic alternative could be selected. For instance, when AT&T was reorganized, thousands of Southwestern Bell employees and their families were linked via satellite and treated to a televised discussion about the planned changes. Although the cost was considerable, the benefits were great: deeper employee understanding of the change, greater commitment to the vision, and less employee anxiety. These results could not have been achieved through a less dynamic channel like an employee newsletter. Why? Because the dynamic channel allows for more timely and effective feedback. Moreover, the very expense of a dynamic channel sends a powerful secondary message that management cares about effectively communicating with employees.

Second, multiple channels should be used to communicate nonroutine changes. Such a practice helps ensure that everyone gets the word. Additionally, different media are more useful for presenting certain aspects of a change. A print medium can show a new office design better than oral channels. Yet, oral channels can be more useful in fielding employee questions. Hence, the different channels should be used so as to exploit their various strengths. Moreover, the redundancy helps to continually remind employees of the vision behind the change.

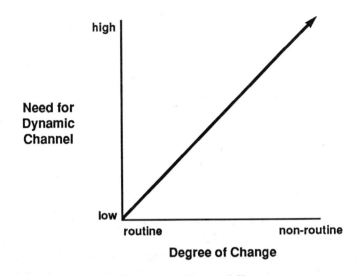

Figure 7.2 Channel Selection Based on Degree of Change

(8) Anticipate possible resistance points.

As noted above, not all changes are going to be resisted. Nevertheless, the more nonroutine the change is perceived as being, the greater the probability that there will be some resistance (see Figure 7.3). While change often is initiated by management, it only can be sustained by employees. Prudent managers recognize this and prepare accordingly. One note of caution should be mentioned. The issues perceived by management as possible concerns may not be the actual concerns of employees. A destructive self-fulfilling prophecy is a potential result.

Generally employees are most concerned with the following issues when confronted with major changes:

- fear of economic loss
- social disruptions
- anxiety over the unknown
- inconveniences

Clearly managers should anticipate these issues and develop appropriate responses to each concern (Lawrence, 1969). There is another way to foresee the potential resistance points. Organizations, like nations, go through various developmental stages. Some researchers have suggested that different

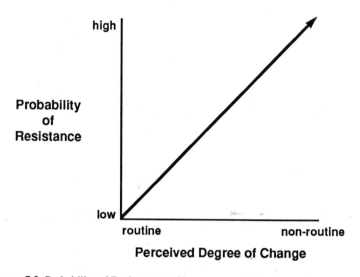

Perceived Degree of Change

Figure 7.3 Probability of Resistance to Change

impediments to change appear at each stage (Gray & Ariss, 1985). Therefore, the wise manager also assesses an organization's developmental state, anticipates the resistance points, and assimilates a plan of action (see Table 7.2).

One useful tactic is to respond to each potential objection point by point. One CEO of a small telemarketing firm used this approach in announcing a plan to change the telemarketers' responsibilities. In one part of his speech he said:

> Some of you may be concerned about wages under the new system. This is a legitimate concern. But let me assure you that there will be no wage reductions under this new plan. In fact, our projections show, with the added revenues, your salaries will actually increase.

> Some of you may be concerned about layoffs. This has never even crossed my mind. In every single change we've instituted in this company's 20-year history, we have always ended up adding personnel.

Note that the CEO accomplished four very important objectives in this excerpt. First, he clearly identified the potential resistance points, which legitimized the employees anxieties. Second, he categorically denied each one. Third, he not only denied them but said exactly the opposite would happen. Finally, he provided some kind of evidence to back up each of his claims. The speech must have worked, because the CEO reported that this

Table 7.2 Resistance Points and Organizational Developmental Stage

Organizational Stage	Identifying Characteristics	Possible Resistance Points
Birth and Early Growth	• Emphasis on entrepreneurship • Heavy influence of "founding fathers"	• Speculation over CEO's reaction • Diminish CEO's control • Impact on corporate vision
Maturity	• Creation of standard operating procedures • Institutionalizing vision • Solidifying departmental responsibilities	• Interdepartmental differences • Protection of "turf" • Control of resources • Budgetary allocations
Decline or Redevelopment	• Dramatic change in competitive environment • More bureaucratic structure • Quest to reshape corporate vision	• Indifference & lethargy • Impact on established careers • Power relationships • Waiting for "crisis" to institute change

NOTE: Developed from work by Gray & Ariss (1985)

change was implemented more smoothly than any of the others in the company's history.

In a variation on this theme, some companies simply issue a set of common questions asked about the change and provide answers to each item. Either approach is extremely powerful at counteracting resistance and building support for a change.

(9) Carefully consider the timing of the messages.

Employee perceptions of change will be greatly influenced by the timing of their receipt of certain information.[1] No one likes to receive information about a major change through the grapevine; it gives a signal that the employee was not considered important enough to be told firsthand. Typically, major changes should be announced so that everyone hears about them close to the same time, thus partially restraining the grapevine. This also is a chance to impart the strategic vision behind the change. After a major change has been announced, there should be an immediate provision for some follow-up. Typically, all employees involved in the change should be allowed to forward questions to a liaison within 24 hours and have a written response to those questions within 24 to 36 hours. This helps ensure that there are no misunderstandings and creates a vehicle through which employee concerns

---

Memo from New Vice President

Date: Monday

To: All Personnel
From: New VP

Re: Mandatory meeting

There will be a mandatory meeting of all personnel at 7:30 a.m. on Friday to discuss the new employee benefits program.

Hourly employees will be paid overtime for coming in early.

Figure 7.4 Memo from New Vice President

can be handled. There is also a powerful secondary message to employees that their anxieties are legitimate.

One of the best ways to learn about timing is by examining what *not* to do. A recently hired VP of a 250-employee paper manufacturer was given the task of redesigning a comprehensive benefits program. He did a brilliant job and worked out a way to increase employee coverage while cutting corporate costs. He worked in virtual seclusion until it came time to announce the plans to the employees. On Monday he sent around a memo to all employees announcing the meeting for the following Friday (see Figure 7.4).

The vice president thought the employees would be excited about his new plan. Since they had never met this man, they did not know what to expect and many were apprehensive. To make matters worse, a short article appeared in a local newspaper about a rollback in benefits by a plastics plant located in the same industrial complex. Then rumors started to circulate that benefits were going to be cut back. The vice president began the meeting by dwelling on the benefits of the plan to the company. While he did mention that there would be "increased benefits" to all employees, he never specified what they were. He ended by saying that all employees would receive written documentation of the plan in two weeks. He did not ask for questions. That was it. The meeting was over. Employees were bewildered. By the following Monday, wild rumors were flying. Employee satisfaction and productivity was at an all-time low (see Figure 7.5). It took another two meetings called by the CEO and months of reassurances to quell employee anxieties.

	MON	WED	FRI	SAT/SUN	MON
managment's actions	memo	**KATO POST** **BENEFITS ROLLBACK!**	formal meeting		
employee actions & perceptions	memo	newspaper article	formal meeting (no interaction)	employees talk to family & friends	productivity down

Figure 7.5 The Impact of Timing on Meaning

What went wrong? First, there was probably too much time between the announcement of the meeting and the actual meeting. Employee suspicions and fears naturally were aroused, particularly when dealing with a virtually unknown vice president. Second, the vice president was insensitive to the employees' context of interpretation, which was influenced by unrelated events (the newspaper story) during the week. In fact, he could have used the story to his advantage by opening his presentation with a reference to the story and then saying that just the opposite was happening here. Third, by dwelling on the benefits to the corporation, he implicitly communicated that the organization's interests were more important than the employees'. Fourth, in addition to not having a feedback vehicle, he compounded the problem by having a meeting on Friday. Employees were desperately searching for more information, but over the weekend the only place they could turn was to friends and relatives, who no doubt exacerbated the issue with their own fears. There was no official place to get formal information during this time period. Rumors were bound to spread. Fifth, the written summary of the information was released too late to answer employee questions. In sum, with the exception of setting a single time to disseminate the information, this vice president completely failed to communicate the change in an effective and timely manner.

Final Thoughts

The Kennedy Center is one of the most beautiful and magnificent buildings in Washington, D.C. In some ways it is a miracle that it ever got built, for there were objections from all quarters as well as troubling financial diffi-culties. In large part the structure owes its very existence and continued success to one man, Roger L. Stevens. He fought most of the battles, and has some perceptive comments on change and success:

> There's an irony implicit in anything that succeeds. From the vantage point of success, it looks as if it couldn't possibly have failed. So with the Center. Twenty years ago, there were any number of people here in Washington eager to tell us that the Center wouldn't work — that even if we could manage to get it built, it would stand idle most of the time. At the moment, the doomsayers are silent, but they haven't gotten away. Maybe I'll get a chance to rouse them one more time. (Gill, 1981, p. 52)

As change goes from the stage of one person's dream, to "our" dream, to "the way it always was" or "should be," the obstacles seem to slowly fade into hindsight. What will eventually be seen as inevitable can only begin as a dream that is inconceivable.

References

Blake, R. R., & Mouton, J. S. (1976). *Consultation.* Reading, MA: Addison-Wesley.

Boeker, W. (1989). Strategic change: The effects of founding and history. *Academy of Management Journal, 32,* 489-515.

Gill, B. (1981). *John F. Kennedy Center for the Performing Arts.* New York: Abrams.

Gray, B., & Ariss, S. S. (1985). Politics and strategic change across organizational life cycles. *Academy of Management Review, 10*(4), 707-723.

Kanter, R. M. (1983). *The change masters.* New York: Simon & Schuster.

Kissinger, H. (1982). *Years of upheaval.* Boston: Little, Brown.

Kubler-Ross, E. (1969). *On death and dying.* New York: Macmillan.

Lawrence, P. R. (1969). How to deal with resistance to change. *Harvard Business Review, 47*(1), 4-8.

Lewyn, M. (1985, June 27). The votes are tallied: Firm to take on IBM. *USA Today,* p. 1B.

Liddell Hart, B. H. (1967). *Strategy.* New York: Signet.

Manchester, W. (1983). *The last lion: Winston Spencer Churchill.* Boston: Little, Brown.

Miller, K. I., & Monge, P. R. (1985). Social information and employee anxiety about organiza-tional change. *Human Communication Research, 11*(3), 365-386.

Nadler, D. A., & Tushman, M. L. (1989). Organizational frame bending: Principles for managing reorientation. *Academy of Management Executive, 3*(3), 194-203.

O'Reilly, B. (1990, January 29). Quality of products. *Fortune,* pp. 42-43.

Our bosses aren't very responsive, most workers believe. (1989, October 3). *Wall Street Journal,* p. A1.

Paul, W. J., Robertson, K. B., & Herzberg, F. (1969). Job enrichment pays off. *Harvard Business Review, 47*(2), 61-78.

Pinchot, G. (1985). *Intrapreneuring.* New York: Harper & Row.

Prahalad, C. K., & Hamel, G. (1990, May-June). The core competence of the corporation. *Harvard Business Review, 90*(3), 79-93.

Rogers, E. M. (1983). *The diffusion of innovations.* (3rd ed.). New York: Free Press.

Shook, R. L. (1988). *Honda.* Englewood Cliffs, NJ: Prentice-Hall.

Swasy, A. (1989, September 21). Slow and steady. *Wall Street Journal,* pp. A1, A14.

Trachtenberg, J. A. (1988). *Ralph Lauren: The man behind the mystique.* Boston: Little, Brown.

Tuchman, B. W. (1982). *Practicing history.* New York: Ballantine.

Uttal, B. (1985, August 5). Behind the fall. *Fortune,* pp. 20-24.

8

Interdepartmental Communication

> I can hardly consider specialization, in itself, evil. On the other hand, I am thoroughly convinced that much of the evil of our times is related to specialization and that we desperately need to develop an attitude of suspicious caution toward it. I think we need to treat specialization with the same degree of distrust and safeguards that we bring to nuclear reactors.
>
> M. Scott Peck

The final memo was terse but lacked the previous punch, like a boxer's weary jab at the end of a long bout: "You guys just can't get it right, the lid still leaks." What began as a routine and friendly exchange of memoranda between the research and marketing departments was ending more like a slugfest with the heavyweights trading insults as if they were punches. Marketing wanted a plastic lid for their new frosting mix. And the research department dutifully developed one which, quite frankly, they were proud of because it was both inexpensive to produce and structurally sound. So the new plastic lid was ceremoniously sent off to the marketing department to be tested on the cans of frosting mix. The research team was soon to be disappointed.

Two days later, memo one was received by the research team. The tone of the memorandum was pleasant enough, but it was greeted with a mixture of puzzlement and disbelief.

> Good work guys! The lid looks great and is plenty sturdy, but it leaks! Our "lovely" white frosting turns brown after a few hours with the lid on it. There must be something in the lid that leaks out. Can you see what you can do?

Despite their obvious predilections, the researchers tested and retested the lid. The results: negative. The lid did not and, indeed, *could not* leak. In due course, an equally magnanimous memorandum to marketing was drafted suggesting that something might be wrong with the frosting.

The second round was not long in starting. Suddenly "greats" became "terribles," "the lid" became "your lid," and the friendly tones were replaced with hostile ones. The researchers chose not to respond in kind but proceeded to conduct still more tests. Again, nothing. An appropriate though less congenial note was sent to marketing providing the "final" results of their tests. Unfortunately, marketing did not choose to respond with such restraint and a three-month battle ensued in which neither side showed a great deal of wisdom or professionalism.

This kind of incident is in no sense unique. Skirmishes like this occur in countless organizations between an ever-changing variety of departments. Indeed, about 65% of the organizations we have surveyed had significant problems with interdepartmental communication. In fact, I feel that with continued specialization of jobs and job duties in the workplace, interdepartmental communication will be one of the greatest challenges facing management in the future. William Ouchi, (1981) author of the widely acclaimed book, *Theory Z,* puts it this way:

> An economic organization is not a purely economic creation: it is simultaneously a social creation. Like any social system, a work organization involves a subtle form of coordination between individuals. Each person and each group within an organization is indeed like an organ in the body. If the coordinating mechanisms between the eyes and the hands are disrupted, then harder work by either the eyes or the hands will fail to improve their joint productivity. Industry does not need managers or workers to toil more assiduously. Instead, the mechanisms of coordination between them must be more attuned to subtlety of relations that are essential to their joint productivity. (p. 199)

In sum, while communication between departments is problematic in most companies, it also is an essential source of productivity.

Therefore, the purpose of this chapter is to explore the nature of interdepartmental communication problems and provide a series of useful tactics to address this issue. Incidentally, the mysterious "leaking lid" controversy was resolved — more on that later. A little hint, though: a key part of the message involved the use of the term "leaking lid."

The Nature of Departmentalization

Departments in an organization are what rooms are to a house. Departments divide. Departments separate. Departments specialize. And departments create barriers. The word "department" comes from the Middle French word "departir," which means to separate. Four particular "separations" are critical when examining interdepartmental communication problems.

First, generally, departments perform separate functions. The success of Henry Ford's production methods forever changed the way organizations do work. Before mass production, cars, like most products, were built one at a time. Henry Ford, of course, changed all that. For example, using old technology it took 18 minutes to assemble a flywheel magneto, but by using an assembly line the time was cut to 5 minutes. The inevitable by-product of these spectacular results was the adoption of similar techniques throughout the United States and Europe.

Obviously, tremendous benefits have been reaped through the use of mass production techniques. Efficiency has increased. Production has increased. Yet, as with any change, there are certain benefits of the old order left by the wayside. In this case, the advantages of the preindustrialized society included (a) employees who had an intimate knowledge of the entire product, not just a portion; (b) employees who psychologically identified with their job, not merely with a paycheck; and (c) employees who naturally made suggestions, not simply followed orders. These are the great communication challenges wrought by mass production techniques. In short, communication was simpler and more efficient before the assembly line.

Mr. Ford's ideas find their way into all modern organizations through the functional division of responsibility often masquerading under the rubric of a departmental name. Rarely will any one person in an organization be able to describe in any degree of detail the responsibilities and duties of personnel in other departments. Even when departments think they are using the same procedures, they can in fact be using very different ones. For example, controllers in one department of Pitney Bowes found that their version of Lotus 1-2-3 software was different from their colleagues in other departments. Because they worked with different versions of the spreadsheet, they could not combine their results. In frustration, they turned the whole business over to an outside vendor (Carroll & Wilke, 1989). This is a far cry from the days before Mr. Ford and his Model T. Ironically, the production efficiency gained through simplicity and standardization decreased the efficiency of communication by creating complex networks of departments that have to coordinate their actions in spite of their uniqueness.

Second, generally, departments are physically separated. Usually the accountants work in one part of the building and the marketing representatives work in another location. Frequently, departments will be separated by walls, stairs, or other physical barriers. The net result is that the physical setup serves to facilitate communication within the department by creating barriers between departments. Interdepartmental communication is often sacrificed for the advantages of intradepartmental communication. Consequently, employees from different departments are only vaguely familiar with each other and they have only a minimal understanding of the equipment, ideas, and difficulties of their colleagues.

Third, typically departments are separated through accounting procedures. Each department has separate accounts and separate budgets. Most expenses are charged to departmental accounts, not general accounts. One production-line employee, when questioned about her reluctance to help fellow workers in another department, said, "It don't count" (sic). Further probing revealed that she received no compensation on her daily production quota sheet for such activities. In fact, such activities had to be recorded in a column designated as "down time." Hence, her efficiency rating and the department's decreased whenever she "committed" interdepartmental communication. Such accounting procedures create a startling set of conceptual blinders that profoundly alter the relationships between departments.

Fourth, departments separate employees through the authority structure. Generally, the chain of command is set up so that employees report to a single individual, the boss. Accordingly, among other activities, the boss evaluates the employee performance and often determines pay scales. It is, of course, not very surprising that given such circumstances most employees have an allegiance to their supervisors. In some cases, the commitment to the boss is so great that corporate goals are sacrificed at the expense of departmental goals (Eisenberg et al., 1982). What is good for the department is not necessarily good for the company. Yet employees must please the boss in order to get promoted. Indeed, the federal bureaucracy is a perfect example of departmental allegiances being valued more than corporatewide commitments.[1] Waste, conflict, and poor decisions are the natural consequences. It is not surprising that the word "department" was first used in governmental circles. In short, the authoritative structure of most organizations is such that employees lack the incentives to communicate across departmental boundaries and, in many cases, are punished for doing so.

Problems of Departmentalization

There are benefits gained by organizing around departments, such as efficiency and the effective management of complex tasks. Yet, managers also must recognize the potential consequences. If efforts are not made to bridge the inherent gulfs between departments, then a variety of serious problems can ensue. Lack of coordination creates difficulties in organizations in the same way it does in a dance studio. A few of these difficulties are discussed below.

Poor Performance

One of the most serious consequences that can occur when departments fail to communicate is that the customer walks away dissatisfied. In one analysis of an airline's communication networks, we found that customers frequently would call the reservations agents and ask about new fares only to be informed that the fare did not exist. Upon further analysis we found that the marketing department would send out advertising about new rates to customers and the media. Marketing belatedly informed the reservation agents of the change, or, in some cases, failed to inform them at all. Marketing perceived their primary function as communicating to the public and felt only a secondary responsibility to communicate to departments internally. Clearly the department fulfilled their primary responsibility at the expense of the broader and more important concern: customer relations. For some very obvious reasons, the net result was that customers chose other airlines. Amazingly, marketing was bewildered as to why the company lost customers when they offered such low fares. Thus the internal communication problems were reflected in the external image of the company.

Unnecessary Conflict

Recall the "leaking lid" episode. What began as a typical exchange of memos between departments escalated into full-scale hostilities. In many ways the conflict could have been avoided if each department had followed some simple steps that will be discussed below. In fact, the situation could have been handled in a manner that promoted greater understanding and mutual respect. Instead, polarization was the result.

This is not uncommon. One creatively designed study examined how employees tended to handle conflict during intradepartmental as opposed to interdepartmental conflicts (Putnam & Wilson, 1982). The results: conflicts between departments were highlighted by strategies that were more confrontive and controlling, which can lead to greater antagonism. In one sense, such expression might be useful if critical issues that were not normally brought out were discussed. On the other hand, frequently such arguments result in bad feelings. Then the departments may take a myopic view of the problem in a win/lose frame of mind. While one department might "win," ultimately the organization, as a whole, loses.

Lack of Innovation

As a consultant, probably the most disheartening words one can hear from employees are: "I just do what I'm told." The inescapable conclusion is that these employees are utterly unmotivated and in some cases deeply bitter. Their potential is being squandered away. Why? There are many reasons, but one of the most frequent involves a rigid adherence to the departmental structure. These employees are not encouraged to offer suggestions for improvements and they rarely know what their colleagues actually do. They may question why the company has certain procedures and policies. The corporate response: "That's company policy." Employee reaction: Work to minimal standards. Reasoning: I cannot see why we do things the way we do, so why try? Analysis: A tragic cycle of wasted human potential.

Overlapping Responsibilities

As a consumer, few events are more frustrating than getting the "run around." Why does this occur? Primarily because people in the different departments know only about their own particular functions and responsibilities. But, ironically, the source of confusion can be that the duties of one department overlap those of another.

In one firm that we assessed, the interviews revealed considerable tension between the customer service department and the telemarketing department. A typical complaint from the telemarketing employees was: "Customer service is interfering with our accounts and it seems underhanded; taking our accounts when they shouldn't be." When customer service employees were questioned, they were equally upset: "They keep transferring calls down here that they could easily answer themselves." One interviewee pinpointed the problem by noting that the telemarketing reps were forbidden to communicate with customer service employees except by memo, which often took too long. In this instance, as with many interdepartmental communication problems, the departmental responsibilities were not clearly defined, and the problem was exacerbated by the lack of an adequate communication channel across the divisions.

Wasted Time

Excessive departmentalization often results in a company wasting a tremendous amount of time. In the airline company discussed above, one individual reported this intriguing incident:

> During the first part of February, several man-hours were spent by the schedule change department as well as the data service department developing a computerized method to analyze aircraft seating capacities. When ready to implement the changes, it was discovered that most of these changes already had been handled in a manual mode. Thus all our efforts were negated. One hand did not know what the other was doing.

Such lamentations reveal that not only did the company waste the time of all those employees, but also that they were quite frustrated with the difficulties. Thus the price of interdepartmental communication problems is paid at the individual and corporate level.

Safety

Employee safety is also at stake if communication between departments goes awry. Mr. Hinojosa, a father of two, was working for a contractor at a gas well and was attempting to dismantle a 15-foot tower by placing a chain around the tower. But the 22-year-old Hinojosa did not know that another contractor had removed two of the four bolts holding up the tower. The result: the tower fell, permanently paralyzing him. The judgment: a jury subsequently awarded him $64 million. The tragedy not only destroyed a man's life but also financially devastated the company (Langley, 1986). The lesson: effective interdepartmental communication is not a luxury but an obligation.

Contributing Factors

A number of conditions tend to accentuate the problems inherent with departmentalization. The factors discussed below create even greater barriers between departments, something like adding a hedge of roses to a fence already separating two homes.

Language Differences

Even today the haunting Biblical story about the Tower of Babel still provides insight.[2] The tale records that God wanted to ensure that his people did not dishonor him by building a monument to themselves.

> Now the whole world had one language and a common speech. . . . But the Lord came down to see the city and the tower that the men were building. The Lord said: "If as one people speaking the same language they have begun to do this, then nothing they plan to do will be impossible for them. Come, let us go down and confuse their language so they will not understand each other." So the Lord scattered them from there over all the earth, and they stopped the city. (Genesis 11.1, 5-8)

The instrument used to stop the building was not some divinely ordered thunderbolt or meteor shower or even a ghastly plague. Rather it was a singularly effective and powerful tool — compelling the people to speak different languages. Equally, though less deliberately, language dissimilarities prohibit modern organizations from achieving their goals.

The difficulty of communicating in an unknown language like Chinese immediately comes to mind when talking about language difficulties. Yet, what I am speaking of is a far more subtle and pervasive, if a no-less formidable, barrier. Accountants have a language of their own. They speak of debits, credits, liquidity, and yield. Computer programmers have their own vocabulary of bytes, bits, CPU, hardware, and software. Even communication scholars have their own obscure language including words like homophily, cybernetics, and the Burkean Pentad. These are the critical language barriers within organizations. People in different departments quite literally speak a different language. They use different jargon, acronyms, and even describe the same things in different ways. This is not all bad. Jargon, acronyms, and specialized meanings for words are all ways for specialists to communicate efficiently and precisely with one another. The problem occurs when trying to communicate with the nonspecialist.

Priority Differences

In addition to the formidable barriers caused by language differences, departments also have different priorities. What may be the first priority for department X may be the last priority for department Y. Ordinarily this may not be a problem except when department X is dependent on department Y.

A destructive sequence of impatience, tension, and distrust may even be set in motion.

One industrial laundry firm we investigated had gone through this exact sequence of events, which eventually lead to lower productivity and employee morale. Industrial laundry firms are in the business of delivering clean linen to other businesses like hotels or hospitals. The operation can basically be broken down into three interdependent phases. The dirty towels, rugs, and uniforms are brought into the plant by the drivers (phase 1); cleaned (phase 2); and delivered back to the clients (phase 3). The main priority in phase 2 is to make sure all the laundry is properly cleaned. The priority of drivers (phase 3) is to make sure the right items are delivered to the proper clients. In order to do this, the drivers like to precisely arrange the items in the trucks before the actual delivery, much like a mail carrier. In this company, the phase 2 personnel loaded the trucks for the drivers. There was constant tension between the two groups because the drivers felt the laundry was not arranged "properly." Tension lead to distrust, which lead to even further problems. Simply, the employees who did the cleaning were not sensitive to the priorities of the drivers.

Rewards and Punishments

One of the most obvious outcomes of a company with a rigid departmental structure is that employees are held accountable to only one boss. The power to either reward or punish employees is in the hands of the boss. When communicating across departmental boundaries there are few direct rewards or punishments that can be meted out by supervisors in other departments. Thus communication efforts across departmental boundaries have less urgency for employees.

Pat, an engineer in a large firm, simply refused to share information with a colleague in another department because Pat felt the other engineer, Sean, would take the credit for developing a more efficient technique. Did Pat incur any punishment for the refusal? No, because Sean's boss had no power over Pat. Only when Pat's boss asked for the requested information did the engineer comply. Meanwhile, valuable time had been lost. Moreover, Pat was not even warned about such behavior. Why? Sean's supervisor could not complain about Pat without Pat's supervisor being understandably protective. Thus the reward/punishment structure inherent in most companies actually creates barriers to interdepartmental communication. Even when the communication climate is more positive, sharing information across divisions is seen as a favor and ultimately can lead to a bartering of information.

Category Dissimilarities

One of the characteristics that distinguishes an expert from a nonexpert is that the expert has more specific knowledge and makes more precise distinctions than the novice. For instance, Eskimos have seven words for different kinds of snow while most people have only one word. Eskimos have a more detailed conception of snow. In a literal sense, experts perceive phenomena differently than nonexperts. They see things that nonexperts do not see. They use names and categories the novice does not use. In short, the experts recognize more specificity in their area of specialization than nonexperts. Similarly, departments act as resident experts in their organizational domain. Hence, they experience the same problems that all experts have when communicating with nonexperts.

Purchasing agents face an unusual challenge in this respect. They are constantly ordering materials that have an almost infinite variety of peculiarities. One agent, for instance, received a memo from the engineering department requesting ten 3/4" screws because the 7/8" screws "didn't work." Sounds simple or at least it did to the engineers. Now consider the purchasing agent who has to thumb through an assortment of catalogs, select a vendor, and decide on these kinds of features:

1. Left or right twist
2. Flat head, round head, or hex
3. Type of alloy used
4. Head type screwdriver or Phillips
5. Tolerance/strength
6. Length
7. Used for metal, wood, or plastic

The engineers in this particular company simply had no idea about the degree of specificity needed to order a seemingly "simple" item. To the engineers, "screw" represented a single concept. To the purchasing department, "screw" was a multidimensional concept. In this instance, the agent had to call the engineers to get answers to all these questions. But this was no easy matter because of the difficulties contacting the engineers. The net result: a needless delay for both the purchasing and engineering departments. Being sensitive to the category dissimilarities between departments is an exceedingly difficult task but a necessary one if communication is to be efficient.

Rigid Procedures

Frequently, past abuse of open and free communication between departments results in rigid managerial control of the communication channels. One communication audit of a small telemarketing firm revealed that the procedures used in communicating between departments were quite restrictive and hindered worker productivity. If a telemarketing representative had a question about a product, they had two options. First, they could ask their managers. This strategy rarely worked because most of the telemarketing representatives knew the products better than their managers. Second, they could draft a written request to the appropriate person in the organization. In practice the policy prohibited direct verbal communication between the persons who had questions and those who could supply the answers. One employee summarized the results of the policy:

> We have to be able to get information about products, credit, and computer runs right away. We used to be able to call most people on the phone but in the last month we have been restricted from doing this and have to send memos. This delays things for hours and sometimes days before we receive an answer. This hinders us in our productivity and sales. We end up taking the static for loss of sales. . . . A lot of things could be solved faster by a single phone call. All this paperwork slows everything down and also loses sales.

When questioned about why this policy was implemented, upper management pointed out two salient factors. First, telemarketing employees were taking too much time from other employees by constantly calling to ask questions. Second, the answers to the telemarketing representatives' questions frequently were contained in the written material that they had at their work stations. In an apparent over-reaction, the pendulum had swung too far to the side of rigidity. In general, most companies have some legitimate need to restrict communication between departments, but these procedures cannot become so rigid so as to hinder achievement of corporate goals.

Addition/Multiplication

Related to the issue of rigid procedures is what could be called the addition/multiplication factor. Deceptively simple, the implications actually are quite profound. Whenever a company adds a department, it multiplies the number of communication linkages. In short, an arithmetical increase in departments geometrically increases the number of communication linkages.

Departments

**Communication
Links**

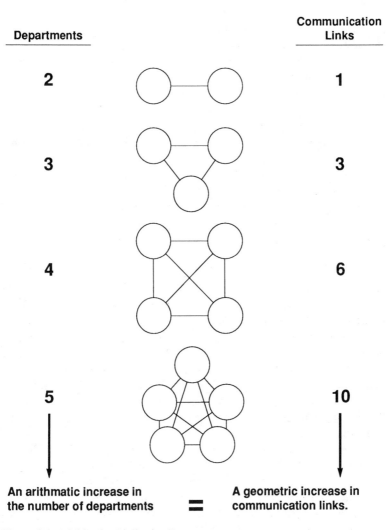

**An arithmatic increase in
the number of departments** **=** **A geometric increase in
communication links.**

Figure 8.1 Addition/Multiplication Factor

For instance, a company that has two departments has only one communication link between the departments. Assume that the company is growing and adds one department. Now the number of communication linkages between departments increases to three. Add another department and increase the linkages to six. Figure 8.1 shows the dramatic increase in linkages that occur when only one more department is added to the organization.

The problem is that many top managers see the addition of a single department as a small structural change, without recognizing the dramatic increase in linkages. Instead of just adding one more department to coordinate with, the company dramatically increases the number of linkages needed to coordinate their activities. Rigid policies to control communication between departments is one possible response to an unwieldy number of communication links, the results of which are reviewed above. The other response could be to open the system up, like the free market, and let each department fend for itself. Information overload, office politics, and information bartering often are the results of this extreme. Thus, by failing to take into account the addition/multiplication factor, many top administrators unwittingly create interdepartmental communication problems.

Office Design

Probably the most subtle barrier that fosters interdepartmental communication problems is office design, which acts as a sort of organizational subconscious restricting certain natural communication impulses. Winston Churchill once said, "We shape our buildings, after that they shape us." Office design to a large degree determines who has access to whom by creating barriers to some departments and bridges to others. In some fascinating research at MIT, Thomas Allen (1967) revealed that people more than 10 meters apart have only an 8% to 9% probability of communicating at least once a week, versus a 25% chance at 5 meters (see Figure 8.2). Of course, this is only one of many studies about the effects of office design on communication (Ornstein, 1989). Because each office is unique, special factors have to be considered in each organization in order to make changes that will facilitate more effective communication between departments.

The same company that had the rigid communication guidelines for the telemarketing representatives also had a unique office design. The telemarketing department was separated physically from other departments to such an extent that the telemarketing representatives would not talk to other employees for weeks. Despite having a joint lunchroom, employees from different departments huddled around their individual tables. The telemarketing representatives vividly characterized the situation: "There is zero communication between upstairs and downstairs. It is like the stairs are a wall or no-man's land. 'The Great Stairwell,' we call it. We up here, can't bother them downstairs."

The Great Wall of China for centuries separated China from the rest of the world, physically, culturally, and intellectually. In much the same way, "The

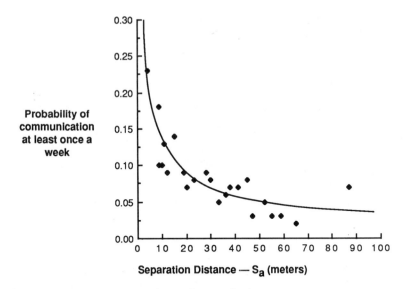

Figure 8.2 The Effect of Location on Communication

Great Stairwell" in this business separated telemarketing from the other departments. This office was designed in this fashion for excellent "functional" reasons, such as telephone hookups, but the layout failed to consider some significant interpersonal communication issues. In any event, such design decisions, whether intentional or not, unfolded into some rather disquieting implicit messages to employees and contributed to the difficulties between the departments.

What To Do?

Diagnosed problems are not solved problems. How can interdepartmental communication problems be effectively managed? Of paramount importance is management's commitment to effective communication between departments. They must be committed not only to short-term projects but also to long-term structural changes. The communication system must not be overly constrained, as is the tendency of Arrow managers. Yet it must avoid the Circuit manager's inclination of a completely open system, which leads to information overload.

To ease interdepartmental communication problems, managers must seek to balance two counteracting forces, just as a dancer balances creative

Table 8.1 Constraints in Sharing Information

Information Providers Concerns	Information Consumer Concerns
Answering questions takes time.	Information is needed to complete tasks.
Information dissemination is a responsibility.	Sometimes it is easier to call or ask someone than look up the answer.
My priority should be answering nonroutine inquires.	Sometimes a routine request for information is a way to legitimately get someone's attention I couldn't normally contact.
Providing information also facilitates receiving information.	They might tell me something I don't know.
It takes time to document everything.	I just want to make sure the information is current.
	I want to confirm the written information.

impulse within musical constraints. One tension point could be called the "sender's concerns," because an effective communication system avoids wasting the time of information providers. It is counterproductive for a system to be so open that employees are expected to answer the same question 10 to 15 times a day. Employees get weary answering the same questions day after day, especially when the information is readily available in a written form. The second tension point could be termed the "inquirer's concerns." Employees need sufficient information to get their job done. Hence, the system needs to be open enough to answer and process legitimate information requests (see Table 8.1).

The perfect system would block all redundant information requests but allow every unique or special inquiry. This ideal will no doubt prove elusive, but as a starting point, department managers need to be aware of the inherent tension between the concerns of senders and inquirers. The objective is to develop a sensitivity to the needs, desires, and problems of other departments. After all, today's requester may be tomorrow's provider. Frustration by either party ultimately results in discontent for all.

Minor Effort Projects

Most employees realize that, to some extent, they affect the productivity of their coworkers. One particularly diligent receptionist at Krueger Incorporated put it this way:

I must screen each incoming call to make sure it is directed to the proper department. In doing this I save my coworkers time, since most calls end up with the proper person. Also, I keep a list of who is in and who is out. By taking messages for people who are not available, I help the others near this "missing person's" phone by not putting any calls through. I must keep things running smoothly when it comes to phone calls.

In this situation, it is apparent that the receptionist is sensitive to how she can affect the productivity of workers in other departments. Many managers would love to have such a receptionist. If every employee displayed this degree of dedication and sensitivity to others, then more organizations would be running smoothly. In many instances, however, employees are unaware of how a specific action or inaction may affect another department. The projects discussed below can help foster a deeper sensitivity on the part of employees, as well as provide more specific information about departments across the organizational boundaries.

Job Switching

Few projects can more effectively force employees to come to grips with their colleagues' work situations than job switching. The basic idea is that employees from various departments switch jobs for one or two days to get a feel for the other person's job. Employees can see firsthand how their actions impact another department.

The industrial laundry discussed earlier used this technique with remarkable success by having plant workers ride with the drivers who delivered the linens to customers. After five out of the 60 plant workers participated in the program, some dramatic changes occurred. The tension between the department slowly dissipated. Amazingly, without any explicit appeal, the plant workers started to arrange the linens in the trucks in a very precise way so as to make it easier for the drivers to do their job.

Small businesses are not the only ones using this technique with success. Hyatt Hotels shut down their corporate headquarters for an entire day and everyone in the home office, from the president to the receptionists, were sent into the field to work. After a two-hour training session, the 375 corporate employees made beds, carried bags, and served as bartenders in 67 different hotels across the nation. President Thomas Pritzker worked as a doorman and waiter (Carroll, 1989). This costly exercise not only helps foster more effective communication between departments, but also provides unique insight into how to effectively serve patrons. The power of such quick and vivid firsthand experiences can replace hundreds of rules, exhortations, reports, and countless hours of training.

Companywide Seminars

A companywide seminar that involves first-line employee as well as top management personnel can provide a rich and unique opportunity to foster effective interdepartmental communication. Many topics are of interest to personnel at all levels of the corporation, like conflict resolution or basic communication skills. Skillful seminar leaders can help bring out the perspectives of the various departments and organizational levels in a way so that everyone develops greater sensitivity to the big picture. If the seminar involves some sort of case study or project in which there is group work, the wise seminar leader should encourage people to work together who would not normally get the opportunity to do so.

For instance, a basic communication skills workshop was conducted for all personnel at a savings and loan association. In each session there were employees from various departments representing tellers as well as top-level managers. This was one of the few opportunities for employees from across the organization to get together. One employee reported that such seminars allow time to develop a "lingo link" that helps bridge departmental barriers. Although not one of the major objectives, a pleasant benefit of the seminar was that top management became aware of a particular issue that tellers were facing on a day-to-day basis. Changes were made that may not have been considered had the tellers' concerns been forwarded through normal channels. Additionally, management, by their presence, subtly communicated that they valued training of this type and that they still were learning, just like their employees.

Interdepartmental team building also can prove useful. Bank employees from two departments that were consistently experiencing communication difficulties found this to be a successful experience. They began the session with the administration of a personality profile, the Myers-Briggs Type Indicator, which revealed some intriguing differences between employees in each division in terms of behaviors and thinking styles. The profile proved to be an excellent primer for a more detailed discussion of the interdepartmental difficulties. Why? Because it legitimized the differences and provided a more objective way to discuss the difficulties. The result: an action plan was developed by the departments to help ease tensions.

Coauthored Articles

Developing opportunities for people of two different backgrounds to work on a project frequently can provide the impetus for departments to change their attitudes toward each other. This project is simple in design but more difficult in execution. Employees from two different departments are asked to coauthor an article on a topic of interest. The article could be published in a scholarly or trade journal or even the corporate newsletter. The higher the prestige of the publication, the better.

In one chemical research firm, a member of the marketing division coauthored an article with the researcher who developed the product. The article was published in a trade journal. Both individuals reported a renewed respect for the other's expertise. Furthermore, the marketing department now had an important advocate *within* the research department who was able to explain a marketing perspective. The reverse also was true, which, in the long run, aided in the overall coordination of corporate policy.

New Product Presentations

A presentation to employees about new products or services can provide a marvelous occasion to foster interdepartmental team building as well as demonstrate corporate pride. Making employees from the various departments responsible for different aspects of the presentation forces the presenters to coordinate their plans. The discussions prior to the presentation generally help the presenters learn about other aspects of the project.

One company tried this idea and was ecstatic about the results. Members of marketing, sales, computer systems, customer service, and even the president participated in the 90-minute presentation to employees that was complete with all the trimmings: overhead transparencies, flip charts, and printed outlines. Not only did the presenters have a sense of cohesiveness and feeling of accord about the new project, but the employees who would be involved at a much later point became equally excited about the project. They even offered a number of useful suggestions. Perhaps the real benefit was that future interdepartmental problems were avoided early in the process.

Brainstorming Sessions

Many times other departments can provide useful insights into the difficulties that another department is experiencing. Setting up sessions between departments in which each unit shares its problems can be a creative experience. The agenda need not be formal. Temporary or permanent companywide task forces can be equally useful.

The marketing department of a research firm noted that the plastic animal carriers used to transport cats and dogs on airplanes often chipped and broke on the corners. They recognized the marketing possibilities and mentioned this to research in a brainstorming session. Subsequently, a new and simple animal carrier was designed and the company scored a nice little success in the marketplace. What makes this case extremely interesting is that normally the research department either thought up their own ideas or, more often, top management developed project ideas. In this case, the communication pattern was reversed, and with convincing results. Many executives might be quite surprised at the workable ideas that could be generated in the various "corners" of their corporate world.

Travel

Often the source of corporate gossip, a company car pool can be a place where employees can easily exchange information across departmental boundaries. It is a natural, easy, and cost-effective way to encourage inter-departmental communication. Company-financed van pools can have the same effect and become a potential place for the spontaneous generation of new ideas. Moreover, trying to arrange corporate airline schedules so that people from different divisions travel together can be equally useful. The same holds true for travel by car during the day to a corporate function. Why take separate cars? It saves money and fosters effective interdepartmental communication.

Companywide Gatherings

Social gatherings of company personnel held on an annual or semiannual basis can provide wonderful opportunities to foster effective interdepartmental communication. Employees make contact with those they would not normally associate with. The nonthreatening atmosphere of a company banquet or picnic often encourages free information sharing across departmental boundaries. The old adage says "It's not *what* you know, but *who* you know that counts" — but one might add, "and *where* you go." Employees will find it difficult to be narrowly concerned with only their department when they share a common experience with everyone else in the corporation. The event becomes a point of possible conversation for any person they see in the hall over the next few weeks. Drill sergeants know that esprit de corps is partly a function of experiencing and surviving a trying event. No doubt some employees feel like they have been through boot camp after a company picnic, but it does give them an important shared experience. In short, a company gathering can provide just the right background to build effective interdepartmental communication.

Show-and-Tell

Most school children eagerly look forward to show-and-tell day. On those days, their excitement is unbridled and their curiosity overwhelming. What new electrical gizmo will Elton bring in? Can Taylor's bow shoot real arrows? Will Martha's cat really dance? The premise is simple: Each child brings in something of interest to show the class and then talks about it. At that age "talking about it" is almost as much fun as bringing something. That changes, of course, with age, as self-consciousness weaves its inhibiting spell.

Many an organization would do well in reviving this old Friday afternoon tradition. I never cease to be amazed at how little we actually know about what our colleagues are doing on a day-to-day basis. In many cases a university professor knows far more about a former colleague at a college a thousand miles away than someone from another department whose office is right next door. But this is the nature of the modern organization.

Recall the plastic lid case at the beginning of this chapter. The problem was solved in short order through a show-and-tell session. After the research department was thoroughly disgusted with marketing and vice versa, they decided to have one final bout. Each brought their respective documents to show how the other side was wrong and misguided. Predictably, the arguments that had hitherto been expressed in other forums were vented in the face-to-face encounter. At one point, someone from marketing pulled out a can of frosting, removed the vacuum-sealed aluminum covering, and placed the plastic lid on the can. The meeting concluded indecisively with both sides claiming victory and neither admitting defeat.

As is often the case, what is communicated unsuccessfully with statistics and arguments can be communicated clearly and vividly with one simple demonstration. By happenstance, research took the can of frosting back to the office. Lo and behold — it turned brown over night. The very next day, research had the answer. What had happened was that the lid was porous to air molecules and the air had interacted with the frosting, causing it to discolor. Research was right; the lid did not "leak." Marketing was right; there was a problem with the lid and frosting. Yet both were wrong. Neither department attacked the problem in the most effective manner. One simple but powerful demonstration could have resolved the difficulty without needless strife, frustration, and wasted time. So it was that the grade school game of show-and-tell stopped the adults from arguing like little children.

Major Effort Projects

For many firms, the projects reviewed above may be the only solutions needed. Yet, for other businesses, more radical measures are needed because the interdepartmental communication problems are more deeply ingrained within the current organizational structure.

Job Rotation

As distinguished from job switching, job rotation involves becoming familiar with another department's jobs and responsibilities and actually performing them over long periods of time. There are no specialists. This year's production manager was the personnel manager three years ago, and this year's marketing manager was the previous production manager. And so it goes. "At Canon, critical people move regularly between the camera business and the copier business and between the copier business and the professional optical-products business" (Prahalad & Hamel, 1990, p. 91). Why? It is a quest to develop "core competencies." The central idea is that the company seeks to develop fundamental "know-how" that can have a wide variety of applications. The key is for the company to strategically bring together corporate knowledge in order to develop or enhance products and services. The impact of this approach has been remarkable: between 1980 and 1988 Canon grew 26.4% (Prahalad & Hammel, 1990). This kind of program provides managers and employees with an amazing amount of detailed knowledge about functions of departments and the company as a whole. Beyond sensitivity, managers develop a commitment to the company instead of their specialty. Moreover, researchers have shown that changing jobs actually can result in increases in employee performance, innovativeness, and job satisfaction (Keller & Holland, 1981).

William Ouchi (1981) describes how the Japanese utilize such a program:

> Sugao will enter in a management training position, spending perhaps a year just meeting people and learning his way around while working on various assignments. Then he will be sent out to a branch to learn bank operations including working with tellers and managing the flow of information, paper, and people. From there he will be brought back into headquarters to learn commercial banking, the process of loaning large sums to major firms with whom the bank maintains relations. Then back to yet another branch. . . . Ten years will have passed and Sugao will gain his first major promotion, perhaps becoming a section chief. In this capacity he will move again. . . . By the time he reaches the peak of his career, Sugao will be an expert in taking every

function, every specialty, and every office of the Mitsubeni Bank and knitting them together into one, integrated whole. (pp. 29-30)

In such a program a lateral move is not seen in the typically negative light, but rather as a radiant opportunity to learn more about the complexities of the company. While, at first thought, it may seem that employees in rotated jobs might experience more ambiguity about their rules than those who do not rotate, researchers found exactly the opposite (Keller & Holland, 1981). Perhaps, by knowing more about the big picture, employees know more about their specific role in the organization.

Redesign of Accounting Procedures

Most accounting systems simply are blind to the necessity of interdepartmental communication. Generally, employees are not rewarded for such efforts and the budgetary constraints actively discourage such attempts. At Legal Sea Foods restaurants, however, the waiters and waitresses work as teams. One of the critical ways in which the restaurant encourages the team atmosphere is that all employees pool their tips. Hence, customers never have to look for "their" waiter or waitress because everyone works together. Such a simple change in accounting procedures has a tremendous impact on the level of customer service (Keidel, 1988). In short, if a company chooses to become serious about interdepartmental communication then some major changes will be needed in the accounting procedures that will reward employees both monetarily and in terms of performance evaluations.[3]

Change the Office Design

As previously discussed, the physical layout of a business can dramatically alter communication patterns. Whether intentionally or unintentionally, office design fosters certain communication events and discourages others. The overriding issue managers should consider is whether the office layout is conducive to communication between departments. Frequently, the changes can be quite minor but have a relatively major impact.

The telemarketing company that had some interdepartmental communication problems (aided and abetted by the "Great Stairwell") could not at the time take out the stairwell or change buildings. Yet there was one saving grace; all employees ate in the same lunchroom. Even here the office design conspired in the downfall. The lunchroom had 20 small round tables that could seat four or five people. Guess who sat with who? The telemartketing representatives sat with telemarketing representatives, the marketing personnel sat with marketing personnel – upstairs with upstairs, and downstairs with downstairs. The "Great Stairwell" was still intact even in a common lunchroom. Solution: put in longer tables, like long picnic benches, and stagger lunch hours so employees would have to eat lunch with people in other departments. Informing the employees about the purpose of this change, accompanied with the development of a strong communication policy, proved successful.

Robert B. Reich (1989), who has taught at Harvard and held various senior-level jobs in the government, insightfully notes one major barrier to United States technological preeminence:

> Most U.S. corporate researchers and design engineers work in laboratories that are separated geographically as well as culturally from factories, warehouses, and distribution facilities where their ideas might eventually be implemented. Research facilities typically occupy modern, campuslike buildings in bucolic surroundings. Researchers and design engineers are often considered to be doing more important or prestigious work than their compatriots on the factory floor. (p. 45)

Reich goes on to point out that one of the reasons that the Japanese have been so successful is that there is rarely a geographical, and thus cultural, distance between research and production. Research is not expected or encouraged to develop fully formed ideas. Indeed, there is a continual give and take between the two departments, in part because they are located on the same grounds. In sum, most organizations need to give further thought to the symbolic messages relayed to employees via the use of physical space.

Communication Policy

At the very heart of any attempt to ease interdepartmental communication problems should be a corporate communication policy. Most organizations simply do not have one. Although the philosophy behind a communication policy already has been discussed, one of the critical parts of that policy should include ways to foster useful communication across departmental boundaries. The central dilemma that such a policy needs to deal with is to reconcile the information provider's concerns and the inquirer's concerns. That is, the policy needs to allow all necessary communication but screen unnecessary and redundant communication. One such policy is outlined in Appendix C.

Ultimately the policy should be based on corporate values. Employees need to develop a commitment to corporatewide goals instead of a deep commitment to a particular department. This means that the training done in the initial stages of employment should stress a corporatewide responsibility for interdepartmental communication. Employees, especially new employees, need to be shown that communication across departmental lines is to be encouraged. There is no better place to begin than with training on a well-articulated policy statement.

Changing Job Descriptions

Few organizations have interdepartmental communication built into job descriptions; American Express is one exception. They require that senior managers develop strategic plans that include collaboration with other departments. The result has been a synergistic use of resources as well as some notable cost reductions (Keidel, 1988).

In most companies there is a big rivalry between the sales and marketing staffs. One analyst put it this way: "Good salespeople are concerned with individual accounts, good marketers, with aggregates of accounts; it's up to good managers to bring those concerns and talents together" (Levine, 1989, p. 36). Merrill Lynch tries to do this. For instance, one of the routine functions of the marketing department is to conduct surveys of the needs of the sales force. Not only have these kinds of efforts succeeded in minimizing interdepartmental conflicts, they also helped Merrill Lynch respond quickly to customers' concerns after the market crash of 1987. The company was one of the first to introduce "flight-to-safety" investment products (Levine, 1989).

Honda has made an even more dramatic change in job descriptions to inhibit departmental rifts. In their Marysville, Ohio, plant there are only two job classifications — assembly and maintenance. Honda workers perform many different tasks, which is inconceivable in other auto factories that have up to 100 classifications (Koepp, 1986). This approach permeates everything Honda does. Job descriptions purposely are left vague:

My boss gave me the best advice I've ever received. During my first week, I commented on how difficult it was for me to understand what my actual job was. He looked at me silently for a few seconds and then said in a low voice, "Your job is everything." That was it! Not another word and he walked away. It took me a while to realize what he meant and how right on target he was. (Shook, 1988, p. 129)

Such job descriptions may induce some degree of anxiety but are unlikely to create departmental blinders. Typically, job descriptions are narrowly confined to departmental responsibilities, not corporatewide ones. In sum, job descriptions may send the clearest messages to employees about the organization's commitment to effective interdepartmental communication.

Changing the Organizational Structure

Perhaps the most extreme step that could be taken would be to alter the organizational structure in some way to facilitate communication. Some organizations have found that a change in reporting relationships can indeed provide the impetus for more effective interdepartmental communication. Sometimes combining departments, altering job responsibilities, or even splitting some departments may prove to be effective strategies.

A highly successful insurance firm, Aid Association for Lutherans, for years had three separate sections: health insurance, life insurance, and support services. The result was that agents calling the home office frequently talked to dozens of different personnel in order to make minor changes in a policy or check the status of a claim. A corporate reorganization was designed that allowed one team of 20 or 30 employees to serve a certain geographic group of field agents. Thus all 167 tasks that used to be performed by a seemingly faceless group of corporate employees are being done by a team dedicated to a particular agent. Now the 1,900 agents deal with only a small team and are not overwhelmed by a bureaucracy of over 500 employees in the home office. The results: a reduction in processing time of applications from 20 days to just 5 days, and a 20% increase in productivity. By changing and expanding job responsibilities, corporate employees experience slightly more stress, but agents and clients clearly experience less (Hoerr, 1988). This dramatic change in corporate structure helped the organization coordinate its efforts more effectively, which should be the focus of interdepartmental communication efforts.

One of the more radical proposals that has been used is called the matrix organizational structure. The idea is relatively simple. Certain employees in the organizational report to two managers instead of just one. A marketing specialist, for instance, might report to both a manager on the West coast and one on the East coast. Or a quality control engineer might report to the production manager as well as the product manager. There is one top manager who oversees the entire process. Certainly this facilitates communication between departments, but it takes a special organization and unique individuals to make the idea work. Training is a must because of ambiguity over responsibilities and a tendency to manage for the short term. Companies in the aerospace industry were the first to try the concept and now it is used in a wide variety of organizations including hospitals, banks, and research firms. It is a serious step, though, and needs to be thought out carefully.

Final Thoughts

Most organizations to some degree have difficulties with interdepartmental communication. Unfortunately, the problem frequently is overlooked and, even when recognized, often the symptoms are treated instead of the causes. To a large extent the problems are unavoidable in North American business because of the penchant for rigid departmentalization. Even under these conditions, however, some significant changes, as outlined above, can be made that will enhance communication between departments.

Avoiding unnecessary conflict, low performance, time delays, and decisions that work at cross purposes are compelling reasons for taking active measures to improve interdepartmental communication. Yet one question remains: At what cost? Are there any dangers in encouraging interdepartmental communication? In a word, yes. An overly integrated organization can stifle creativity and innovation, and develop a tendency for "groupthink." Frankly, given the ingrained belief in the wisdom of departmentalization, these possibilities are remote.

The other disadvantage of this is time. As many Japanese businesses have discovered, decisions typically will take more time to make because all the departments have to be consulted and allowed input into an impending change. But that time often is more than compensated for by swift and smooth implementation. Nevertheless, a more rigidly departmentalized company will frequently be able to react more quickly than one that is not.

On the balance, though, the benefits of effective interdepartmental communication far exceed the costs. Misunderstandings can be reduced, antagonisms avoided, cooperation encouraged, and sensitivity promoted. And, in the end, a supportive communication climate can be developed and maintained.

In a sense, communicating across departmental boundaries is like taking a voyage into an unknown land. Daniel Boorstin (1983), in his magnum opus *The Discoverers,* writes passionately about the real goal of the "discoverers":

> The ability to come home again was essential if a people were to enrich, embellish, and enlighten themselves from far-off places. . . . Getting there was

not enough. The internourishment of the peoples of the earth required the ability to get back, to return to the voyaging source and transform the stay-at-homes by the commodities and the knowledge that the voyagers had found over there. (p. 158)

So too, communication between departments seeks to enrich the lives of individuals throughout the entire company.

The frontier these days is not geographical but, rather, technological. The Macintosh personal computer emblazoned a new frontier of sorts by coupling extremely potent hardware with extraordinary graphics software. The result: a powerful computer that was amazingly simple to use. How was it designed? One member of the design team puts it this way: "The great thing about the Mac as a product is that it really wasn't designed as just a piece over there and this piece over there and this other piece. . . . All of it was designed in parallel, everybody knowing what everyone else's job was" ("Interview," 1984, p. 68). Steven Jobs, cofounder of Apple, said of the project that this was the first time that hardware people had gotten together with software engineers to design a computer. Imprinted in the plastic inside the Mac are the names of all the design team members, formally from different "departments." This is what effective interdepartmental communication is all about. The result: Apple's initial sales of the Macintosh exceeded even their highest expectations. These are the kinds of benefits that are possible with effective interdepartmental communication.

Notes

1. For an excellent example, see Henry Kissinger's *The White House Years,* 1979, p. 887.

2. In Hebrew the word "Babel" sounds like the word for confused.

3. For an excellent and thoughtful piece on how accounting systems often deceive managers, see Kaplan (1984).

References

Allen, T. J. (1967, October-November). Communication in the research and development laboratory. *Technology Review.*

Boorstin, D. J. (1983). *The discoverers.* New York: Random House.

Carroll, D. (1989, September 25). Hyatt execs check out how the other half works. *USA Today,* p. 1B.

Carroll, P. B., & Wilke, J. R. (1989, August 15). Calculated move. *Wall Street Journal,* pp. A1, A6.

Eisenberg, E. M., Farace, R. V., Monge, P. R., Bettinghaus, E. P., Kurchner-Hawkins, R., White, L. L., & Williams, K. I. (1982, May). *Communication linkages in interorganizational systems: Review and synthesis.* Paper presented at the annual meeting of the International Communication Association, Boston.

Hoerr, J. (1988, November 28). Work teams can rev up paper-pushers, too. *Business Week,* pp. 64-72.

Holy Bible: New international version. (1978). Grand Rapids, MI: Zondervan Bible Publishers.

Interview: The Macintosh design team. (1984, February). *Byte,* pp. 58-80.

Kaplan, R. S. (1984, July-August). Yesterday's accounting undermines production. *Harvard Business Review,* 62(4), 95-101.

Keidel, R. W. (1988, November 27). Going beyond 'I'm O.K., you're O.K. *New York Times,* p. 2F.

Keller, R. T., & Holland, W. E. (1981). Job change: A naturally occurring field experiment. *Human Relations, 34*(12), 1053-1067.

Kissinger, H. (1979). *The White House years.* Boston: Little, Brown.

Koepp, S. (1986, September 8). Honda in a hurry. *Time,* pp. 48-49.

Langley, M. (1986, May 29). Generous juries. *Wall Street Journal,* pp. 1, 20.

Levine, R. (1989). Overcoming sibling rivalry between sales and marketing. *Management Review, 78*(6), 36-40.

Ornstein, S. (1989). The hidden influences of office design. *Academy of Management Executive, 3*(2), 144-147.

Ouchi, W. (1981). *Theory z.* Reading, MA: Addison-Wesley.

Peck, M. S. (1983). *People of the lie: The hope for healing human evil.* New York: Simon & Schuster.

Prahalad, C. K., & Hamel, G. (1990, May-June). The core competence of the corporation. *Harvard Business Review, 90*(3), 79-93.

Putnam, L. L., & Wilson, C. E. (1982). Communicative strategies in organizational conflicts: Reliability and validity of a measurement scale. In M. Burgoon (Ed.), *Communication yearbook 6* (pp. 629-673). Beverly Hills, CA: Sage.

Reich, R. B. (1989). The quiet path to technological preeminence. *Scientific American, 261*(4), 41-47.

Shook, R. L. (1988). *Honda.* New York: Prentice-Hall.

9

Communicating the Innovative Spirit

Everything that can be invented has been invented.

Charles H. Duell, Director of U.S. Patent Office, 1899

Loyalty to petrified opinion never broke a chain or freed a human soul.

Mark Twain

He was like so many innovators who yearned for change and looked to the future with a wide-eyed eagerness. He was young, energetic, a bit brash, and had an infectious enthusiasm for life. He had a favorite saying that inspired not only him but all those around him: "Some men see things as they are and say, why. I dream things that never were and say, why not?" This is the spirit of innovation. And it was the spirit that emboldened the thousands who supported him. Tragically, his life was cut short at the hand of an assassin.

Yet, even in the anguish and despair of that moment on June 6, 1968 there was a glimmer of hope. The vision — his vision — still lived. Even today, there are those who dream dreams and have the courage and tenacity to bring them to reality. Robert F. Kennedy never had that chance. But he would cheer on those who do.

At the time of the Kennedy assassination, the United States was at a historical crossroads. There was social tension and a political crisis. Many people believe that now the United States is an another historic crossroads. This time the crisis is in American business. The rising trade deficits, aging industries, and increased competition from abroad all lead to one indisputable conclusion: those organizations — and indeed countries — that will survive in the future will be the ones that are innovative. But many managers do not really understand the innovative process or how to foster the spirit of innovation. That is the focus of this chapter.

Misconceptions

A host of misconceptions plague the innovative process. Some of the more important ones are discussed in detail below.

Myth 1 — Innovation is risky.

Innovation often is resisted by managers and organizations alike because of a fear of the unknown. Innovative practices, by definition, are not tested, tried, and proved; they are not traditional. Results cannot be guaranteed. There can, in fact, be "failures." The safe course appears to be in continuing to do what the organization does well. Thus it is assumed that tampering with past successes can incur unnecessary risks. Why change if everything is going well?

This is begging the question, however. That is, the answer is implicit in the question. Logically, one could just as easily ask: Why not change? After all, the successful company or manager is in a better economic and political position to experiment than those who are less successful. Indeed, those who ask "Why change?" are already standing on shaky ground, for they do not really understand the source of their success.

Entrepreneurs tend to be highly innovative. But contrary to popular belief, entrepreneurs do not tend to be big risk-takers. The press often covers those who are, but careful research on the attributes of entrepreneurs generally reveals that their propensity for risk taking is not much different than the general population (Brockhaus, 1980). Other characteristics, like the need for achievement, autonomy, self-esteem, and independence tend to be far more predominant in entrepreneurs. A tolerance for ambiguity, high energy levels, and assertiveness are other unique attributes of the entrepreneur (Collins & Moore, 1964). In short, entrepreneurs may be robust and exciting human beings, but they are not some kind of organizational Evil Knevils.

Moreover, in the long run it is more risky for corporations to not innovate than it is to innovate. The near collapse of the U.S. steel industry is a case in point. For years, new technology was passed up by U.S. manufacturers while competitors in Japan embraced the innovations. The result: a market that was once thoroughly dominated by domestically produced steel is now dominated by foreign-produced steel.

But the risks of not innovating go beyond the domination of this or that market. The very survival of the economic system is dependent on innovation. Around 1909, Bell Telephone conducted a study of how many telephone operators would be needed if telephone usage continued to increase at the present rate at the time. They concluded that between 1925 and 1930 every female in the United States between the ages of 17 and 60 would have to become a telephone operator (Drucker, 1985). That scenario, of course, was untenable. Within two years, however, automatic switching devices were developed. The lesson is simple: innovation is a necessity, not an option. Innovation involves some risk, but the risk of not innovating is far greater.

Myth 2 — Innovation is always the product of the revolutionary "big" idea or grand scheme.

In fact, there are some innovations that appear to be of this ilk, such as the Wright Brothers' airplane. But these tend to be the exception rather than the rule. The "little" ideas, the minor modifications here and there, or the addition of this or that feature, are the greatest source of innovation. Here's a sampling:

One employee at a Texas Instrument plant suggested using larger spools of wire so as to decrease the number of trips made to replace the used spool. The result: a time study showed an annual increase in productivity of approximately 15%. ("Organizing," 1981)

An employee at a small paper converting plant suggested that someone begin work one half hour early in order to warm up the cutting machines. The result: the elimination of five man-hours a week of idle time for that division.

During the 1950s, Allen Grant, the president of Glen Raven Mills, asked his wife, Ethel, "How would it be if we made a pair of panties and fastened the stockings to it?" She thought it was a grand idea. The result: pantyhose. ("Nights," 1989)

In each case, these seemingly minor innovations have reaped huge dividends.

Likewise, many of the greatest scientific discoveries were the product of the seemingly inconsequential. For instance, Louis Pasteur became intrigued by an experiment that had gone "bad" when his calcium tartrate solution became turbid because of some mold. "Most chemists would have poured the liquid down the sink, considering the experiment as entirely spoiled" (Dubos, 1976, p. 107). Not Pasteur, who used such a seemingly trivial event to launch his prodigious innovations of pasteurization and immunizations for contagious diseases. Pasteur once reflected on "the infinitely great power of the infinitely small" in the world of bacteria, fungi, and the like. (Dubos, 1976, p. 45). Perhaps he spoke in another sense as well and was characterizing the entire process of innovation.

Myth 3—Innovation is solely the product of a few great minds.

Tangled in the web of the "big idea" theory of innovation is the belief that innovation can be done only by a select set of gifted individuals. Certainly some innovations, like genetic engineering or the silicon chip, would not have been possible without the genius of a select few. But this does not mean that all innovations are the product of the gifted. Examples abound of the "ordinary" individual coming up with some special and useful new innovation. Even the supposedly uninformed customer can sometimes be the source of useful innovation. For instance, Clearwood Building Incorporated, a San Francisco based construction company, simply listened to customers' complaints about their competitors. Then the company revamped their service to alleviate the more common complaints about contractors, like poor manners, beat-up trucks, and workers who track dirt across the carpet. Their service level became the epitome of professionalism, with spotlessly clean trucks and employees dressed in jacket and tie. All of this may sound a bit obvious, but it worked. Within two years, annual revenues jumped from $200,000 to $1 million (Galante, 1986).

Another problem with the "great mind" theory of innovation is one of perspective. Rarely are the "great minds" recognized as such in the beginning of their careers. In fact, it is usually just the opposite. Who would have thought that two college dropouts tinkering with electronic components in a garage would have launched the personal computer revolution? Of course, that is exactly what Steven Jobs and Steven Wozniak did with Apple computer. The label of "innovative genius" is almost always attached after the fact.

Innovators may not necessarily be blessed with an apparent intellectual prowess. Rather, intellectual curiosity and drive are more important. Most great scientists have an IQ score of at least 120. Yet, after that point, there is little relationship between IQ and scientific success. "A scientist with an IQ score of 130 is as likely to win a Nobel Prize as one with a score of 180" (Beveridge, 1980, p. 93). Moreover, grades in school may not be a useful predictor of potential. Einstein and Darwin are two classic examples of poor students who clearly achieved some scientific fame. On the other hand, there are those who carried straight As in school but never had a creative idea in their life.

Organizations that wait for the "great minds" to propose innovations almost always wait until the innovation proves to have a high likelihood of success. By then the competitors recognize it and also jump at the chance. By virtue of the fact that "great minds" are labeled after the fact, most companies fail to exploit a host of innovative opportunities within grasp. For nine years Chester Carlson tried to sell his idea of xerography to more than 20 companies such as RCA, Kodak, and IBM. All rejected the innovation, reasoning that there was no need for a machine that does the same thing as carbon paper (Jacobson & Hillkirk, 1986). Of course, Xerox is now a corporate giant. The crux of the matter is that innovative opportunities abound in organizations, whether at Xerox or the local flower shop. Potentially, anyone could propose a useful innovation. Hence, the great challenge is to encourage the innovative spirit in employees but still be able to separate the wheat from the chaff.

Those who by word or deed endorse either the "great mind" or the "big idea" theory of innovation frequently are seeking to justify their own complacency. They are trying to deny their responsibility to innovate. They will not accept the burden of an occasional "failure." The logic behind this is that one cannot fail if one attempts nothing. They seek the safe course. Ultimately they do so at their own peril and the company's as well.

Myth 4—Innovation is product-focused.

Most discussions of innovation center on the invention of new products, like the electric light bulb or personal computer. The entrepreneurial heroes who typically are praised tend to have invented some gadget or device. The school history books take note of the genius of Alexander Graham Bell, Benjamin Franklin, Eli Whitney, and Robert Fulton. This is understandable for they have contributed greatly to our lives. This is, however, only one narrow band on the entire innovative spectrum.

There are other great innovators who, while not heralded in the history books, have equal significance. Few Americans would recognize the name of Rowland Hill. Yet he is often credited with "inventing" the modern postal service in 1836. Postal systems existed since antiquity, but Hill suggested a new approach: a postage rate that was uniform across Great Britain. He also proposed that the sender pay the fee and attach a stamp to the letter, just as it is done today. But it was not always that way. Previously, the cost was computed according to the weight and distance and paid by the recipient. Such service was, at the least, inconvenient and costly. Hill's proposal changed all that and was a smashing success. He invented no product or new gadget; rather, he invented a new method, a new service that has been enjoyed by countless millions since then (Drucker, 1985). Surely he deserves mention in the innovators' Hall of Fame.

Or, consider what Hanes did with L'eggs pantyhose. Hanes did not invent pantyhose, but it was the first ones to sell them at the grocery store. Like most manufacturers Hanes sold pantyhose at department stores, which women visit on the average once every six weeks. However, marketing research found that women visit grocery stores about twice a week. Thus by placing those oddly shaped plastic eggs filled with pantyhose next to the razors and candy at the checkout stand, Hanes greatly increased the probability of purchase. And that is exactly what happened: the stock increased sixfold after the introduction of L'eggs (Lynch, 1989). This is a delightful tale of an innovation that involved a new marketing approach.

Each year in Japan an award called the Edward Deming Prize is given. This highly prestigious award is given for the best quality improvement of the year. Deming, an American, introduced to the Japanese a variety of concepts developed by scholars in the United States. Deming (1986) and his followers developed the concept of quality circles, which allow the workers actually doing the job to come up with more productive ways to complete the task and solve other job-related problems. Deming might be said to have "metainnovated," for he introduced a new way to encourage innovation.

In sum, innovation that is not product-based is a vital part of the economy. New approaches to service, learning, marketing, management, advertising, and even innovation are equally essential. In fact, despite all the press about high technology, I believe the most unexpected innovations in the future will be in the area of these so-called "soft sciences."

Myth 5 — Creativity is the same as innovation.

There are those who argue that the reason new ideas never surface in their organizations is that their employees are not creative enough. Sometimes these very employees are then dutifully packed off to some seminar to give them a dose of creativity. Here the employees learn of their latent creative powers that have never been tapped. And, sure enough, the employees find that they are indeed more creative than they ever thought. How can one fault such an approach? Yet, this method falls short on two accounts.

First, lack of ideas rarely is the problem in organizations. In fact, the problem is usually just the opposite. Employees, if given the chance, have too many ideas to act on effectively. In fact, this is precisely why so many ideas can be generated at these creativity seminars. Most human beings are naturally creative if properly challenged. In the organizations we have assessed, the employees almost always have numerous ideas to improve operations. Not all the ideas are feasible, but many are. When asked why they do not share their ideas with anyone, however, the most frequent response is that management does not listen.

Second, some employees erroneously believe they are innovative if they can think up a lot of new ideas. This may be the essence of creativity but not of innovation. Rather, innovation means carrying the idea to fruition. Nothing is more frustrating than talking to an "idea man" who has no idea about how to implement one.

Professor Lindeman, one of Winston Churchill's long-time advisors, knew the difference between creativity and innovation. In 1916 many airplane pilots died in violent nose dives. "The Prof," as he was called, worked out the mathematics of a new maneuver that would bring the planes out of a tailspin. "The pilots said it wouldn't work. The Prof taught himself to fly, took off without a parachute, deliberately set the aircraft down in a spin, and brought it out so successfully that mastering his solution became required of every flier" (Manchester, 1983, p. 781). Here is a man who was a true innovator, for he was willing to stake his very life on an idea.

In the final analysis, those who believe creativity is innovation are fundamentally unclear about the true nature of innovation. To this issue we now turn.

What Is Innovation?

Innovation is more than a good idea. It is a process that can be thought of in four phases: (1) idea generation; (2) feasibility analysis; (3) reality testing; and (4) implementation. The process is one of winnowing down the possibilities to the select few that can be really useful to the organization (see Figure 9.1).

Idea Generation

The first stage is the one most typically associated with innovation. It is the point of pure creativity. The emphasis is on the generation of novel ideas. One of the more effective techniques that can be used at this stage is brainstorming, which means to develop a multitude of ideas in a nonevaluative setting. Often done in a group setting, people are encouraged to think of wild, bold, and new ideas. The more far out, the better. Feasibility, logic, and practicality are not to be guides. Instead, intuition, ambiguity, and speculation are to reign supreme (e.g., Oech, 1983).

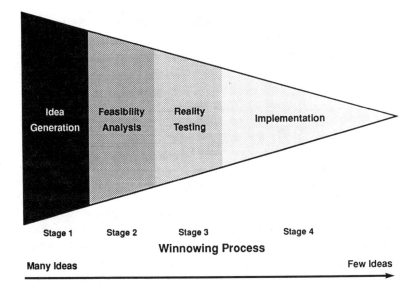

Figure 9.1 Innovation Process

As mentioned above, the problem in most organizations is not at this stage. Most employees have a wealth of creative ideas that could prove useful. Indeed, after extensive study of creative and noncreative research and development employees, a group of psychologists have concluded that the greatest difference between the groups was that, "The creative people thought they were creative and the less creative people didn't think they were" (Oech, 1983, p. 122). Organizations stifle creativity in a variety of subtle ways, like not recognizing employees who have useful ideas or not having a forum to make suggestions. The central challenge for managers is not to demand inventiveness but to release employees' latent creativity by removing the inhibiting factors. Ingenuity must be cultivated in the organizational culture, like tending a garden. Ideas will not sprout instantly, but under the right conditions and with proper care a rich harvest can be reaped.

Feasibility Analysis

At stage two the question becomes, which of the multitude of ideas generated are really feasible? Is it possible to actually create the product or execute the idea? Many of the ideas generated at stage one will be eliminated at this point because they fail to meet this test. Experiments or test runs often are conducted at this juncture in order to determine if a product can actually be made. For example, computer simulations of design changes of an airplane may be used. Prototypes can be built and tested. A new advertising campaign could be test marketed. Frequently, the results indicate that the basic idea or design needs to be rethought and the entire process can begin again. Whatever strategy is used at this point, fundamentally the tests are designed to determine if the idea is a real possibility.

For example, in the early 1970s a Dutch company, N. V. Philips, suggested that it might be possible to use lasers to play audio and video recordings. Many U.S. corporations such as RCA and Zenith worked for years only to abandon the project as hopeless. Sony and Philips did not, and they launched the entire compact disc revolution that will no doubt make vinyl records a collector's item. For most companies the idea never got past the feasibility stage. For Philips and Sony, persistence paid off; they not only introduced an innovation, they introduced a revolutionary one (Browning, 1986).

Reality Testing

The most difficult hurdle of all for any idea is what might be called "reality testing." Are corporate resources available to produce the innovation? Can the new service be rendered with a reasonable profit? Does the new procedure really save money or improve productivity? These are the toughest questions of all. The fundamental concern is over a reasonable return on investment; however, this is not always an easy question to address because the information usually will be incomplete. Some innovations that are introduced into the marketplace take a long time to be "reality tested." A new automobile is a case in point. The feedback lag is fairly long. New ideas that are introduced internally may prove more successful than objective evidence indicates because of the "placebo effect." That is, employees often will make something work simply because they thought up the idea.

Organizations also have their own idiosyncratic "reality tests" that are determined by the unique corporate culture. An idea that might be embraced in one culture may not stand a chance in another organization that does not have the culture to sustain the idea. Moreover, the political structure of the organization may be part of the reality test. An idea needs to be filtered to the right people at the right time in order to succeed. Indeed, someone who develops a successful innovation not only needs a workable idea, but also the political backing in the organization to push it through to the implementation phase.

Implementation

Seemingly, if an idea has survived the feasibility and reality tests, then implementation would be a foregone conclusion. Experience does not bear out this conclusion. In one organization we found that only 60% of the ideas formally accepted actually were implemented. Another study suggested that the nature of the innovation itself as well as its symbolic significance had a major impact on whether an idea actually got implemented (Meyer & Goes, 1988). The ideas that are victims frequently are those generated at the lowest levels of the organization. This is because implementation usually depends on other people to initiate the action. For example, one paper mill employee suggested a change in the way a drum was cleaned in order to increase productivity. The idea was evaluated and deemed cost effective. Approval was given and budget allocations made. But for some reason the purchase never was made and the idea never implemented. Neglect, time constraints, and other priorities take their toll. The irony, of course, is that an idea that has survived the most difficult hurdles fails to become a true innovation because someone neglects to finish the last few yards of the race.

Implications

There are four important implications of this process view of innovation. **First, there are differing criteria of evaluation used at the various stages of the innovative process.** In the first stage, judgments tend to be made in terms of novelty. Creativity often is measured in terms of how bizarre or different the idea is. This is perfectly acceptable at this stage, but does not mean the idea will translate into innovation.

For instance, for years railroads have tried to deal with the curvature of the countryside by blasting through mountains and blowing up hills and slowly rounding the tracks. Even with these measures, trains were notoriously slow. Why not develop a train that could take the corners at a high rate of speed while keeping the passengers upright and riding like a cork in a bottle of water? Why not develop a tilting train? Now that is a truly novel idea, and that is exactly the "innovation" the British government funded. No other train had been designed along these lines. It was an exciting and new concept. But it never really worked. The British government sunk 15 years and $75 million into the project with little or nothing to show for it (Newman, 1986). Novel idea, yes; a successful innovation, no. The tilting train failed to meet the important test of feasibility.

Even if an idea proves feasible, that does not guarantee workability. For example, the oceans contain billions of tons of gold. There are polymers available that can harvest the gold from the sea waters. However, to date, the expense has proven prohibitive. Thus the idea is novel and possible, but not workable. It fails on the third criteria. The point is that an idea can become problematic at any juncture. One alternative is simply to deem the idea not useful. Another alternative is to start the entire process again until eventually the idea crosses all the hurdles.

Second, organizational barriers can occur at any point in the innovative process. The problems encountered at one stage are not the same as the ones at another stage. In fact, the organizational policies or attributes that allow seeming success at one stage of the process may actually inhibit the process at another stage. Typically, organizations that are high in complexity, and low in formalization and centralization, provide a rich environment for innovation in the initial stages but present difficulties at the implementation stage. This seems reasonable as complex but loosely organized companies would allow frequent and varied communications across departmental and organizational boundaries. Thus a great number of ideas should be spawned in such interactions. Getting the employees together to do something different would prove difficult, however, because of the very same diversity. On the other hand, a more centralized and controlled structure does not fully encourage communication across organizational boundaries and therefore inhibits idea formation. Such a structure would, however, be able to immediately implement a new idea if one should be approved (e.g., Lawrence & Lorsch, 1969). A major managerial challenge, therefore, is to simultaneously encourage new ideas and maintain a structure that can implement the ideas quickly.

What this means is that a manager must use different tactics at each juncture of the innovative process. Indeed, the Circuit manager tends to excel at the initial stages of the innovation process, while the Arrow manager excels at the latter stages. The effective manager must become a kind of idea shepherd, protecting them from various attacks along their journey. Flexibility and savvy are the key weapons. Table 9.1 reveals some of the more common difficulties encountered at each stage. In stage one, the difficulties tend to revolve around developing an environment of creativity. Communication across departmental boundaries is essential as is receptivity on the part of supervisors. In stage two, the issue becomes getting the ideas on an agenda to actually be tested or seriously analyzed. At stage three, the central concern is building commitment for the idea. There is a need to demonstrate that the idea actually will work in a cost-effective way. In the final stage, the challenge is to get people to actually do what they have approved.

Table 9.1 Barriers to Innovation

Stage	Evaluation Criteria	Critical Questions	Organizational Barriers
Idea Generation	Novelty	Is the idea novel?	• Highly structured organizational climate. • Authoritarian communication style. • Too many rules and regulations.
Feasibility Analysis	Possibility	Is the idea possible?	• Cost of determining feasibility. • Lack of corporate resources to dedicate to research. • Lack of commitment to research.
Reality Testing	Practicality	Does the idea produce a reasonable return on investment? Does the idea fit with organizational objectives? Does the organization have the start-up capital for the idea?	• Short term focus. • Inadequate research on the potential return or marketability of idea. • Resistance to change.
Implementation	Activity	Has the idea been acted on?	• Too many priorities. • Nobody has responsibility for the implementation • Over-consultation with involved parties. • Highly unstructured organizational climate.

Third, the time line for the innovative process is elastic. In some cases, the four stages can take a matter of days. In other cases, the process may take years. A new office filing system may take only a week from conception to implementation, while the design of a new microship may take years. As J. A. Morton (1971), a former vice president at Bell Telephone laboratories, says: "Innovation is not a single, simple act" (p. 49). The implication is that the cost of innovation will vary greatly depending on the type of idea. The filing system, if a failure, can be easily changed, while an entire company's well-being may be based on a new microchip. Therefore, the degree of thoughtfulness needed at each stage changes in proportion to the time invested. More prudence and thought is required for innovations with a longer time line. Service organizations, such as marketing or advertising firms, can try a wealth of new ideas with less concern for failure than an automobile manufacturer. Their proper emphasis is on encouraging creativity (stage one). A traditional manufacturing firm proposing a new product has to be more careful; consequently, the emphasis should be on proper research and development (stages two and three).

Fourth, an overemphasis on any one stage can become problematic. If innovation is more than just a lot of novel ideas, it is also more than research on possibility testing. Innovative corporations must also face the tough questions of reality testing and implementation. Campbell Soup Company, for instance, bought into the lure of the creativity panhandlers and introduced 334 new products in a five-year period. While there were successes, there were some dismal failures. The Pepperidge Farm division, for example, lost $9 million in 1983. The CEO, Gordon McGovern, decided that, "Campbell may have done too much innovating too fast" (Schwadel, 1985, p. 1). In short, the products were creative and possible, but failed at the implementation stage because of some inadequate reality testing. In a broader sense, the problem was an overemphasis on the creativity part of the innovative process.

Measuring Success and Failure

Artificial Intelligence (AI) is the next great frontier in the computer industry. The very term creates awe in many, disbelief in others, and fear in some. That need not be. The basic idea is very simple: try to teach computers the rules by which human experts make decisions. The people who are currently trying to accomplish this task are called knowledge engineers. The knowledge engineer goes about this task by interviewing an acknowledged expert in some area (Schank, 1984). The goal is to understand how the expert makes decisions so this can, in turn, be programmed into a computer. For instance, how does a physician go about determining what type of blood disease a patient might have? Or how does an investment counselor decide the type of financial portfolio a client needs? These are the kinds of questions a knowledge engineer tackles by extracting a series of decision rules from the expert. Numerous AI programs like this already have been developed.

The most intriguing part of the entire process has been where the problems or bottlenecks tend to occur. It might seem reasonable to assume that the greatest difficulty would be with developing the proper software; that is, translating the expert's knowledge into a programming language the machine can understand. Or, at first glance, the great difficulty may appear to be one of developing proper hardware to handle all the complexities. But neither concern has proven all that problematic. Rather, the really tough problems have been to get the experts to articulate what they know. Apparently most experts operate on the basis of an intuition gleaned from years of experience. The experts know how to make the proper responses but do not always know how they arrived at those responses. In a nutshell, they do not always know what makes them successful.

Most organizations face the same dilemma. Survival depends upon at least a modicum of success, but corporations are not always clear about what is the source of their success. Even more opaque to corporations than their failures is a deep understanding of their successes. Ultimately those companies that desire a long-term innovative spirit must have a proper perspective on both success and failure.

Whenever some new idea is tried there can be failures. Even with the most carefully tested notions, failure is still a possibility. In 1962, Bell Laboratories launched the Telstar I satellite. It was thoroughly tested and retested in the best of their tradition. Yet, one day before the launch, the Soviets secretly conducted a high-altitude test of a nuclear device. The satellite was shut down with seven months because it was not resistant to radioactivity. A failure, yes; a complete failure, no. Why? Because Bell Labs learned from the "failure." A year later they launched a satellite, Telstar II, that could successfully function even with radioactivity in the atmosphere (Morton, 1971).

What, then, is failure? What is success? Perhaps the most useful perspective is to look at success and failure along two dimensions instead of just one. Figure 9.2 diagrams four possible quadrants in which a given innovation might fall.

Potential Success

The first quadrant is labeled potential success because one learns from the "failure." Certainly the Bell Labs satellite falls in this category because Bell Labs eventually produced a successful innovation. Likewise, in 1989 Sony surprised many Americans with its purchase of Columbia Pictures for $3.4 billion (Castro, 1989). But the purchase makes a great deal of business sense in light of Sony's "failure" with the Beta format for videotape players. The Beta format offered superior quality compared to VHS players. Yet, Beta never really took off with consumers because so few movies were available

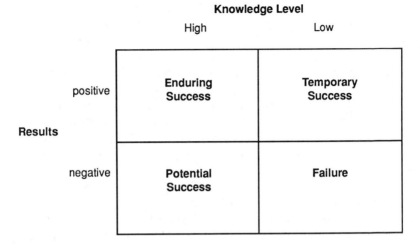

Figure 9.2 True Success and Failure

in the format. In purchasing Columbia, they have insured that they will have the software to go with their new hardware like the 8-millimeter video (Gross & Holstein, 1989). The Beta format was an expensive "failure," but Sony learned a valuable lesson. In fact, independent analysts predict the 8mm format eventually will claim 50% of the market (Armstrong, 1990).

In every "failure" there is some knowledge to be gained. This may sound like some platitude of a motivational speaker. But the cold hard facts remain that those organizations and people who ultimately prevail learn from their "mistakes." And those who do not are doomed to happenstance.

Enduring Success

The sources of enduring success are both producing useful ideas and knowing why they are successful. Certain people seem to have this uncanny ability, like Thomas Edison or Benjamin Franklin. Organizations, even more than individual inventors, need to understand their successes in order to pass along their knowledge to others. The corporation that most exemplifies this pattern is IBM. They have shown over the years a sustained growth and development. They continue to produce new and successful products despite occasional "failures" like the PC junior, which really is another example of a potential success. But one aspect of IBM's continued success is that they show a deep understanding of the corporate values necessary for success. The thorough employee training in the "IBM way" helps ensure that the attributes of success are sustained. This is not to say that enduring success can only come from IBM's approach. There are countless other approaches. But the key is to know what makes a particular person or company successful.

IBM is constantly conducting research even on the products that are successful. They seek to understand their successes as well as their "failures." Why is this so important? Because companies are not always successful for the reasons they think they are successful, which leads to the third quadrant.

Temporary Success

A temporary success is one in which the results obviously meet or exceed expectations but there is no true understanding of why the success occurred. Temporarily, money — maybe lots of money — can be made, but the results are not enduring. The Arab oil cartel, the American steel industry, and some oil companies are excellent examples of originally innovative ideas falling by the wayside. The gains were only temporary. Huge profits were generated at one point but there were failures at another.

So what? It could be argued that temporary success is better than no success at all. True enough. But that is a false dichotomy. The real question is: Why have temporary success when it is possible to have enduring success? The problem with temporary success is that no one knows how long the results can be sustained. Organizations that are temporarily successful do not have the corporate intelligence to cope with change. They are caught flatfooted when some change in the business climate occurs, just as the American steel industry was when it passed up new technologies that the Japanese adopted. Temporarily successful people or organizations can only pass along money, not knowledge — the true source of future innovation (Gilder, 1981). There also seems to be an ethical obligation for an organization to provide its employees as much employment security as possible. The costs of temporary success may not be felt too deeply by those in top management but are borne by the employees and families of those who work for the company.

Failure

True failure only can result when there is no knowledge gained from an innovative experiment. Such a situation is almost always avoidable. When the space shuttle tragically blew up on January 28, 1986, it was properly labeled a "major setback" not a "failure" because, as devastating as the results were, still something valuable was learned.

The movie industry has had an almost sustained rate of box office "bombs" over the years. Is this the nature of the business? Maybe. Yet, little research has been put into the characteristics of these box office failures other than on an individual basis. The collective knowledge yielded from such research could at least alter the probabilities of future box office failures. This state of affairs seems like a failure, not only in terms of results, but also as regards knowledge.

Implications

First, results do not determine if a new idea is a success or failure. Rather, it is what is done with the results. If innovation is only thought of in one dimension, a novel idea can only be a winner or loser. If innovation is thought of two dimensionally, there are three "chances" to win and only one to lose. Of course, a temporary success is not really a long-term gain but ultimately can be transformed into one, a kind of second chance. Hence, the innovative manager and company aim at positive results, but they focus on developing a deep understanding of either success or failure. A negative result is only fatal if not understood. Likewise, success only can be sustained if it is comprehended.

Second, present success is no guarantee of future success. Just because an innovation has proven successful under one set of conditions does not mean it will continue to be. The violent economic swings that are so much a part of the Silicon Valley companies provide one clear example. The flexibility to change is the only true way of survival. And this only can be done by having the best understanding possible of why an innovation is successful.

Continued results cannot be assured by sticking to traditions. Oscar Wilde said it best: "Consistency is the last refuge of the unimaginative." For instance, in the electronics market there has been a tremendous turnover in the industry leadership from the vacuum tubes of 1955 to the present day. Many of the companies are no longer even in business (Foster, 1986). It may seem safe to keep doing what one does well. And there is a certain wisdom in this. However, there is another pull as well: the need to continue to change. Keeping a proper balance between the traditional successes and future potential successes is one of the important challenges facing management. After all, tradition often is the enemy of innovation.

Third, the actual innovation is only the tip of the iceberg. The knowledge base underneath the idea is the key to further growth and innovation. Even "failures" can add to the knowledge base. When conditions change a new idea can spring forth from that knowledge base, which substitutes for the old.

There may not even be an awareness of all the knowledge that sustains a successful innovation. But there should be a continual push to get at even deeper levels of understanding. Vaccines have been used for years to prevent deadly diseases, but only in more recent years have scientists begun to understand why a vaccine actually works. So it is with most innovations. Indeed, this is precisely the challenge facing the knowledge engineer.

Stop and Go Signs

Stop signs regulate the flow of traffic; they tell people when and where to stop. With too few stop signs the streets are unsafe; with too many progress is impeded. Either extreme is disastrous.

Organizations also have stop and go signs. They may not have red, yellow, and green lights but they are just as real and have just as much effect on the flow of organizational events. The corporate policies, rules, regulations, procedures, organizational structure, the day-to-day interactions in meetings, conversations, and memoranda are all varieties of these organizational traffic signals. If there are too many stop signs, then innovative efforts come to a grinding halt. If there are too few, then there is chaos. The objective, then, is to design a system that (a) does not impede the flow of innovative ideas; (b) increases the probability of a safe and speedy passage for useful ideas; and (c) decreases the probability that the poor ideas get through to the implementation stage. Only through careful and thoughtful planning can each of these goals be achieved. The more important guidelines for successfully setting up the organizational traffic signals are discussed below.

First, develop a formal corporate policy on innovation. A policy statement in the employee handbook can be a useful starting point. Here a commitment to innovation can be made in black and white. The very process of developing this policy statement forces management to articulate goals and commitments. The initial training of employees also can stress the necessity for innovation. Even the corporate philosophy should have a sentence or phrase about the organization's position on innovation.

But policy statements are no guarantee of action. There must be mechanisms for implementation, some of which are reviewed later. Employees must see the link between the specific programs and the policy. This demonstrates that the company is willing to practice what it preaches.

Second, require innovation. One of the more radical steps an organization or manager can take is to make innovation a requirement of the job. For example, at 3M, the company known as the "Masters of Innovation," there is a 25% rule. This means that 25% of a division's sales must be from products developed in the last five years (Mitchell, 1989). Bonuses also are tied to this yardstick. It works. 3M markets more than 50,000 products worldwide, ranging from scotch tape to blood filtration systems. Rubbermaid has a similar program but raises the figure to 30% in five years. Managers can institute a similar program by requiring that innovation be part of the formal evaluation system.

Third, develop company programs that encourage innovation. Some companies, like IBM, allow their employees to take sabbaticals to work in a new environment or teach in a college. The program can last anywhere from six months to years. By placing employees in different environments, they can meet new people, come across new ideas and, hopefully, generate their own novel approaches.

Along these same lines, employees can be encouraged to attend conventions or off-site training. By coming into contact with new people, ideas, and situations, an employee may come up with a new approach that is useful for the corporation. The payoff may not be immediate. But these opportunities allow the employee to build up a useful base of knowledge that will pay dividends in the long run. Perhaps, at a later point, a novel combination of ideas will spring forth as a result of finding the missing piece to a puzzle. The value of face-to-face or personal contact is that ideas can be exchanged, questions asked, and nuances noted. Company financed journal and magazine subscriptions are a less effective but inexpensive alternative.

Another alternative that has proven especially beneficial for high-tech companies is the weekend retreat. Microsoft sponsors "Innovation Retreats" every few months. Up to 16 employees gather on a remote island in Puget Sound in order to develop new product ideas. The retreat begins with structured presentations about new ideas, which are followed by more informal small group discussions. Ideas are critiqued, modified, and enhanced. It is a simple idea but an effective one. For instance, the new operating system for the IBM Personal Computer, OS/2, was hashed out in several Innovation Retreats (Field, 1988).

By financing and sponsoring these kinds of activities, a company sends a message to employees that it is willing to invest the money necessary for innovation. The financial backing shows that innovation is more than just rhetoric. While these programs provide no guarantee that employees will come up with useful ideas, it does increase the probabilities. That is what management must count on.

Fourth, make every employee an innovator. One of the worst situations that can develop is when employees feel that "good" ideas can come only from the outside. Companies can communicate this message implicitly by overly depending on outside consultants or review boards. When the innovations of outsiders continually are adopted over in-house ideas, the organization has again communicated this message. The statement, "That's the way they do it at company X," translates into, "Good ideas are *not* generated here." The result is that employees think, "What's the use, they will only get something 'better' somewhere else." In short, the modern equivalent to the old adage, "A man cannot be a prophet in his own village," seems to be, "Employees cannot be innovators in their own company." But this need not be the case.

One program that has been successful involves keeping a written record or log of all suggestions and the actions taken on those ideas. The list is then circulated around the company. Timeliness also is important. Walter Scott of Motorola, Incorporated said, "Any employee's recommendation for new methods or change should get a reply in 72 hours or less" (Barks & Bennett, 1979, p. 35). Both the timeliness of the response and providing a written record demonstrates a corporate resolve to harness the innovative potential of its employees. The Marriott Corporation has carried the idea one step further and lets stockholders into the act. They reward the best ideas with stock at their annual meetings (Freedman, 1986).

Fifth, allow "secret" persistence. All organizations have open secrets — practices that are tacitly forbidden but tolerated. Persistence is a necessity if the innovative process is seen through to the end. This is particularly true at the possibility and reality stages at which there usually are setbacks. For instance, K. Alex Mueller and J. Georg Bednorz were two of the principal scientists who set off the frenzy for superconductors, which are substances that conduct electricity without resistance. They toiled away on the project at their Swiss IBM lab in between their normal duties and without "official approval" from management. At one point Bednorz was so excited about the project that he was spending up to 30% of his time on it. Finally, they told not only management but the world about this revolutionary idea (Hudson, 1987).

3M also has a model program that allows secret persistence by way of its 15% rule. Most employees in the organization are allowed to spend up to 15% of their time working on their own innovative project with little or no direct managerial control. Indeed, the almost ubiquitous *Post-it* notes are a direct result of this rule and now account for an estimated $300 million of revenue. And 3M takes it one step further with its Genesis grants. Employees can apply for up to $50,000 of seed money to get a project going (Mitchell, 1989).

How can something be officially off-limits but unofficially condoned? There are a host of ways, some of which are industry specific. Allowing employees to work on a pet project at home or in "off hours" is just one. Another example is to be tolerant of a certain amount of "leakage" in supplies or materials in order to foster experimentation. If control is too tight and everything is too organized then there is nothing with which to conduct the possibility and reality tests.

The added benefit of allowing secret persistence is that it helps the winnowing process. Employees are going to have to set their own priorities and decide which ideas really are important. These are the ones that will be secretly pursued. Allowing secret persistence even after a project has been officially rejected is like placing a large "Proceed with Caution" sign on the employee's path. Some people will turn back; the ideas will not be pursued. Others will take the detour and brave the rocky course. These ideas may indeed reach the implementation state. But the "Caution" sign is not some kind of "Do Not Enter" posting. In essence, secret persistence increases the probability that the useful notions will survive the rigors of the innovation trek, while decreasing the probability of pursuing the unfruitful ones.

Sixth, eliminate lengthy proposal procedures. The paperwork involved in proposing or even pursuing a project can be a major roadblock to innovation. Particularly in the initial stages it is stifling to ask for too much justification for ideas. In the first place, many of the questions cannot be fully answered until later in the innovation process. In the second place, many relevant questions cannot even be anticipated. Moreover, the message sent to employees by requiring extensive paperwork is that results must be guaranteed and failure will not be tolerated. There is no need for 150 pages of detailed justification for the project when six pages could do the job.

Documentation is not the only place where streamlining is needed. The administrative procedures for proposing and implementing an idea can become cumbersome. On the average, how many levels of the organization does an idea have to go through to get the green light? Can any of these levels be eliminated? Can some ideas simply be approved and initiated on the spot? How long does an idea take to wind its way through the administrative process? Months? Weeks? Days? What can be done to speed up the process?

These are the kind of tough questions about administration that can help eliminate the natural barriers to innovation and smooth the bumpy road.

Seventh, foster informal communication. Paperwork and administrative regulations often are initiated in organizations to provide some control of organizational events. What will be the regulative mechanism if these are scaled down? Informal communication can fill the gap. Managers can keep up to date by informally communicating with employees about projects or new ideas. Often this kind of "checking up" is more informative than endless reams of paperwork.

Informal communication encourages discussion across departmental boundaries and formal lines of authority. The benefit is that more useful ideas seem to emerge in such a free-flowing environment. Why? In part, because these discussions expose organizational problems, concerns, and needs — all of which are begging for innovative solutions. Employees need to know where the hitches are before they can creatively address them. Additionally, employee ideas can be informally critiqued by colleagues in a supportive environment. This helps the employee save face because no formal rejection is recorded. Moreover, informal criticism is a useful tool because it provides valuable information about where improvements are needed and, at times, the solutions to the dilemmas.

Bill Gates, the innovative founder of Microsoft, credits the use of electronic mail as one of the keys in keeping his company on the creative frontier. If someone has a brainstorm, they can immediately flash the idea to others for their reactions. He says, "It sparks interest" (Field, 1988, p. 86). Adding blackboards, sketchpads, and small conference rooms in the workplace has also proven helpful in encouraging more informal communication (Peters & Waterman, 1982). Electronic mail, blackboards, and sketchpads have one common characteristic: mistakes can be corrected quickly and easily. Therefore, speculation, change, and creativity are encouraged. Deletions or additions can be readily tried. This is the spirit of informal networks — quick feedback with little fear of change. There are few repercussions when changing an idea in an informal situation. Formal documents are less easily amended. And that is why it so important to set up an informal communication environment.

Eighth, reward innovation. Companies reward that which is valuable to them. Employees know this and react accordingly. Financial rewards have proven successful but there are other, and often more meaningful, rewards. Personal recognition is one such example. Innovators can be recognized in company newsletters, trade publications, and even the local media. Stories about innovators not only provide recognition, but also show others in the organization what the company really values.

Rewarding individual innovators is not the only tactic that can be employed. After all, the objective is to spur on the spirit of innovation throughout the entire organization. Why not recognize an entire unit, department, or division that is particularly innovative? This might encourage the teamwork so necessary for successful innovation. Why not carry it a step further? Could the entire company be recognized for its innovative spirit? It might seem like tooting your own horn, but that is exactly what Allied-Signal Incorporated did with a full-page spread in the *Wall Street Journal* (see Figure 9.3). This ad sends a clear message, not only to the public but also to Allied-Signal employees, that innovation is valued by the company. Moreover, the ad is a clever way to recognize the authors of the patents. One can easily imagine Allied-Signal's scientists looking up their patent number in the newspaper, circling it, and showing the spread to family and friends.

One of the ironies about rewarding innovation is that it is often more meaningful for those who have not been rewarded than it is for those who are rewarded. The reward acts as a target for those who have not won, and it tells them what the attributes of success are at this company. Hence, it is not the size of the reward that really matters. Rather it is the impact of rewards on the company as a whole. A large award may implicitly send a message that the organization is only interested in the "big ideas."

Ninth, learn how to properly reject novel ideas. For example, Dr. Orlando A. Battista was asked to develop a fine structure of nylon fibers to be used in tires. Instead he came up with a white powder that was in a crystal form. His boss wanted to fire him. As it turned out that would have been a major blunder. Other minds prevailed and allowed him to pursue his strange substance, Avacil. The results: today Avacil is used as a clotting agent for blood, in beauty creams, salad dressings, and a host of other products (Battista, 1984). All of this from a "bad" idea.

There is a certain art in dealing with a "bad" idea that is based on a simple philosophy: An idea may fail but people are not failures. Too many times employees who introduce ideas that do not work out are ostracized or labeled as kooks; in essence they are treated as failures. Such practices send strong and discouraging messages to others who might have a useful idea: "The cost of an idea failing is very great." The logic continues: "It is therefore safest not to suggest anything." The result is that innovation is stifled. One wonders how many potential Battistas have been lost because a manager rejected the person along with the novel idea.

THE WALL STREET JOURNAL, WEDNESDAY, NOVEMBER 20, 1985 **21**

There's strength in numbers.

Every one of these patents represents an original idea. A way to advance technology. Allied-Signal is proud to say that we own over 25,000 of these patented ideas. With 10,000 more pending. Last year alone, we were granted more U.S. patents than any other American industrial company except IBM and GE.

Allied-Signal is a research leader in such diverse areas as aerospace propulsion and guidance systems, automotive electronics, high-strength fibers, high-performance alloys and ceramics, and video graphics.

And we intend to stay a leader. With our thousands of scientists and engineers working constantly to advance advanced technology. Because one good idea leads to another.

Allied Signal

Figure 9.3 Example of Praising Corporate Innovation

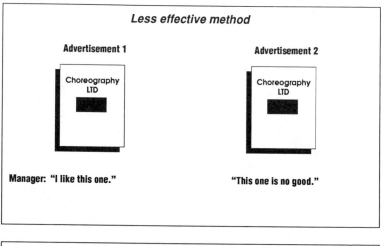

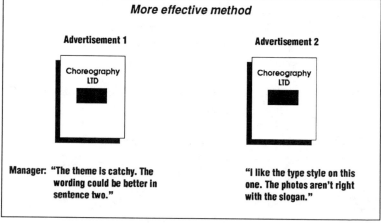

Figure 9.4 Approach to "Bad Ideas"

The typical way of dealing with a new idea is to evaluate it in terms of whether it is good or bad, useful or useless, effective or ineffective. If an idea has problems then it is rejected out of hand, just as Avacil initially was. This kind of evaluation process creates a false dichotomy where an idea either hits or misses the target. Far too many ideas go unheeded and untried because of this kind of simple-minded thinking.

A more useful way is to look at an idea in terms of attributes or character-istics, some of which are good and some bad.[1] As seen in Figure 9.4, there are two primary ways to evaluate an idea. In the first case, some useful ideas, like a diamond in the rough, may be quickly cast aside because they do not appear in final form. In the second case, the idea is examined more closely, the characteristics of the idea are refined and discussed, just as a jeweler cuts and polishes the diamond.

Inevitably, managers will have to flatly reject some ideas. The worst possible method is to ignore the suggestion. There are countless ways of ignoring suggestions: changing the subject when the idea is brought up, nonverbally communicating disgust, or simply not taking the time to fully listen to the idea. Ignoring an employee's idea not only discourages pursuit of one idea but also any other ideas that might be really useful. The broader message is, "I don't have time," or "I don't care about your new ideas." An honest, straightforward appraisal of how the idea is flawed is much more easily handled by employees. Then they know precisely what criteria are being used in evaluating an idea. And they may even find some solution to the precise objection, thereby making the notion viable. Perhaps the greatest benefit of a straightforward appraisal is that while it may discourage pursuit of a certain idea, it does not hinder the general pursuit of innovation. That is, indeed, precisely the message you wish to communicate.

Tenth, educate employees about the innovative process. Employees need to become aware that innovation is more than a good idea. Rather, as outlined above, it is a process fraught with different challenges at each stage. Employees who do not understand this are more likely to propose useful as well as responsible ideas. They must know the objective standards by which to judge an idea. Understanding the process also is a way for employees and managers to save face. An idea can be judged novel but not practical, or practical but not feasible. People who propose ideas that make it through the entire process truly can be proud. Those whose ideas are stopped at various stages can also feel a certain amount of fulfillment and should be encouraged to keep trying. Moreover, training about innovation demonstrates that the organization takes innovation seriously. And this may be the most important message of all.

Innovation is a matter of probabilities. Failures are to be expected, just as every batter expects to strike out. The only losers are those who do not get up to the plate in the first place. Even then, a batting average of .400 is considered exceptional. So too with ideas; a certain percentage will always go awry. The key is to keep trying. Certain financial loses are to be expected, but they are necessary in order to have a chance at winning. Thus, if an idea does not exactly pan out, there need be no recriminations. Everyone hits foul balls.

In sum, implementing only one of the ideas suggested above is not going to transform a logjammed organizational system. The entire set of organizational traffic signals has to be examined. With a proper balance of incentives and policies, the organization can become a kind of innovative superhighway that creates a system in which ideas are exchanged quickly. The case study presented below summarizes the dilemmas as well as the challenges associated with innovation.

Blue Ribbons and Red Tape

Sir Winston Churchill is best known as a great statesman, author, or perhaps a painter. Few know that he was also a successful innovator. His special genius led to a navigational tool used to guide pilots: the idea of dropping tin foil to confuse enemy radar, armor-plated buses, and even the artificial harbors used on D day (Manchester, 1983). He was also known as the father of the modern tank. It was Churchill who, during the bloody trench warfare of World War I, thought of the tank as a practical means to end the madness. Although Churchill said that no single man could be said to have invented the tank, it was known at the time as "Winston's folly." And with good reason; he was the one who provided the idea and the money for the endeavor. But no one today scoffs at the transformation of warfare wrought by "Winston's folly."

The invention of the tank is instructive on several counts. First, as Churchill freely acknowledges in his memoirs, the idea was not entirely novel. H. G. Wells had speculated about such a vehicle as early as 1903. But, as suggested above, a novel idea — even a fictional one — is not an innovation. It is, however, a start. Second, the tools used for the innovation already were well known. The technology for armor plating had been used in ships and the internal combustion engine had proven reliable, as had caterpillar tracks. The key was to combine the various devices into a new and useful weapon. This was no easy task. Similarly, many innovations are the product of new combinations of already existing ideas. Moreover, "Winston's folly" provides a splendid example of the hurdles faced by most innovators. He discusses the project at length in his memoirs of the first World War:

> I thus took personal responsibility for the expenditure of the public money involved, £70,000. . . . It was a serious decision to spend this large sum of money on a project so speculative, about the merits of which no high expert military or naval authority had been convinced. The matter, moreover, was entirely outside

the scope of my own Department or of any normal powers which I possessed. Had the tanks proved wholly abortive or never been accepted or never used in war by the military authorities, and had I been subsequently summoned before a Parliamentary Committee, I could have offered no effective defense to the charge that I had wasted public money on a matter which was not in any way my business and in regard to which I had not received expert advice in any responsible military quarter. The extremely grave situation of the war, and my conviction of the need for breaking down the deadlock which blocked the production of these engines, are my defense; but the defense is only valid in view of their enormous subsequent success. (Churchill, 1931, pp. 316-317)

First, this passage illustrates the speculative nature of any innovation. The idea had been rejected by any number of different experts and commit-tees. No one thought it would work except Churchill. In a similar fashion, innovators in organizations are plagued by disbelievers. Innovators naturally seem to first run into the scoffers, then the cynics, followed by the critics, and finally the surprised.

The problem for the innovator is to sift the rhetoric from the reality. Often the corporate policy says: "We want innovative ideas." But the real meaning is "We want innovative ideas *that work.*" Countless papers have to be prepared justifying the project. Prolonged analyses about the potential impact have to be drafted. In some cases, doing the paperwork takes more time and money than the actually testing of the notion. For instance, the Israelis installed rearview mirrors in their F-4 Phantom jets. One American pilot remarked that in the United States it would take four-and-a-half years of research and development just to put in that rearview mirror. It took the Israelis one week. They just tried it out (Weisman, 1986).

Churchill, like all successful innovators, recognized that there were no assurances. Someone had to take a chance, albeit a calculated one. Compa-nies that refuse to take such risks, often by tying up the process with endless red tape, are stifling innovation. Moreover, they are operating under the delusion that the red tape will provide certainty when, in fact, there can be no such thing. There must be room for "failure," and no amount of red tape can remove that basic risk. Campbell (1977) sums up the matter best: "The demand for predictable outcomes deprives many companies of unusual outcomes" (p. 90).

Second, note that Churchill was the First Lord of the Admiralty at the time when he proposed and financed the tank. Here was a man, whose primary responsibilities concerned sea warfare, backing the research and development of a land-based weapon. He obviously strayed very far afield. Organizations that believe in innovation cannot stick to rigid departmental responsibilities. Often the very best creative ideas come from the cross-fertilization that occurs between departments. Sometimes a person from another department can have a perspective on a problem that no one in the department would even think of. Effective interdepartmental communication is a necessity for any organization that wishes to innovate.

Many organizations tacitly communicate that innovation is only to be done within the narrow confines of a particular job. Ideas are rejected out of hand because they come from the wrong department. Managers do the same with comments like, "That's not really your concern." Sometimes the approach appears more reasonable, but the results are the same. Confining all innovation to the research and development department is one of the frequent practices of this ilk. Often, when companies are asked if they are committed to innovation, they respond by boasting about the number of dollars spent on research and development. Certainly, research and development are an integral part of the innovative process, but they are not the sole source of organizational innovations. The front line of innovation consists of supervisors in contact with their employees. If new ideas are not harvested at this level, then the company cannot be said to be truly innovative. New ideas are like wildflowers; they can crop up anywhere, even in the Admiralty. Innovation is not the sole province of any one department or person, rather it should be a commitment of everyone in the organization.

Third, the saga of the tank demonstrates the necessity of someone being the champion of the idea. Somebody must clear away the red tape and take the chance. Furthermore, the person must be powerful enough or the organization flexible enough to allow this person the financial wherewithal to sponsor the endeavor (e.g., Meyer & Goes, 1988). There must be some "slack resources" to commit to the idea even when it is clearly outside the province of one's primary concern. Churchill committed a considerable sum of money as well as the time and effort of dozens of people to the development of the tank. This is what it takes to transform an idea into an innovation. There must be more than a good idea; there must also be money and time. The champion, while clearing away the red tape, also provides this.

Conclusion

At county fairs across the land, blue ribbons are given for the best breads, jams, chili, and a host of other goods. The prizes do not go to those who follow the book; they go to those who dare to "fail." After countless attempts and admitted "failures," they succeed. Why? Persistence is part of it. But freedom — freedom to dream — is the critical factor. There is the freedom to change, to try something new and different. There are no real boundaries. Unfortunately, tinkering is not encouraged in most organizations — red tape is. And no one is truly free if tangled in the red tape. In the end, the result is paralysis; the red tape chokes off any chance for the blue ribbon. But the red tape can be cut, procedures streamlined, and innovation can triumph. Churchill did it, and dedicated managers can as well.

Note

1. Theoretically each attribute could even had a valence attached to it. Thus a weighted score could be computed that would allow the innovator to further work on those features that are most problematic.

References

Armstrong, L. (1990, June 11). How Sony became a home-movie superstar. *Business Week*, p. 72.

Barks, J. V., & Bennett, K. W. (1979, October 1). Why America can't afford to overlook. *Iron Age*, pp. 28-50.

Battista, O. A. (1984). Research for profit: The chief executive officer connection. *Accounts of Chemical Research, 17*(4), 121-126.

Beveridge, W. I. B. (1980). *Seeds of discovery*. New York: Norton.

Brockhaus, R. H. (1980). Risk-taking propensity of entrepreneurs. *Academy of Management Journal, 23*(3), 509-520.

Browning, E. S. (1986, February 27). Sony's perseverance helped it win market for mini-CD players. *Wall Street Journal*, pp. A1, A11.

Castro, J. (1989, October 9). From Walkman to showman. *Time*, pp. 70-71.

Campbell, D. (1977). *Take the road to creativity and get off your dead end*. Allen, TX: Argus.

Churchill, W. S. (1931). *The world crisis*. New York: Scribner.

Collins, O. F., & Moore, D. G. (1964). *The enterprising man*. East Lansing: Michigan State University Press.

Deming, W. E. (1986). *Out of the crisis*. Cambridge: Massachusetts Institute of Technology, Center for Advanced Engineering Study.

Drucker, P. F. (1985). *Innovation and entrepreneurship*. New York: Harper & Row.

Dubos, R. (1976). *Louis Pasteur*. New York: Scribner.

Field, A. R. (1988, October). Managing creative people. *Success*, pp. 85-87.

Freedman, A. M. (1986, May 20). Marriott Corp.'s new form letter: Thanks very much, Mr. Czul, but . . . *Wall Street Journal*, p. 33.

Foster, R. (1986). *Innovation*. New York: Summit.

Galante, S. P. (1986, March 3). More firms quiz customers for clues about competition. *Wall Street Journal*, p. 17.

Gilder, G. (1981). *Wealth and poverty*. New York: Basic Books.

Gross, N., & Holstein, W. J. (1989, October 16). Why Sony is plugging into Columbia. *Business Week*, pp. 56-58.

Hudson, R. L. (1987, August 19). Scientific Saga: How 2 physicists triggered superconductor frenzy. *Wall Street Journal*, pp. 1, 10.

Jacobson, G., & Hillkirk, J. (1986). *Xerox*. New York: Macmillan.

Lawrence, P. R., & Lorsch, J. W. (1969). *Organization and environment*. Homewood, IL: Irwin.

Lynch, P. (1989). *One up on Wall Street*. New York: Simon & Schuster.

Manchester, W. (1983). *The last lion*. Boston: Little, Brown.

Meyer, A. D., & Goes, J. B. (1988). Organizational assimilation of innovations: A multilevel contextual analysis. *Academy of Management Journal, 31*(4), 897-923.

Mitchell, R. (1989, April 10). Masters of innovation. *Business Week*, pp. 58-63.

Morton, J. A. (1971). *Organizing for innovation*. New York: McGraw-Hill.

Newman, B. (1986, April 7). The tilting train: Movable monument to British persistence. *Wall Street Journal*, pp. 1, 9.

Nights of the garter are over. (1989, August 25). *Wall Street Journal*, p. B1.

Oech, R. (1983). *A whack on the side of the head*. Menlo Park, CA: Creative Think.

Organizing for productivity. (1981, February 9). *Industry Week*, pp. 55-60.

Peters, T. J., & Waterman, R. H., Jr. (1982). *In search of excellence*. New York: Harper & Row.

Schank, R. C. (1984). *The cognitive computer*. Reading, MA: Addison-Wesley.

Schwadel, F. (1985, August 14). Burned by mistakes, Campbell Soup So. is in throes of change. *Wall Street Journal*, pp. 1, 15.

Weisman, A. (Producer). (1986, March 9). [Interview with Morley Safer, reporter of *60 Minutes*]. New York: CBS News.

10

Communication Ethics

> I think that failures in ethics and integrity here are less excusable than errors in performance.
>
> Frank T. Cary, former chairman, IBM

> It is strange that social scientists, who are by profession devoted to the application of reason to man's affairs, have been more impressed by the use and misuse of power than by the use and misuse of knowledge.
>
> Harold Wilensky

If one peered into a crystal ball of managerial consciousness, how often would ethical concerns filter into major decisions or even minor ones? What shape would those concerns take? Would they be clear visions or hazy apparitions? Ethics is a subject that if approached at all is done so with great fear and trepidation. Only in the last few years have business schools added courses on ethics to their curriculums. Almost all textbooks in organizational communication completely avoid the topic. There may not be an active conspiracy of silence, but there seems to be a tacit one. Why? What is the source of this reticence? There are many reasons, but three stand out in particular.

First, many people believe that discussing ethics will inevitably lead to imposing one's morality on others. The heritage of western civilization is one that seeks to give people the widest possible freedom and individual discretion in forming moral opinions. Hence, even seeking to persuade someone of the rightness or wrongness of a particular decision can be seen as a first step onto the sacred ground of individual discretion and responsibility. Thus, it often is assumed the safest course is to avoid the discussion all together.

Governments, however, have always imposed a type of morality on their citizenry. Laws are designed to prohibit and prescribe certain behaviors even though a practice may be seen as ethical by some members of that society. The Mormon faith, for instance, at one time condoned polygamy. The government of the United States said otherwise and enforced the law of monogamy. Similarly, organizations have certain rules and regulations that may be contrary to a person's ethics, such as prohibiting alcohol consumption on the job. Organizational rules and regulations, like laws, impinge on individual freedom. In short, organizations and managers do indeed impose their ethics on others.

While philosophers may enjoy debating the question, "Do we have the *right* to impose our values on others?", managers do not have that luxury. They must ask: "In this instance is it right to impose our ethics on others?" The crucial issue is how this control can be managed ethically. Surely, in keeping with Western values, employees should be given the widest possible discretion for individual freedom. The fundamental point is that to avoid ethical discussion because "one does not impose one's views on others" is, ironically, an unethical cop-out.

Second, ethics often are seen as irrelevant to the fundamental purpose of business. Do ethics have an impact on the bottom line? It would be nice to say that ethical behavior always results in increased profits or productivity. But that is simply not the case. Many corporations with high ethical standards have been overwhelmed by unscrupulous competitors. Employees who, altruistically, "blow the whistle" on unethical corporate practices frequently suffer financial strain, social ostracism, harassment, and medical problems (e.g., Kleinfield, 1986). Sometimes it is said that "in the long run" ethical behavior pays off. But if one does not survive the short run, there can be no long run.

Researchers have tried to link organizational ethics to performance measures. One measure of a corporation's ethical stature that has been developed is an index of an organization's corporate social responsibility (CSR). One study found only a "weak link" between an organization's CSR and financial performance (Cochran & Wood, 1984). Results from other studies have been mixed (e.g., Reidenbach & Robin, 1989). Therefore, a strong argument cannot be raised that ethical behavior clearly is linked to increased profits.

The tendency then may be to dismiss all arguments of an ethical nature as irrelevant. Yet, simply because ethics may have little or no impact on the bottom line does not mean the issue is unimportant. After all, employee job satisfaction has little discernible impact on productivity, but that does not mean it is unimportant (Locke, 1976). Many researchers have said that job satisfaction is a legitimate organizational goal in and of itself. Likewise, an ethical standard of organizational behavior appears to be a legitimate corporate objective. Even though a concern for ethics may not be strictly justifiable in terms of the bottom line, there is ample reason on other grounds. Namely, ethical behavior can be valued for its own sake, just like job satisfaction and profits.

Businesses are not simply cold, grinding money-making machines. Organizations are not merely bastions of plenary productivity. People are the heart and soul of organizations. And these uniquely human communities also must be concerned with the human condition. Behaving ethically is one of the continual human struggles. Organizations cannot ignore such a fundamental human dilemma. To do so is to deny part of the human essence. There is more than the "bottom line." And, ironically, one of the most famous champions of the "profit motive" came from a professor of moral philosophy — Adam Smith.

Third, ethical discussions are avoided because of the "it depends" philosophy. When confronted with case studies of ethical dilemmas, the most frequent response is to probe for further information. No doubt, in most cases this is justifiable. But frequently an erroneous inference is drawn from such an exercise: Because every situation is unique, discussions of fundamental ethical principles that apply across situations are doomed to triviality.

A deep-seated belief in the "situational ethic" would clearly obviate much discussion of fundamental ethical principles. Yet, upon further examination, the "it depends" philosophy breaks down. Physicists have long known that the weight of an object depends on the gravitational field in which the object exists. A 180-pound person on earth weighs 30 pounds on the moon. Physicists, however, did not stop looking for fundamental principles of physics because weight varied with gravitational field. Indeed, they became intrigued by the problem. In the same way, it is frustrating to come to grips with the fact that the same action can be deemed ethical in one circumstance and unethical in another. Physicists did not give up when faced with such complexities — why should anyone else? To be sure, there are difficult issues, and all the answers are not discernible at this juncture in time. Yet we must seek to understand. The secrets of the universe lie behind physical complexities. Perhaps the secrets of the human condition lie behind the ethical complexities.

The purpose of this chapter, therefore, is to unravel some of those complexities and explore a few fundamental principles behind ethical conduct.

Foundations

There are three fundamental assumptions that shape this discussion of ethics.

First, every communication decision has some ethical dimension to it, whether acknowledged or not. There are countless complexities involved in the communication process, but the communicator initially is faced with only three simple choices: to speak, to listen, or to remain silent. In each choice there is an ethical decision.

In speaking, a communicator chooses to disclose information, motives, or feelings to someone. Judging whether or not this communication should take place is partly an ethical decision. Ivan Boesky, the infamous trader of insider information, certainly has shown that. But should one share a rumor about an organizational change with a colleague? Such actions are commonplace and appear to be less objectionable than insider trading. Additionally, there are questions not only of *what* but also *how* and *when* the information is shared. Is it ever wrong to "tell the truth"? Can one be too blunt? Is it always wrong to lie? It is ethical to use ambiguity? In short, people inevitably are making ethical judgments in choosing the timing, the subject, and mode of their communications.

Few would doubt that ethical concerns are inherent to the act of speech, but what about the act of listening? Alexander Solzhenitsyn, having experienced both the oppression of the Soviet Union and the immoderation of Western society, is in a rare position to comment on the distinctive problems encountered in each society. In an address at Harvard University he cast his discerning eye on American society:

> Because instant and credible information has to be given, it becomes necessary to resort to guesswork, rumors, and suppositions to fill in the voids, and none of them will ever be rectified, they will stay on the readers' memory. How many hasty, immature, superficial, and misleading judgments are expressed every day, confusing readers, without any verification? The press can both stimulate public opinion and miseducate it. Thus we may see terrorists turned into heroes, or secret matters pertaining to one's nation's defense publicly revealed, or we may witness shameless intrusions on the privacy of well-known people under the slogan: "Everyone is entitled to know everything." But this is a false slogan, characteristic of a false era: people also have the right not to know, and it is much more valuable one. The right not to have their divine souls stuffed with gossip, nonsense, vain talk. A person who works and leads a meaningful life does not need this excessive burdening flow of information. (Solzhenitsyn, 1978, p. 680)

His insight and remarkable candor seem lost on most people. He addresses not only the responsibilities of the speakers but also the listeners. Simply because someone is willing to tell us does not oblige us to listen. In the very act of listening one is making a moral stand.

Remaining silent may seem like the safest way to avoid ethical dilemmas. But even here there is no safe harbor. For remaining silent in the face of unlawful behavior or a potentially harmful situation is a serious ethical decision. Silence signals acquiescence or perhaps tacit agreement, as many of the Watergate defendants surely found out. In sum, there are ethical considerations whether communicators choose to speak, listen, or remain silent.

Second, communication ethics inevitably involves both motives and impacts. It is easy to condemn people who lie to pull off swindles. Their motive is deceit and the results are immoral. But what happens when the motives are good but the impact is bad? For instance, one manager wanted to boost United Way contributions in his unit. A noble motive, no doubt. He proceeded to attain salary information about each employee from the personnel department. On each employee's check he attached a note suggesting a "fair percentage gift." The means used to attain this noble goal are, at best, questionable. Indeed, most employees felt this action was a violation of their privacy. The old adage, "The road to hell is paved with good intentions," still rings true. In short, noble motives are not enough; the ultimate impact of the actions also must be considered.

Third, the ethical nature of communication must be considered within the context of "who, what, when, and where." Suppose fellow employees discussed a project they were working on. This may seem perfectly ethical on the surface. After all, such discussions actually foster effective interdepartmental relationships. A worthy goal indeed. The problem may be that the discussion took place in a crowded bar and a competitor overheard the conversation. When the employees are confronted, they may well reply: "What did we say that was wrong? We weren't talking to a competitor." But this is, of course, the wrong question. The issue is not what was said or even to whom it was said. The ethical issue is *where* the conversation took place. One of the reasons ethical issues are so complex is that evaluations must be made on more than one dimension. Communicators who are deemed ethical are not concerned with just *who* or *what* or *where* or *when* but with all four dimensions simultaneously, just as a physicist looks at the movement of a particle in four dimensions.

Ethical Dilemmas

There are many ethical dilemmas facing the manager. Some of the more vexing ones are discussed in detail below.

Secrecy

Secrets are held for honorable and dishonorable reasons. Sissela Bok (1982), in the insightful book, *Secrets,* defines secrecy as "intentional concealment." There is no moral judgment implied in that definition. Indeed, she comments that

> secrecy is as indispensable to human beings as fire, and as greatly feared. Both enhance and protect life, yet both can stifle, lay waste, spread out of all control. Both may be used to guard intimacy or to invade it, to nurture or to consume. And each can be turned against itself; barriers of secrecy are set up to guard against secret plots and surreptitious prying, just as fire is used to fight fire. (p. 18)

Here then lies the challenge for the manager: to determine when secrets are justifiable and when are they not.

The engineer who remains silent about potentially catastrophic failures in a product has in the same way abrogated moral responsibility. Such a duty should not be taken lightly by managers and employees. The makers of asbestos who knew of the potential health hazards of their product were morally culpable. Secrets can have a clear and detrimental impact on decision making and consumer safety. On the other hand, secrecy can be essential in order to make successful decisions or encourage innovation. There is a need for managers, for instance, to discuss the projected promotional prospects of employees or even salary projections with a personnel manager but not inform the employees. The employees may not live up to expectations; leeway is needed. Simply because employees are not privy to all corporate information does not imply the intent to deceive.

Corporations also have a legitimate need to protect certain information from competitors. Many corporations invest millions of dollars for research to develop new products or procedures. If other companies gain access to that information, they can produce that product for a much lower net cost because they do not have to pay the research and development costs. The net effect is that there is no incentive for the corporation to be innovative. Trade secrecy has implications not only for individual corporations but also for the general technological advancement of society.

Yet there must be limits even to trade secrecy. Too much secrecy about trade practices creates just as many problems as too little. One of the most vital aspects of the innovative process is having access to new ideas. Dr. An Wang (1986) believes that the great speed with which computer technology developed in the United States and Great Britain can be attributed to the openness of laboratories and the lack of secrecy clamps imposed by the governments of these countries. It is in the haphazard ricochet of one person's ideas against another's, against a third person's, and so on that new insights are gained. Innovation is the product of the carom of ideas whizzing through a community, as they bounce from conferences, to the university, to the business world, to government laboratories, to private research facilities, to publications, and back again. When the clamp of secrecy is too tight, the interactions are too few, too restricted. And the net results are all too predictable — lack of innovation. The innovative heritage of the Soviet Union and China are the quintessential examples.

Thus problems are evident at either end of the spectrum. Too much secrecy bogs down the creative process. Too little secrecy removes incentives. There is a middle ground of sorts. Patents and copyrights allow for information to be used and generally circulated while providing a modicum of protection for researchers and authors; but even with these devices there are problems. Changing some minor aspect of a product may be enough to circumvent a patent infringement lawsuit. Moreover, litigation is time consuming and costly. In fact, fewer than 30% of patent-infringement lawsuits are settled for the plaintiffs. However, about 50% of suits involving trade secrets have stood up to judicial scrutiny (Bok, 1982). Hence, many companies have started using trade secrecy agreements to protect innovative ideas. Therefore, one of the continuing dilemmas for Western society is how to avoid the stifling effects of either extreme of the secrecy continuum.

Whistle-blowing

Any employee who goes public with information about corporate abuses or negligence is known as a whistle-blower (Westin, 1981). The most important issue for the manager is to find ways to make whistle-blowing unnecessary. Corporations and managers legitimately expect employee loyalty. Only under extraordinary circumstances should such obligations be cast aside.

Some whistle-blowers are motivated by greed, jealousy, and revenge. That does not mean they are necessarily wrong, but it does cast doubt. Some are simply misinformed. Some confuse public interest with private interest.

Certainly the community has a right to know about corporate practices that are potentially hazardous. Yet an overly ambitious courtship of the whistle-blower can be problematic. After all, Stalin, Lenin, and almost every despot encouraged widespread "whistle-blowing."

Stifling criticism through autocratic measures, as in the tendency of the Arrow manager, may work in the short term but is disastrous in the long term. The objective then is not for the organization to squash dissent but rather to have some procedure whereby complaints, concerns, and criticism can be handled internally rather than externally. The "open door" policy is the typical approach taken. This policy allows employees to take a grievance to their supervisor first and then up through the chain of command until they get satisfaction. But more than once the open door has become a trap door through which employees tumble at their peril. For example, three engineers working on the San Francisco Bay Area Rapid Transit System (BART) in 1969 complained to their managers about potential safety problems but to no avail. Theoretic predictions proved ominously accurate. In 1972 the control system failed and one of the trains crashed into a parking lot for riders. After further pursuing the matter the engineers were fired. They had trouble finding jobs elsewhere and experienced a host of other hardships. Sadly, these were the consequences of criticism that was right on the mark (Baum & Flores, 1978).

On the other hand, some employees choose to "swallow the whistle" rather than discuss matters with a manager who may be part of the problem in the first place. The result is that potentially valuable information is lost by the organization and the public at large. With the wholesale default of many savings and loans in the late 1980s, one has to wonder how many employees "swallowed the whistle" (e.g., Berg, 1987). While the open-door policy is useful in many situations, it does not really meet the needs of the potential whistle-blower. Open-door policies inherently stress power relationships rather than corporate citizenship. That is, grievances tend to be considered in the context of how they affect the chain of command rather than on the propriety of the individual case. Hence, appeals rarely are investigated or impartially considered. In short, either "swallowing the whistle" or "blowing it" can be problematic. Therefore, the central challenge for organizations is how to properly channel employee dissent.

Leaks

A leak is a kind of anonymous whistle-blowing. The accused does not know who chose to release certain information or why they have done so.

Politicians have used leaks for years to send up trial balloons, stall a plan, or even defame an opponent. Employees also may leak information to the press for honorable or dishonorable reasons. Leaks may cause organizational plans to be altered or abandoned. Leaks can be a form of political maneuvering in the organization or a way to sabotage the career of a colleague competing for a job.

Are leaks ethical? In one sense the ethics of leaking information is the same as whistle-blowing. Indeed, the preventive measures are about the same. However, there is one distinction between the two that casts a dark shadow over the propriety of the leak. Namely, the person who leaks information cannot be cross-examined. For example, a supervisor at Georgia-Pacific Corporation received an anonymous letter accusing a worker of being drunk in public. The supervisor fired him and reported the incident to 100 employees at a meeting. The state appeals court awarded the employee $350,000 for defamation of character (Hoerr, 1988). Clearly, this worker never had a chance to respond to the charges. This hit-and-run tactic makes it difficult to assess the veracity of any claim and the motives of the accuser. Therefore, using a leak is particularly dubious in nature and should be undertaken in the rarest of circumstances.

Rumors and Gossip

Is there anything inherently wrong with sharing news about the birth of the supervisor's baby? What about speculating on an affair the supervisor is supposedly having with a secretary? Or what about passing on an unconfirmed report of a corporate takeover? Rumors and gossip seem to be an inevitable part of everyday corporate life. Even though rumors and gossip often travel through the same networks, there is a distinction between the terms. Rumors tend to focus on events and information, while gossip focuses on people. To the manager the ethical dilemma is twofold: (1) Should gossip about other employees be listened to? and (2) What should be done about rumors in the organization?

Managers appear to be on slippery ethical ground when they listen to gossip about fellow employees. Even though the information is often treated as "yet to be confirmed," there is often a tendency for the gossip to cloud judgments about that person. The information has a way of creeping into performance evaluations and promotion decisions, even if unintentionally. Moreover, the information may be completely inaccurate. Why would someone want to make a decision on the basis of inaccurate information? One young manager heard about one of his employee's sons having a drug problem. He decided not to promote the employee, reasoning that if this mother "couldn't control her kids, then how could she manage a department?"—a dubious assumption at best. (I wonder if a father would be held equally accountable?) Of course, the manager never said that, per se, but the assessment of her "leadership skills" was considerably lower than the other candidates. Such practices appear unethical on several accounts. First, the employee could never confirm or deny the information, even if it could be shown to be relevant. Thus there was no mechanism for correcting the inevitable distortion. Second, the manager did not have access to the same type of information about all the other candidates. What if the manager found out that the son of another candidate was a drug dealer? No doubt such information would have altered the rankings of the other employees. The supreme irony was that this employee's son was not on drugs but helping other kids get off drugs.

The other added benefit in avoiding gossip is that it engenders trust among employees. If they know that the boss will not listen to gossip, then they can be assured that such information will not somehow enter into decisions and unfairly influence the outcome. Employees who are confident their boss wants to hear the best about them are highly motivated. What then should a manager do when he begins to hear employee gossip about another employee? Perhaps the easiest approach is to interrupt the employee and ask a simple question: "Are you telling me this in order to help solve a problem? If not, then I don't want to hear about it." If there is some problem between employees, they should be instructed to try to work it out between themselves first. As a last resort they should come to the manager. The wise manager does not encourage the "tattle tale."

In fairness, there is another school of thought. Blythe Holbrooke (1983), the author of *Gossip: How to Get It Before It Gets You*, says, "A commanding knowledge of gossip and gossips give you the edge in conversation and helps keep you clear of potentially damaging situations at work" (p. 5). Other social critics have argued that gossip is one of the means by which people develop their moral sensibilities. By gossiping, people both develop and expose their moral judgments. Gossiping about the boss's affair surely indicates a moral condemnation. Lance Morrow (1981), *Time* magazine's social commentator, states that

> in gossiping, people try to discover their own attitudes toward such behavior and the reactions of others. It is also a medium of self-disclosure, a way of dramatizing one's own feelings about someone else's behavior, a way of asserting what we think acceptable or unacceptable. . . . Gossip is the layman's

mythmaker and moralist, the small, idle interior puppet-theater in which he tries out new plays, new parts for himself. (p. 98)

If so, this moral training is often done at the expense of running roughshod over other people's reputations. Is this really fair? Moreover, gossip is often the product of boredom. There must be a better antidote.

Indeed, rumor mongering could be justified on similar grounds. Rumors can have a disastrous effect on corporations. Proctor & Gamble spent years and thousands of dollars fighting a rumor that their corporate symbol represented the devil. Rumors that McDonald's added worms to its meat in order to increase protein content lowered sales in some states. Both rumors were unequivocally false. But clearly the impact was great (see Rosnow & Fine, 1976). Passing along such hearsay seems ethically unjustifiable. The seminal research in the area was done by Allport and Postman (1947), who studied rumors during wartime. They found that rumors were passed from person to person and hence distortion was inevitable. Allport and Postman identify three fundamental ways in which the information is distorted. First, leveling may occur, which means that details of the original message are left out. Second, sharpening may occur, in which certain parts of the message are overly highlighted. Finally, assimilation may happen, in which case the information is twisted to fit some preordained prejudice or predisposition. Which process is most likely to occur depends on the people comprising the network. Thus no one can really be sure what type of distortion has taken place. But the critical point is that some distortion is inevitable — and this leads to the ethical dilemma.

Rumors are more apt to occur in ambiguous situations in which people have a high interest in the topic. Announcing that "changes" are forthcoming in an organization without any specifics is the perfect environment for rumors to flourish. Passing along unverified information in these circumstances may seem to be an effective way to cope with anxiety. Controlling rumors is no easy task and never will be met with complete success. Nevertheless, timely information probably is the best antidote to rumors, even to the point of admitting when something remains unknown. In a crisis situation the key is to immediately develop a highly credible channel of information that people believe will provide accurate and timely information. Such an approach characterized the exemplary handling of the Tylenol tampering by Johnson & Johnson. Some organizations even have rumor-control hotlines where employees can call to check out any unconfirmed reports they have heard. Training on the negative effects of rumors and gossip may also be helpful approaches.

Maybe some of these ideas sound a bit idealistic. Employees find rumors and gossip almost as irresistible as the mythological Sirens whose beautiful voices lured sailors to their death. The allure seems inevitable. Perhaps. But remember the sailors in Homer's *Odyssey* easily resisted the temptation. They had plugs in their ears.

Lying

Of all the ethical dilemmas discussed thus far, lying would appear to be the least morally perplexing. Most would agree that, "One ought not tell a lie." A lie is a false statement intended to deceive. Yet lies in business are more common than many would care to admit. A letter similar to the one in Figure 10.1 was sent to a small group of executives in a major organization by a corporate lawyer. Within days, hundreds of employees had "mysteriously" received copies. The bold-faced admission of past deception had a predictable effect on morale — anger, cynicism, and apathy. Those who dealt with this lawyer, no doubt, questioned the veracity of all his past comments. He moved ever so close to the linguistic "black hole" discussed in Chapter 2. Like most lies, this one harmed both the deceiver and those deceived.

Yet one of the most frequent justifications for duplicity is that the intent was good. The "white lies" that are uttered to flatter or to avoid hurting someone's feelings are of this ilk. Some people even argue that certain "little lies" are inconsequential and have "little" actual impact. However, the very people who vigorously defend a falsehood on such grounds rarely are comfortable with others telling them "white lies." Moreover, there can be some long-term unintended consequences. The "broccoli soup" tale can easily become a reality. A couple, married for 35 years, sought the help of a marital counselor. In one of the final sessions with the counselor the following conversation took place:

Husband:	And another thing — why do we always have broccoli soup on Tuesday nights? I hate broccoli soup!
Wife:	I hate it too!
Husband:	Then why do you make it?
Wife:	I only make it because I thought you liked it. Don't you remember the very first meal I ever cooked you? It was broccoli soup. I asked if you liked it. You said you loved it.
Husband:	I only said that to be nice to you.

For 35 years they ate a broccoli soup they both hated. I wonder how many "broccoli soup" management practices are the result of little white lies.

ACME Oil Company

Law Department

December 1, 1989

In re: Pension Litigation

During the pendency of this litigation, we have had numerous inquiries about the status of the case. Recently, rumors have surfaced that the case has settled. These rumors were further fueled by a misleading broadcast on CNN reporting that settlement had been achieved. In the past, when calls were received from former employees, we suggested that ACME respond by saying that no settlement negotiations are underway between the parties.

On November 28, the plaintiffs tabled their first settlement proposal....

If you have any questions on this matter, please call me directly.

Wm. G. Howard

Figure 10.1 Example of "Objectionable" Corporate Memo

Therefore, even "white lies" should be avoided. There are almost always more ethical alternatives. For instance, Judith Martin, "Miss Manners," once counseled a reader about how to handle inquiries about her rather large diamond wedding ring. The reader was often asked by inquisitive acquaintances: "Is it real? How many carats is that? What does your husband do?" Such questions often are met with little white lies, anger, or bewilderment. Miss Manners offered a "gem" of a response. She advised that the answer to the first two questions would be, "I'm so glad you like it," and to the third, "Charming things, as you can see." These are more than clever responses. They are at once honest and polite, while effectively communicating that the information is "none of your business." When faced with situations that might invite some little falsehood, managers would do well to think of such appropriate and effective retorts.

Even if some lies are used for the best of intentions, there is a great deal of evidence to indicate that most falsehoods are uttered for less altruistic reasons. In one study researchers found that 76% of the lies were of benefit to the liar, while only 22% benefited the person lied to, and 2.5% were told for a third party (Camden, Motley, & Wilson, 1983). Equally alarming was the finding of another researcher who determined 75% of the lies told are directed at superiors (Hample, 1980). Since most falsehoods are self-serving, supervisors might well question the validity of the information received from subordinates. One of the greatest harms of a lie is that potentially valuable information is not made available to change a policy, alter a procedure, or mitigate potentially serious situations. For example, when an employee lies about actions during a crisis, the true cause of the disaster may never be known; thus, the potential for recurrence is high.

The bottom line is that lying should be resisted. Lying breaks down trust between individuals, shaking the very foundation upon which discourse between people is based. How does one communicate in a community of liars? Which remarks can be trusted? Which can not? Sissela Bok (1978) insightfully summarizes the issue:

> The veneer of social trust is often thin. As lies spread—by imitation, or in retaliation, or to forestall suspected deception—trust is damaged. Yet trust is a social good to be protected just as much as the air we breathe or the water we drink. When it is damaged, the community as a whole suffers; and when it is destroyed, societies falter and collapse. (pp. 26-27)

In short, when words lose their power only force remains.

Euphemisms

Lenin reportedly once said: "If you want to destroy a society, corrupt the language." By definition, a euphemism is using a less offensive expression instead of one that may cause distress. Using the expression "passed away" instead of "died" is one of the more common examples. This usage is no doubt understandable. Yet frequently the euphemism is but a first cousin to the lie. A purchasing agent has a far easier time accepting a "consideration fee" than a "bribe." Petty office theft often is passed off merely as "permanently borrowing" the item instead of "stealing." The use of such terms is meant not only to obscure the truth from others but also from oneself.

Euphemisms cannot be universally condemned. Yet, the user's motivations and the impact of such language need to be carefully evaluated. When used to rationalize unethical activity such as bribery or theft, there is little justification. The deeply contemplative Dag Hammarskjöld, former secretary general of the United Nations, poignantly writes of what should be our attitude towards language:

> *Respect for the word* is the first commandment in the discipline by which a man can be educated to maturity — intellectual, emotional, and moral.

> Respect for the word — to employ it with scrupulous care and incorruptible heartfelt love of truth — is essential if there is to be any growth in a society or in the human race.

> To misuse the word is to show contempt for man. It undermines the bridges and poisons the wells. It causes Man to regress down the long path of his evolution. (1978, p. 112)

Ambiguity

Since all language contains some degree of vagueness, there might be some question as to why the topic is even discussed in a chapter on ethics. Yet, ambiguity, like secrecy, can be used for ethical or unethical purposes (e.g., Bavelas, Black, Chovil, & Mullett, 1990).

For example, an employee asked his superior about the possibility of promotion and was told, "We have the very best in mind but we can't discuss it now." The supervisor implied that the subordinate would in fact be promoted. That is at least one possible interpretation. But what the manager actually meant was that he had "the best" in mind for the company, which meant that the employee was eventually to be fired. That, of course, is another possible interpretation. There can be no doubt that only the most cynical of employees would come away with the latter interpretation. Was such a statement an ethical way to stall further discussion? When later confronted with the true facts, the employee justifiably felt lied to. Indeed, the *effect* was one in which a falsehood was perpetuated through the use of equivocation. Technically it may not have been a lie because it was not a "false statement." Yet, the intent clearly was to deceive.

With a lie the onus of responsibility for veracity clearly is with the sender of the message. And even when someone chooses to remain silent, the onus of responsibility lies with the secret keeper. But with ambiguity, who is actually responsible is not altogether clear. There can be no question that in the example above, deception was the obvious intent and indeed the effect. In this sense, the manager's action was unethical. Moreover, there were legitimate alternatives open to the manager. If he wanted to stall on the issue, then he could have simply said, "We will have to discuss it later." Such an expression implies no commitment and doesn't lead the employee astray.

Yet, what about a manager who does not purposely intend to deceive? Take, for example, the case of the secretary of the Air Force who concurrently was a special partner in an industrial engineering firm. Using official Air Force stationery, he wrote letters to companies who had contracts with the Air Force, urging them to use the services of the industrial engineering firm. When the incident was reviewed by a congressional committee, the secretary quite honestly could not see how the letters could be interpreted by the corporations as a message saying essentially, "You do business with them, I'll do business with you." The conflict of interest never occurred to him (Austin, 1961). But that is indeed one highly probable interpretation of that message. Even though the secretary had the very best of intentions, the ambiguity of the message had an undesired effect. The congressional committee rightly held him responsible for this legitimate misinterpretation.

Therefore, whether there is the intentional use of ambiguity (as in the first case) or there is not (as in the second case), communicators are to some extent held responsible for possible misinterpretations. This means that it is imperative for a manager to be aware of the probabilistic nature of communication and to consider not only how the message is intended to be understood but also how the message might be misunderstood. Communicators have a responsibility to anticipate at least *some* of the possible interpretations of their remarks. This does not mean that speakers are responsible for *all* possible misinterpretations, for any remark can be twisted into thousands of different meanings. There is a responsibility, however, to look at the *legitimate* possible interpretations.

There are ethical uses of purposeful vagueness or equivocation. Managers may equivocate when setting up certain tasks in order to encourage creativity. Employees are more likely to come up with new ideas when asked to come up with "a new marketing strategy" than when told in highly specific terms what the strategy should be like. Equivocation can be an effective and legitimate persuasive tool. Professor Lee Williams (1976) of Southwest Texas State University has done extensive research on the topic. His conclusions include the following:

> In contrast to the tenet advocated since antiquity that all issues should be addressed clearly, this study indicated that under certain circumstances the speaker might be wiser if he used deliberate vagueness. . . . If the speaker knows that certain issues are disagreeable and if he feels that the circumstances seriously limit the probability of successful persuasion, then equivocation appears to be the best alternative available. It provides the speaker with an effective means for avoiding premature exposure of his innermost feelings, it leaves the receiver with a neutral to moderately favorable disposition, it minimizes the chance of recalling the disagreeable issues, and it avoids negative connotations which might jeopardize future persuasive attempts. (p. 17)

Managers, when considering difficult issues might, therefore, legitimately use equivocation as a strategy.

Equivocation also serves a useful function of uniting people while allowing diversity. Corporate slogans are one of the best examples. The company with a "commitment to excellence" has thousands of different ways in which the commitment is expressed, and the slogan allows for some semblance of corporate unity. Ambiguity also allows for freedom to maneuver when circumstances change. Dr. An Wang, the founder of Wang Laboratories, encouraged employee commitment with the philosophy, "providing specific solutions to clients problems." He did not make a commitment to a specific product per se. Thus when he decided to move out of the calculator market in which the company had enjoyed great success and into the computer market, he was being completely consistent (Wang, 1986). If the change had been perceived as a total shift of corporate position, then the strategic move would have been met with even more resistance than it was. Indeed, Wang's move proved prescient. While values are necessarily ambiguous, the commitment to the values endures long after the passing fancy of a marketplace. Such commitments engender trust and stability amid the turbulent seas of technological change. The challenge for the manager and the CEO alike is to determine when ambiguity is necessary and when it is not. There is no magic formula to fall back on — only sound judgment.

Apology

Inevitably, managers and organizations are involved in situations that require an apology. This is a special communication challenge because the motives or reputation of a manager are called into question. Such concerns strike at the very heart of managerial effectiveness. If managers' motives or reputations are suspect, so is their credibility and, ultimately, their ability to influence others.

Every apology is unique. However, there are two basic strategic responses to a perceived or actual offense. First, a manager may seek to *reform* perceptions of the offense by denying the allegations, clarifying the situation, or identifying with independent, credible sources. For example, one manager was accused of making racist comments at an off-site party. When questioned by the vice president, the manager not only denied that the episode occurred, he also encouraged the vice president to question colleagues, who were minorities, about his racial attitudes. Clearly, the manager was seeking some independent verification of his position. Second, a manager may seek to *transform* perceptions by placing an incident in a broader context of events, or show that the incident was an aberration (Ware & Linkugel, 1973).

The fundamental issue in choosing between the "reforming" and "transforming" strategies involves responsibility. Is the manager going to accept responsibility for the incident or not? The appropriate strategy is situationally dependent. But regardless of where the responsibility for the incident lies, the manager or organization must take responsibility for resolving the situation. The Tylenol tampering case began with the death of a woman who took two Extra-Strength Tylenol capsules. An unknown terrorist had perpetrated the crime; Johnson & Johnson was not directly responsible for the mishap. However, Johnson & Johnson did have a duty to respond to the situation in a responsible and decisive way. Tylenol continues to sell well despite the incident because the "apology" was handled effectively (Benson, 1988).

Even when an organization clearly is responsible for a mishap, effective communication can limit the damage and actually build the corporate reputation. For instance, on January 15, 1990, AT&T had major service disruption that affected long-distance service across the entire United States. Clearly, this kind of difficulty threatened AT&T's reputation. However, after a brief period of confusion, AT&T handled the situation with aplomb. The letter in Figure 10.2 was the centerpiece of their strategy. It provides an appropriate model for an apology:

(1) It was a timely response. In less than five days the letter appeared in major U.S. newspapers.

(2) It clearly acknowledged the difficulty. AT&T did not equivocate about the nature of the incident but admitted it in the first sentence.

(3) It unambiguously communicated AT&T's responsibility. The letter cleverly acknowledged that AT&T caused the problem, while simultaneously suggesting that they had higher standards.

Robert E. Allen
Chairman of the Board

550 Madison Avenue
New York, NY 10022
212 644 1000

Dear AT&T Customer:

AT&T had a major service disruption last Monday. We didn't live up to our own standards of quality, and we didn't live up to yours.

It's as simple as that. And that's not acceptable to us. Or to you.

Once we discovered the problem, we responded within minutes with every resource at our disposal. By late evening, normal service was restored. Ironically, the problem resulted from a glitch in software designed to provide back-up in a new signaling system we were installing to bring even greater reliability to our network. It has now been fixed.

We understand how much people have come to depend upon AT&T service, so our AT&T Bell Laboratories scientists and our network engineers are doing everything possible to guard against a recurrence.

We know there's no way to make up for the inconvenience this problem may have caused you. But in an effort to underscore how much we value our relationship with you, we've filed with the FCC to offer a special day of calling discounts on Valentine's Day, Wednesday, February 14:

Discounts all-day for residence and business customers on most out-of-state calls made on the AT&T public network throughout the U.S., and on international calls to all 158 direct-dial countries.

We've also extended the provisions of our AT&T 800 Assurance Policy to cover this extraordinary situation.

For more than 100 years, we've built our reputation on superior quality, reliability and technological innovation. Our goal is to ensure that you <u>always</u> regard us that way.

Sincerely,

R. E. Allen
Chairman

Figure 10.2 Example of a Corporate Apology

(4) It demonstrated that AT&T was taking decisive action to insure that the problem would not recur. This message was vital in securing future customer loyalty.

(5) It was brief. The letter did not go into a lot of detail that could detract from the central purpose of the apology and might make it appear that AT&T was trying to gloss over the situation.

(6) It provided a type of restitution. The Valentine's Day discounts could not compensate for the difficulties consumers experienced, but it did show that AT&T was remorseful. Moreover, consumers were aware that this form of restitution had an impact on AT&T's bottom line, which meant they were willing to pay for a good reputation.

Clearly, the objective of this letter was to vouchsafe AT&T's reputation. They wanted to communicate that the service disruption was an aberration and not an indication of the service quality. In short, the AT&T letter was based on sound principles of an effective apology.

A Strategic Approach to Corporate Ethics

There is probably no way to absolutely guarantee that a corporation or its employees will behave ethically. Yet acknowledgment of occasional failures does not reduce our fundamental ethical responsibility. Organizations, like people, should strive for ethical behavior. This is as much a philosophical position as a moral one. And like all great philosophical statements, it implies certain actions. For the organization, it implies action on three basic levels: (1) cultural, (2) policy, and (3) personal. Ethical organizations are created and sustained by individuals of personal integrity, operating in a culture of principle, and governed by conscientious policies (see Figure 10.3).

Corporate Culture

Throughout the span of history the great philosophers and religious figures have penned works aimed at resolving the moral perplexities that face all human beings. There are a host of ethical quandaries that man has faced since the beginning of time, but there are three central threads running through the great debates: man's relationship to God, to things, and to each other. Cultures have been shaped by our struggles with these fundamental issues. Yet, with modern technical advances in data storage and retrieval, there is a fundamentally new and different arena of ethical concern emerging: man's relationship to information. There is little consensus on the shape of information ethics. In short, there are few agreed-upon cultural values for how information is to be treated.

Building consensus on informational values may be one of the greatest cultural challenges facing CEO's in the future. For example, only in the last few years has an ethic about copy-protected software started to emerge. Another issue involves the concept of "corporate due process," which has a

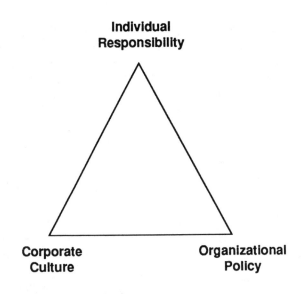

Individual Responsibility

Corporate Culture

Organizational Policy

Figure 10.3 The Ethical Organization

toehold in the business conscience. David W. Ewing (1989), a former editor of *Harvard Business Review,* defines the concept as "effective mechanisms and procedures for ensuring equity and justice among employees" (p. 4). In both cases, values are slowly emerging through the dynamic interplay of practice and philosophy. However, the very existence of an ongoing debate communicates the importance of the ethical concern. Indeed, the ethical organization must have a culture that symbolically signals its commitment. There are a variety of ways to do this, including the development of a set of fundamental operating principles that are widely circulated. For example, when George Bush became president of the United States he read a list of "Marching Orders" at his first informal cabinet meeting that set the ethical tone for the administration (see Table 10.1). But principles are not enough. Principles must be translated into policy. To this issue we now turn.

Organizational Policy

There are three critical policy issues that every organization must face. First, what information should be gathered? Second, how should that information be gathered? Third, how should the information be used? Within the vortex of these circles of concern lies the essence of an ethical policy (see Figure 10.4).

Table 10.1 George Bush's "Marching Orders"

- Think big

- Challenge the system

- Adhere to the highest ethical standards

- Be on the record as much as possible

- Be frank

- Fight hard for your position

- When I make a call, we move as a team

- Work with Congress

- Represent the United States with dignity

SOURCE: W. Safire, "Bush's Cabinet: Who's Up." *New York Times Magazine* (March 25, 1990) 31-67.

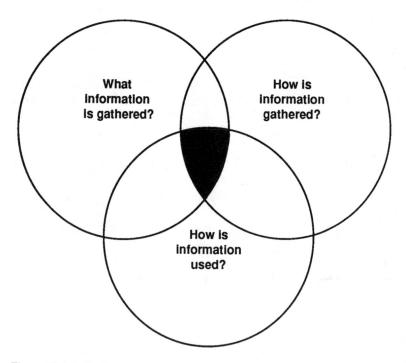

Figure 10.4 Policy Issues

Policy Issue 1: What Information Should be Gathered?

Since the cost of gathering and retaining data has steadily decreased, many organizations routinely gather information for which they have little use. Often the attitude is: "Who does it hurt? Besides, it might be useful someday." Yet, this cavalier attitude often runs roughshod over employee rights to privacy and may unfairly influence decision making (e.g., Burgoon, 1982). There are important ethical considerations when one gathers information, and organizations need to carefully consider the implications of their procedures.

One way to capture the perplexities facing an organization is to examine the tension between who controls access to the information and who desires the information. In particular, three fundamental parties are involved — individual employees or potential employees, the organization, and the community at large. A proper information policy should consider the often conflicting needs and desires of each of these three groups. There are many specific issues that face particular organizations, but some of the more common dilemmas are included in Figure 10.5.

What information does an organization legitimately need about employees? Some points of controversy are pictured in sector 1. Does an organization really need information about a person's marital status, employment of spouse, previous arrests, and off-job behaviors? Organizations routinely collect such information. For example, a society that believes "innocent until proven guilty," could hardly justify making a hiring or promotion decision based on an arrest. Indeed, this is what the courts have ruled. Moreover, in most cases, the health background of an employee has little relevancy to promotion decisions. Thus when making such a decision, a manager should not even have access to this information, so that there is no possibility for it to influence decision making. Of course, the personnel department will need such information to administer health care plans. Therefore, employee files need to be structured in such a way that managers have access only to the information necessary to make proper decisions.

There are a host of other issues that are of potential concern for employees. Organizations that have not set up task forces to analyze the specific records kept on individual employees would be well advised to do so. What is at stake is employee privacy, and all employees like to feel a certain sense of personal dignity. Therefore, the task force should take a good hard look at issues such as the use of Social Security numbers, and personality and IQ tests. *The guiding principle in making such decisions should be relevancy to the decisions that need to be made.* Clearly, in making a hiring decision,

Information Controlled By	Information Desired By		
	Individual	Organization	Community
Individual		• Medical Records • Employment of Spouse • Marital Status • Off-job behaviors • Personality tests • Social Security Number **sector 1**	• Corporate Misconduct • Trade Secrets • Corporate Strategy • Policy Disputes **sector 2**
Organization	• Performance Appraisals • Personnel Files • Salary Projections • Private Management Files **sector 3**		• Recommendation Letters • Product Information • Employee Names, Phone **sector 4**
Community	• Affirmative Action Guidelines • Professional Standards • Legal Rights **sector 5**	• Competitor Strategy • Government Policies • Forthcoming Media Stories **sector 6**	

Figure 10.5 Dilemmas in Gathering Information

managers need access to the educational background of the candidates, but do they really need to know the candidates' date of birth? Many of these changes can be easily implemented by changing the forms used to collect employee information. Gathering more information is not always better; it can be intrusive.

Sector 2 represents the quandary often faced by employees in resolving their respective responsibilities to the community at large and to the company. Employees need to have a clear sense of what they can and cannot discuss with members of the community at large. Organizations need to respect employees' freedom of speech while simultaneously protecting vital information. Employees should be aware that trade secrets, marketing plans, and the like are out of bounds. Making the community privy to internal policy disputes is another questionable activity, although employees of public agencies are allowed a little more leeway in publicly criticizing policy (Sanders, 1986). On the other hand, employees are ethically obligated to tell of corporate misconduct and consumer safety concerns if the corporation proves unresponsive. Many states have followed the lead of Michigan and set up whistle-blower protection acts. Many federal employees are protected under the Federal Whistle-Blower Protection Act of 1989 (e.g., Wald, 1990). The California Supreme Court has ruled that, "The privilege ends where the public peril begins." Managers and employees alike should feel an ethical obligation to inform the public of events that might imperil their safety. The code of corporate secrecy, while important, is subject to a higher code of societal responsibility.

Sector 3 addresses the issue of what degree of access employees should have to files about themselves. As suggested above, there are a few areas in which the company rightfully restricts employees access to their records, like projected promotion prospects or salary plans. IBM has an exemplary policy on this point. Employees are allowed to see almost all job-related and non-job-related information in their files. If they feel an error has been made, they can insert explanatory material. This policy of open employee files may sound burdensome to the organization but few companies have found it so. Fewer than 1% of the employees at AT&T have asked to look at their files (Ewing, 1983). In short, the benefits of such a program far outweigh any costs.

Clearly, organizations need secrecy, but there is little need for metasecrecy — secrecy about the secrecy. That is, employees can be told what information will be screened from them. If informed about why the secrets are needed in the first place, most employees will accept the rationale. Indeed, the case for some secrecy in an organization is undeniable. Of course, this policy should be presented in tandem with a discussion of the organization's communication responsibilities. Most employees can endorse a policy where "almost all information is accessible but when it is not, we know why."

Sector 4 represents the information the community at large desires about the organization. Publicly held corporations have a legal responsibility to provide certain information to their stockholders, like earnings, assets, and liabilities. Product information is another area of concern around which corporations need to make policy. Balancing the legitimate need for trade secrecy and the public's need for information is tricky. Certainly, clear warning of potential hazards must be provided by the company. The precise shape of the warnings and the extent of the warning is an ethical issue that is being hotly debated at present. Another issue of concern is how much information about an employee can be released to outsiders without the employee's knowledge. IBM will verify that a person is an employee, his or her place of work, job title, and date of employment. Any information beyond this requires the employee's consent. This policy is aimed at insuring employee privacy. Bank of America has a specific guideline prohibiting the disclosure of employee names and addresses to any other organization for the purposes of solicitation, even nonprofit solicitation (Westin, 1980). Even the dissemination of company phone books should be considered when examining policies in this area.

Sector 5 concerns information primarily under the control of the community at large that is desired by employees. Corporations have some limited responsibilities to insure that individuals are aware of laws and government policies that affect their well-being. Corporate newsletters often serve this function. Organizations also have a vested interest in allowing their employees access to professional organizations and societies.

Organizations quite legitimately seek information about the community at large. The environment has a tremendous impact on the corporation. Sector 6 lays out some of the ethical decision points for the organization. How far should the organization go in trying to gather information about a competitor, the government's future plans, and the press? The issues here are particularly fuzzy because the restrictions often are more in terms of *how* the information is gathered rather than *what* information is gathered. That is, placing a spy in another organization to steal trade secrets is expressly forbidden (e.g., Ingrassia, 1990). But restraints on the precise data-gathering objectives are unclear. There often appear to be few. The attitude often is "the more information, the better," but this is precisely the kind of stance that has lead to so much concern about employee privacy. Indeed, in late 1989 Boeing pled guilty to receiving unauthorized classified information and agreed to pay $5 million in fines. Some argued that Boeing had an "insatiable appetite" for defense department secrets that would give the company advantages over other competitors (Pasztor & Wartzman, 1990). Hopefully, as corporations grapple with this issue a reasonable consensus will emerge about what the legitimate information needs of the organization are in regard to the government and competitors.

Policy Issue 2: How is Information Gathered?

If information objectives are legitimate but the means used to gather the information are not, then the entire enterprise is deemed unethical. Managers, therefore, must not only be concerned with what information they gather but also the means by which it is gathered. It is legitimate, for example, to appraise employee work, but is it ethical to tape their telephone conversations in order to do so? These are the kinds of issues facing organizations today. There are two basic areas of concern.

First, organizations should have some kind of policy on what methods can be used to gather information about employees. Should an organization carry on investigations about employees without their knowledge? One survey of 126 Fortune 500 companies found that 42% of those organizations would gather information on employees without telling them (Solomon, 1989). Should detectives be used to investigate claims of impropriety? The same survey reported 57% of the companies use private detectives to investigate employees. Should drug tests be administered to employees? If so, under what conditions? Should employee phone calls be monitored? Should polygraph (lie detector) tests be used on employees? These are the kinds of issues every corporation faces. IBM, for example, has an explicit policy of not recording meetings or telephone conversations unless employees are informed of the practice. These vexing issues raise questions not only about employee privacy but also send powerful messages about the degree of trust management has in its employees.

Second, organizations need to develop a clear set of guidelines concerning the methods used to gather information about competitors. There are entire books published about the subject (e.g., Fuld, 1985). To what lengths should a corporation go to secure information? Some firms apparently feel that buying stolen documents is ethical. The law does not. For example, Chien-Min Sung was accused of selling GE's secret formula for making industrial diamonds to a South Korean firm. The possible loss is conservatively estimated to exceed $5 million (Ingrassia, 1990). Tapping into another company's data bank is expressly forbidden. But what about hiring a competitor's key employee? There are legal restraints on what information that employee may reveal, but subtle pressure is often applied. Upon leaving a company employees do not return knowledge, but they usually do return the corporate typewriters. Even consultants can unwittingly provide information on competitors. Some organizations limit employees' memberships to professional organizations for fear of employees unknowingly revealing corporate secrets. Is it legitimate to use personal contacts to gather information? Should trusted clients be pumped for information about the competition? The list of questions could go on and on. The point is that an organization needs to have a clear policy on the matter. Fundamentally the issue comes down to fairness. Most of the information needed about competitors can be legitimately gleaned from published sources that are widely available (Meyer, 1988). That is fair. Other practices decidedly are not.

Table 10.2 Does the procedure make a difference?

---

* Is access to the system a right, not a privilege?

* Is the procedure simple and easy to use?

* Is the board or investigator independent of the chain of command?

* Does the ombudsperson or board have the power to get the facts on both sides of the case?

* Is retaliation kept to a minimum?[1]

* Is the response of the tribunal or investigator timely?

* Is confidentiality preserved?

* Is the system visible?

* Are cases approached rationally and objectively?

* Are the processes and decisions predictable?

* Are staff people ready to help and advise employees with complaints?

* Are the rules clear?

Third, organizations would be well advised to set up "due process" procedures to air employee grievances. "Corporate due process is a dispute resolution procedure whereby a neutral agency or person has the power to investigate, adjudicate, and rectify" (Ewing, 1989, p. 35). Some organizations use an investigator approach, but most use one involving an appeals board. Regardless of the approach, the intent is the same: employees have a vehicle for dealing with grievances outside the normal chain of command. Corporate due process is a kind of organizational safety valve for employees. Why is it needed? Because some problems cannot be resolved fairly through the normal open-door policies. Grievance review boards typically disregard rank and status issues and focus on the merits of an employee's case. David Ewing (1989) has conducted some intriguing research on corporate justice and suggests 13 tests for an effective corporate due process system (see Table 10.2). A small but growing group of corporations—like Honeywell, Polaroid, and John Hancock—are using such systems with great success.

Policy Issue 3: How is the Information Used?

Information, unlike property, can be lost without you knowing it. Unlike the thief who steals jewelry, someone could read a personnel file and leave no clue that a "theft" has even taken place.[2] In this sense, providing security for information is more difficult than protecting property. Once information is released, it is no longer under your control. For instance, mailing in a donation to a worthy cause often means that your name is placed on dozens of mailing lists for other charities, who freely send you their literature and solicitations. Therefore, organizations need to carefully consider three fundamental questions.

First, who is allowed access to information? As has already been suggested, employee files should be classified in such a way that managers have access only to information they really need to make decisions. Federal employees are governed by the Privacy Act of 1974, which allows them to examine their own personnel files. If an employee deems the information inaccurate or misleading there are ways for the employee to correct or explain any of the material in the file. One survey found that 87% of U.S. organizations have adopted similar policies, which often results in a morale boost because of the increased sense of fair play and equity (Solomon, 1989). Typically organizations also have restrictions on the type of channel that can be used to request certain information. It is far too easy for an unauthorized person to pick up the phone and gather classified information. Thus many organizations require written requests for certain information.

Second, when can information be released? The United States federal government operates under The Freedom of Information Act, which sets a clear time line for the release of classified documents. Companies might well consider a sort of "freedom of information act" concerning corporate decisions and future planning. Such openness can help engender that intangible but powerful sense of employee trust in managerial decision making. In a crisis or time of uncertainty, employees feel more secure if there are guidelines about when information will be forthcoming.

Third, when should information be destroyed? Negative information in a personnel file often tags along with a person for years. This may unfairly influence decision making. For example, one executive was not given a promotion because his personnel file contained a note about "larcenous tendencies." It turns out that the characterization referred to a teenage prank (Solomon, 1989). How long should performance appraisals be kept on record? Is there really any need to keep an appraisal from 10 years ago? This might unfairly influence decisions. A manager deciding on two candidates for promotion might base an evaluation on an incident in the distant past, rather than a thorough examination of the candidate's performance in the last four years. Indeed, at IBM most performance appraisals are destroyed after a three-year period. Such a policy acts as a kind of statute of limitations. Employees need to feel that the "slate will be wiped clean" after so many years. No one wants to feel haunted by the past. Even God did not condemn Moses forever because he committed a murder in his youth.

Individual Character

Corporate culture and organizational policy are powerful forces that can mold the ethical spirit of an organization, but they are no substitute for the character of individual employees (e.g., Pastin, 1986). Thorton Bradshaw, a former president of Atlantic Richfield and chairman of RCA, was once asked about how to "infuse ethics into a huge organization." He responded:

> Well, I'm not sure it's a matter of infusing ethics into an organization, because I think most people that any good organization hires come with a set of ethics of their own, and live with because they're their own. What an organization should do — its objective should be not to twist or distort those ethics. (Freudberg, 1986, p. 230)

Most employees want to behave ethically. Indeed, research indicates that when employees behave unethically they believe that others are often the cause. On the other hand, when behaving ethically they cite personal values as the reason (e.g., Baumhart, 1961). Ethics are a product of a rich interaction between people's religious values, family background, and professional standards. Yet one of the most important determinants of ethical values is an employee's supervisor. Raymond C. Baumhart (1961) in *Harvard Business Review* puts it this way: "If you want to act ethically, find an ethical boss" (p. 3). There is a compelling tendency for employees to adopt the values of their supervisors. This places an extraordinary burden on managers to foster ethical behavior. How can this be done? Typically employees are trained in what specific activities to avoid. While no doubt necessary, there is another way. Ethics is more than a list of "thou shalt nots." The positive is a better motivator than the negative. Employees yearn for values they can believe in. "The value of an ideal is that it shifts attention away from what we know does not work and onto what we want to accomplish" (Pastin, 1986, p. 219). A commitment to these ideals, almost by necessity, means avoiding the questionable activities. Below are five suggested tests for communication that should engender a spirit of honorable communication.

Discretion

Sissela Bok (1982) perceptively describes the quality of discretion:

> At its best, discretion is the intuitive ability to discern what is and is not intrusive
> and injurious, and to use this discernment in responding to the conflicts everyone
> experiences as insider and outsider. It is an acquired capacity to navigate in and
> between the worlds of personal and shared experiences, coping with the moral
> questions about what is fair or unfair, truthful or deceptive, helpful or harmful.
> Inconceivable without an awareness of the boundaries surrounding people,
> discretion requires a sense for when to hold back in order not to bruise, and for
> when to reach out. (p. 41)

Respect for our fellow human beings, their privacy, and their dreams requires a sense of discretion.

Relevancy

Communication should be structured around the norm of relevancy. That is, communicators should take care that their remarks are pertinent to the purpose at hand. Private confidential discussions have no place in certain decisions. In this context relevancy means that only information relevant to a specific purpose is collected. It means when the information is no longer pertinent it is disposed of. On the other hand, the norm of relevancy means that all relevant facts be brought to bear on a decision. A manager who sugarcoats an appraisal review has not complied with the norm of relevancy. What is not communicated often is as important as what is. The norm of relevancy aids the communicator in making that kind of critical choice.

Accuracy

A healthy respect for the truth is the foundation of communication. The Biblical adage, "And the truth shall make you free," is more than a religious saying. Only when information is reliable can we be free to make wise choices. Lies and half-truths rob people of fundamental choices. If an employee lies about the true cause of an accident, it prevents the organization from protecting others from harm. Information is sketchy enough in these situations; intended deception not only compounds the difficulty but it may point investigations in precisely the wrong direction (e.g., Oberg, 1986). Therefore, all employees must be committed to the ethic of "accuracy," even when the implications prove personally painful.

On the other hand, the communicator must be reasonably certain that the information will be interpreted in the way intended. William James once said, "There is no worse lie than the truth misunderstood." One could take this line of reasoning even further and claim that it is impossible to have an ethic of "accuracy." Why? Because there is not enough time to communicate the appropriate context, or because information is always incomplete. Yet that takes the argument too far. Employees must strive for accuracy, even if they may never know the complete truth.

Fairness

Many questionable activities easily could be eliminated if one simply asked, "Would I want this done to me?" Ambiguity meant to deceive and lies could hardly be justified. Treating people in a judicious manner would mean elimination of much idle gossip, pain, and sorrow. Fair communication requires us to speak up to correct an inaccuracy, to defend someone's reputation, or to deal with impropriety. To be fair means to avoid the unjust but also to do the just. It is to speak and listen only under the proper circumstances.

Timing

Even accurate information can be useless if communicated in an untimely fashion. Why? Just as with a lie, choice can be restricted. Every day an employer who sits on the news of impending layoffs may deprive some employee of another job opportunity that comes his or her way. Likewise, if someone communicates to the press about an indiscretion before the matter has been discussed internally, the test of proper timing has been violated. How much better to remember a spouse's birthday at the proper time rather than a week later. By timing communication properly one communicates respect for the individual.

An athlete in a pentathlon must successfully compete in all five events. The winner excels in all the events, others do not. In the same way an ethical communicator must run the good race on all five accounts. I can still vividly recall one cold Thanksgiving day from my teenage years. After a sumptuous meal with my family we did what others were doing all across the land — we talked. As families do from time to time, we began to talk about various happenings and people we knew. My grandmother began telling a wickedly funny story about an acquaintance of hers. We egged her on for more juicy tidbits. We all laughed. But then I said, "But Grandma, that's gossip." To which she responded: "No it's not. It's the truth." That caused us to roar all the more. Reflecting on that incident now, I see that truth is not the only criteria by which communication is judged. Information may well be accurate and even timely but fail to be used with discretion. No single one of these criteria is sufficient unto itself. Each criteria must be balanced against the other. There is a dynamic tension in this pentad. Here is where judgment comes into play. Here is where the complexity of communication comes into play. And here is where the true test of ethics comes into play. The only real losers in the pentathlon are those who fail to compete in all five events. So too with communicators.

Conclusion

Discussions of ethics inevitably seem to lead to great philosophical words like "dignity," "freedom," "fairness," "right," and "wrong." For many, these words stay on the mind's bookshelf in the same dusty place where the Bible and the works of Aristotle and Plato reside in most libraries, untouched, unexamined, and unwelcome. But there are times when the force of circumstance or the compelling sense of place inspires one to dust off those forgotten tomes and contemplate these very words.

For me, it happened on a hot, muggy August afternoon in Washington, D.C. One marvels at the Washington Monument, the Lincoln Memorial, and the White House. But upon approaching the Vietnam War Memorial there is a different and inexplicable sense. The monument does not tower; it is carved out of the earth, a wound that is healing. The hard black blocks of granite shimmer. The sun gleams and glares off the names of war heroes that comprise the memorial. Strangely, unlike the war itself, the names on the face of memorial are difficult to photograph. I thought perhaps this was a reminder that even though it was the most televised war in history, no photograph could ever tell of the true horror. There were people solemnly walking by. But there were a few who knelt down, as if to pray. And then they reached out to the cold hard granite and touched the name — the life — of a loved one. They wept. Down through the centuries men and women like these have suffered and died for freedom. Freedom of choice, freedom of speech. These were not some philosophical abstractions to be debated; they were living principles that were bought and paid for in the blood of fighters and the tears of families. One feels a tremendous obligation to not make a mockery of such sacrifice, to not abuse the freedom but use it to pursue the very best in life. We often hear of the freedom of speech, but here on that hot humid day in Washington, D.C. I thought about the responsibilities of speech.

Notes

1. There has been some research indicating that employees who have won grievance suits against their supervisors have been retaliated against in the form of lower-than-expected performance evaluations (e.g., Klass & DeNisi, 1989).

2. The English language does not have an appropriate pejorative term to describe illicit copying of information. "Theft" implies the stealing of property but that is not quite the same as the unlawful perusal of a document.

References

Allport, G. W., & Postman, L. J. (1947). *The psychology of rumor.* New York: Holt, Rinehart & Winston.

Austin, R. W. (1961, September-October). Code of conduct for executives. *Harvard Business Review, 39*(5), 53-61.

Baum, R. J., & Flores, A. (1978). *Ethical problems in engineering.* Troy, NY: Center for the Study of the Human Dimensions of Science and Technology.

Baumhart, R. C. (1961, July-August). How ethical are businessmen? *Harvard Business Review, 39*(4), 6-21.

Bavelas, J. B., Black, A., Chovil, N., & Mullett, J. (1990). *Equivocal communication.* Newbury Park, CA: Sage.

Benson, J. A. (1988). Crisis revisited. An analysis of strategies used by Tylenol in the second tampering episode. *Central States Speech Journal, 39*(1), 49-66.

Berg, E. N. (1987, July 5). Critics fault accountants for not blowing whistles. *New York Times,* p. 3Y.

Bok, S. (1978). *Lying: Moral choice in public and private life.* New York: Pantheon.

Bok, S. (1982). *Secrets: On the ethics of concealment and revelation.* New York: Pantheon.

Burgoon, J. K. (1982). Privacy and communication. In M. Burgoon (Ed.), *Communication yearbook 6,* (pp. 206-249). Beverly Hills, CA: Sage.

Camden, C., Motley, M. T., & Wilson, A. (1983). *White lies in interpersonal communication: A taxonomy and (preliminary) investigation of social motivations.* Paper presented at the International Communication Association, Dallas, TX.

Cary, F. T. (1980). IBM's guidelines to employee privacy: An interview with Frank T. Cary. In A. F. Westin & S. Salisbury (Eds.), *Individual rights in the corporation: A reader on employee rights,* (pp. 214-225). New York: Pantheon.

Cochran, P. L., & Wood, R. A. (1984). Corporate social responsibility and financial performance. *Academy of Management Journal, 27*(1), 42-56.

Ewing, D. W. (1983). *"Do it my way or you're fired!": Employee rights and the changing role of management prerogatives.* New York: John Wiley.

Ewing, D. W. (1989). *Justice on the job: Resolving grievances in the nonunion workplace.* Boston: Harvard Business School Press.

Freudberg, D. (1986). *The corporate conscience: Money, power, and responsible business.* New York: AMACOM.

Fuld, L. M. (1985). *Competitor intelligence: How to get it—how to use it.* New York: John Wiley.

Hammarskjöld, D. (1978). *Markings.* New York: Knopf.

Hample, D. (1980). Purposes and effects of lying. *Southern Speech Communication Journal,* *46,* 33-47.

Hoerr, J. (1988, March 28). Privacy. *Business Week,* pp. 61-68.

Holbrooke, B. (1983). *Gossip: How to get it before it gets you and other suggestions for social survival.* New York: St. Martins Press.

Ingrassia, L. (1990, February 28). How secret GE recipe for making diamonds may have been stolen. *Wall Street Journal,* pp. A1, 11.

Klass, B. S., & DeNisi, A. S. (1989). Managerial reactions to employee dissent: The impact of grievance activity on performance ratings. *Academy of Management Journal, 32*(4), 705-717.

Kleinfield, N. R. (1986, November 9). The whistle blower's morning after. *New York Times,* pp. C1, C10.

Locke, E. A. (1976). The nature and causes of job satisfaction. In M. D. Dunnette (Ed.), *Handbook of industrial and organizational psychology* (pp. 1292-1350). Chicago, IL: Rand McNally.

Meyer, H. E. (1988). *Real-world intelligence: Organized information for executives.* New York: Weidenfeld & Nicolson.

Morrow, L. (1981, October 26). The morals of gossip. *Time,* p. 98.

Oberg, J. E. (1986, May 5). Soviet secrecy may cost future lives. *Wall Street Journal,* p. 15.

Pastin, M. (1986). *The hard problems of management.* San Francisco, Jossey-Bass.

Pasztor, A., & Wartzman, R. (1990, January 15). How a spy for Boeing and his pals gleaned data on defense plans. *Wall Street Journal,* pp. A1, 12.

Reidenbach, R. E., & Robin, D. P. (1989). *Ethics and profits.* Englewood Cliffs, NJ: Prentice-Hall.

Rosnow, R. L., & Fine, G. A. (1976). *Rumor and gossip.* New York: Elsevier.

Sanders, W. C. (May, 1986). *Important and unimportant organizational communication: Public employee freedom of speech after Connick v. Myers.* Paper presented at the International Communication Association, Chicago.

Solomon, J. (1989, April 19). As firms' personnel files grow, worker privacy falls. *Wall Street Journal,* p. B1.

Solzhenitsyn, A. (1978, September 1). A world split apart. *Vital speeches, 44*(22), 678-684.

Wald, M. L. (1990, March 11). Whistle-blowers in atomic plants to be aided. *New York Times,* p. 13Y.

Wang, A. (1986). *Lessons.* Reading, MA: Addison-Wesley.

Ware, B. L., & Linkugel, W. A. (1973). They spoke in defense of themselves: On the generic criticism of apologia. *Quarterly Journal of Speech, 59*(3), 273-283.

Westin, A. F. (1980). A profile of Bank of America's privacy experience. In A. F. Westin & S. Salisbury (Eds.), *Individual rights in the corporation: A reader on employee rights* (pp. 226-243). New York: Pantheon.

Westin, A. F. (1981). *Whistle-blowing! Loyalty and dissent in the corporation.* New York: McGraw-Hill.

Wilensky, H. (1967). *Organizational intelligence: Knowledge and policy in government and industry.* New York: Basic Books.

Williams, M. L. (1976). *Equivocation: How does it affect receiver agreement and recall?* Paper presented at the Speech Communication Association Convention, San Francisco.

11

Conclusion

The distinguishing mark of managers with really fine minds is more in the questions they ask than the answers they give. They ask questions that cut to the heart of the matter. Every question has implicit assumptions that latently structure the answer. For instance, one manager asked, "What training package should we purchase to improve our communication?" There is an assumption in the question that a training package is the proper solution to the problem. There also is an assumption that communication is an amorphous issue and can be dealt with in global terms. As we have seen, there are a variety of different types of communication difficulties that merit various intervention strategies. All too often the perceived communication difficulties are not the actual ones. There is a more fundamental question that should be asked: How does one discern the fundamental communication issues that should be addressed?

One useful starting point is a communication assessment. The objective of this process is to discover the communication strengths and weaknesses of the organization. The problems then can be prioritized and solutions developed. After implementation, the organization should be reassessed to determine if the strategy was successful (see Figure 11.1). What happens in some instances is that managers only ask questions for which they already have answers. For instance, an organization will conduct training and then assess the effectiveness of the training. Clearly this is important, but there is a broader issue at stake: Does the training address a crucial organizational need? The assessment addresses these kinds of broad questions by surveying employee opinions.

There are numerous advantages to an assessment. Greenbaum and White (1976) put it best:

Communication problems in the organization are not unlike the progressive development of a headache. If the initial body cues are ignored or not monitored,

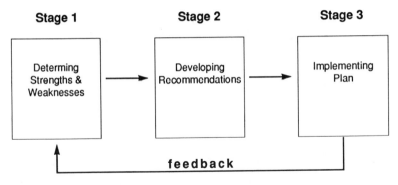

Figure 11.1 Assessment Process

the full "throb" will hit. The result is much more time and effort lost in trying to correct the unbearable condition than would have been needed to prevent the situation in the first place. The communication audit can provide that initial sensoring or monitoring for the organization which will allow for a preventative stance regarding communication problems rather than the typical corrective stance. (p. 5)

The assessment not only identifies potential problems but also communicates to employees that their opinions are valued by the organization.

The downside is both the expense and time involved in collecting the information. However, reputable assessors work by this creed: Gather a maximum amount of relevant information in a minimal amount of time. The other potential disadvantage involves thwarting employee expectations after the assessment. If the organization does not plan to respond to the findings, then it is best to not collect that data in the first place. At minimum, every employee who participates in the process should receive a summary of the results.

There are a variety of methods that can be used to conduct the assessment (Downs, 1988). While each method can prove revealing, each can create blind spots for the assessor. For instance, there are no questions about interdepartmental communication on the Downs and Hazen (1977) survey, which might lead an assessor to erroneously conclude that such problems do not exist in the organization. If interviews are used in conjunction with the survey, these difficulties might emerge. Therefore, it is wise to use a combination of methods. In other words, the best way to assess a company's position is to triangulate between three different assessment tools. Typically, I recommend using quantitative and qualitative survey questions as well as interviews to conduct a thorough assessment. Moreover, a comprehensive assessment should examine at least the basic concerns discussed in these pages:

* corporate culture
* information use
* channels of communication
* personal feedback
* communication about changes
* interdepartmental communication
* innovation
* communication ethics

The administration of the assessment is critical in terms of attaining valid results. First, there is the crucial issue of who should conduct the assessment. In most cases an independent consultant should be used. Why? Employees often are reluctant to share their true feelings to insiders because they fear identification and possibly retaliation. Outside observers also can be more objective in analyzing the results and less influenced by internal politics. Second, it is important to assure all employees confidentiality. This will encourage employees to respond forthrightly. Third, make sure that top management fully supports the assessment because it will bolster the participation rate. Finally, one of the dilemmas in conducting any assessment is being able to isolate problem areas while preserving employee confidentiality. The organization naturally is interested in breaking down the results by department, job type, shift, and demographic variables in order to target corrective measures. While it is important to do this, it is equally important to preserve employees' anonymity. My rule of thumb is to only report results from groups larger than five persons.

After the assessment is completed, the tough work really begins. The organization must grapple with a plan to address the concerns revealed. In 1984, Associated Kellogg Bank faced this very challenge. Like most companies, one of the problem areas was personnel feedback. But they went to work on the issue. They had an employee task force that developed a new corporate strategy for recognizing employees. Managers participated in an extensive training about how to conduct performance appraisals. The form used to conduct performance appraisals was revised. There were a host of other tactics employed that signaled a corporate commitment to an effective feedback system.

In 1990, the assessment was repeated. The result: employee concerns about the feedback system had almost disappeared. This is what the assessment process is all about. When managers ask the right questions, thoughtfully work through the answers, and tenaciously pursue the implications, they near the elusive goal of effective communication — and they become choreographers of organizational excellence.

References

Downs, C. W. (1988). *Communication audits.* Glenview, IL: Scott, Foresman.

Downs, C. W., & Hazen, M. (1977). A factor analysis of communication satisfaction. *Journal of Business Communication, 14*(2), 63-74.

Greenbaum, H. & White, N. D. (1976). Biofeedback at the organizational level: The communication audit. *Journal of Business Communication, 13*(4), 3-15.

Appendix A

Data Bank Composition

Organization	Type	Union Present	N	% Response Rate
Auto Dealer	Service	No	44	100
TV Station	Media	No	79	75
Industrial Laundry	Service	No	62	94
Packaging Plant	Manufacturing	Yes	43	77
Hotel	Service	No	81	87
Insurance Firm	Service	No	44	90
Health Agency	Service	No	28	78
Savings and Loan	Financial	No	78	93
TV Station	Media	No	24	67
Savings and Loan	Financial	No	65	100
Chair Manufacturer	Manufacturing	Yes	116	98
Nuts and Bolt Distributor	Service	No	57	88
Custom Manufacturer	Manufacturer	Yes	57	90
Savings and Loan	Financial	No	90	92
Bank	Financial	No	162	61
Motel	Service	No	63	65

Organization	Type	Union Present	N	% Response Rate
Newspaper	Media	Yes	239	75
TV Station	Media	No	79	92
Trucking Firm	Service	Yes	29	90
Paper Product Producer	Manufacturer	Yes	54	95
Machine Maker	Manufacturer	Yes	92	99
Utility	Service	Yes	169	99
Office Supply	Retail	No	61	93
Savings and Loan	Financial	No	119	87
Communication Service	Service	No	84	90
Building Supply	Service	Yes	83	94

Total N = 2,101 employees
Total companies represented = 26

Appendix B

Results of Communication Assessments

The Communication Satisfaction Questionnaire developed by Downs and Hazen (1977) was one of the primary investigative tools used in the communication assessments referred to in the manuscript. Basically, employees were asked about their satisfaction level with various aspects of communication within the organization. This appendix contains a summary of employee responses collected from the 26 companies cited in Appendix A. The results are presented in three sections. First, a rank order of the items concerned with communication satisfaction are displayed. All means are computed on a 0-10 point satisfaction scale with "0" representing no satisfaction, "5" average satisfaction, and "10" maximum satisfaction. Second, there is a presentation of items that explore employee reactions to factors that impact their personal productivity. A 0-10 scale was used with "0" representing that the item had no influence on performance, "5" indicating average influence, and "10" indicating maximum influence. Third, the demographics of the sample are presented.

Rank of Employee Satisfaction Levels

Rank	Mean	Standard Deviation	Statement
1	7.45	2.44	• Supervisor trusts me.
2	7.14	2.34	• Supervision given me is about right.
3	7.07	2.17	• Work group is compatible.
4*	6.88	2.04	• My employees are responsive to downward directive communication.
5*	6.81	2.04	• Subordinates are receptive to evaluation, suggestions, and criticism.
6	6.79	2.02	• Satisfaction with my job.
7	6.69	2.29	• Supervisor is open to ideas.
8*	6.64	2.12	• Subordinates feel responsible for initiating upward communication.
9*	6.53	2.06	• Subordinates anticipate my needs for information.
10	6.48	2.66	• Information about employee benefits and pay.
11	6.39	2.52	• The extent of grapevine activity in our organization.
12	6.38	2.29	• Horizontal communication with other employees is accurate and free flowing.
13	6.34	2.50	• Information about the requirements of my job.
14	6.34	2.33	• Written directives and reports are clear and concise.
15	6.23	2.83	• Supervisor listens and pays attention to me.
16	6.14	2.68	• Supervisor offers guidance for solving job-related problems.
17	6.13	2.28	• Communication practices are adaptable to emergencies.
18*	6.12	2.23	• Supervisors do *not* have communication overload.
19	6.00	2.56	• Information needed to do my job is received on time.
20	5.87	2.19	• Informal communication is active and accurate.
21	5.73	2.71	• Information about company policies and goals.
22	5.66	2.5	• The attitudes toward communication in the company are basically healthy.
23	5.62	2.73	• Information about departmental policies and goals.
24	5.59	2.58	• Meetings are well-organized clear, and concise.
25	5.56	3.25	• Information on company profits and company standing.
26	5.51	2.46	• Personnel news.
27	5.38	2.56	• Company publications are interesting and helpful.
28	5.34	2.31	• The amount of communication in the company is about right.

Rank of Employee Satisfaction Levels

Rank	Mean	Standard Deviation	Statement
29	5.3	2.38	• People in my organization have great abilities as communicators.
30	5.27	2.86	• Information about accomplishments or failures of the company.
31	5.26	2.58	• Conflicts are handled appropriately through proper communication channels.
32	5.19	2.60	• Company's communication makes me identify with it or feel like a vital part of it.
33	5.18	2.60	• Information about my progress in my job.
34	5.02	2.63	• Information about changes within organization.
35	4.99	2.47	• Company communication motivates and stimulates enthusiasm for meeting its goals.
36	4.86	2.51	• Supervisor knows and understands the problems faced by subordinates.
37	4.86	2.80	• Recognition of my efforts.
38	4.56	2.71	• Information about how I am being judged.
39	4.83	2.60	• Reports on how problems in my job are being handled.
40	4.5	2.81	• Information about government action affecting my company.
41	4.44	2.57	• Information about how my job compares with others.

NOTE: * Designates that only those in supervisory position answered the questions.
$N=2101$
*$N=547$

Factors Influencing Level of Job Performance

Rank	Mean	Standard Deviation	Statement
1	8.77	1.67	• Feelings of personal achievement
2	8.72	1.72	• Job satisfaction
3	8.68	2.14	• Job security
4	7.73	2.09	• Pay
5	7.70	2.81	• Family
6	7.63	2.21	• Immediate supervisor
7	7.56	2.59	• Opportunities for advancement
8	7.18	2.13	• Coworkers
9	5.91	2.71	• Economic conditions

Demographics on Database

Sex:

49.9% = (a) Males   50.1% = (b) Females

Age:

 3.2% = (a) under 21   15.7% = (d) 40-49
38.9% = (b) 21-29   8.9% = (e) 50-59
31% = (c) 30-39   2.2% = (f) 60+

Education:

44.5% = (a) High school or less   20.7% = (d)College degree
22.7% = (b) Some college   2.0% = (e) Graduate degree
10.7% = (c) Specialized Professional Degree

Length of Time Worked for the Organization

18.2% = (a) Less than a year   20.5% = (c) 5-8 years
32.9% = (b) 1-4 years   25.8% = (d) 9+ years

SOURCE: Downs, C. & Hazen, M.D. (1977). A factor analytic study of communication satisfaction. *Journal of Business Communication, 14*(3),63-73.

Appendix C

Imperial, Inc., Communication Policy

Imperial, Inc., developed the communication policy below to encourage more effective communication throughout the organization. At the center of this policy is the simple and easy-to-use flowchart that details how requests for information are to be handled. All employees received a copy of the policy and were briefed on implementation. The changes were enthusiastically received by top management and employees. The results were outstanding. This particular policy seems to work in this company, but this is not to say that the communication policy is a model for every company. Each organization needs to develop its own policy that considers its unique situation. In this way, the special information challenges and problems of the organization can be addressed.

Policy Statement

(1) A communication policy was developed because: (a) orderly communication throughout the company is necessary to keep all departments functioning smoothly and on schedule; (b) it avoids tying up individuals with redundant questions; and (c) it allows for complete, comprehensive answers from the source most qualified to provide the answer.

(2) While an individual may jump at the first opportunity to obtain the answer from another person, this does not necessarily provide the best method of seeking the answer or the best answer.

(3) There are four basic types of communication used in this company: written memos, phone calls, meetings, and informal face-to-face verbal communica-

tions. Our goal is to use these types of communication in the most effective manner to obtain the desired results.

(4) The initiator of the communication must analyze the situation and determine the best method of communicating with other people. This person should first look for answers in the material available to him or her. If this does not provide a satisfactory answer, coworkers and supervisors should be contacted to try to answer the question. There are valid reasons for working through established channels when solving a problem: (a) getting a complete answer; (b) providing those who should know the answer the opportunity of learning the answer, so they can provide the correct information next time the problem arises; (c) limiting the interruptions placed on other people; and (d) handling the follow-up to make sure the problem is taken care of.

(5) Managers are responsible for their departments in many ways, including communication within the department and interdepartmental communication. Part of this responsibility centers around the manager as the focal point for information. The manager should be so familiar with company policies and procedures that the staff is able to use the manager as the first source of information. If the manager can provide the answer, then the communication need is taken care of within the department. If the manager cannot answer the communication need, the manager has the access to sources who can provide the answer. The manager should be involved in the communication process that will eventually bring the answer back to the employee.

(6) This formal structure is not meant to inhibit communication. It is meant to provide an orderly structure that allows the company, as a whole, to function efficiently. Managers have a responsibility to keep their staff informed of what is happening within the company. Notable exceptions to the normal chain of communication do exist for valid situations.

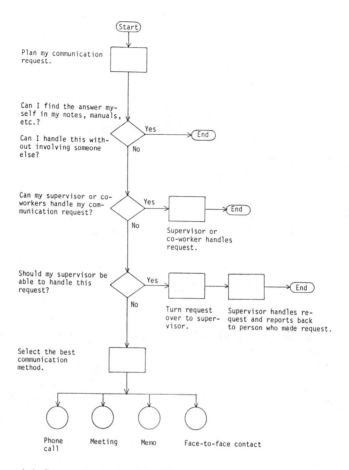

Figure A.1 Communication Decision Flowchart

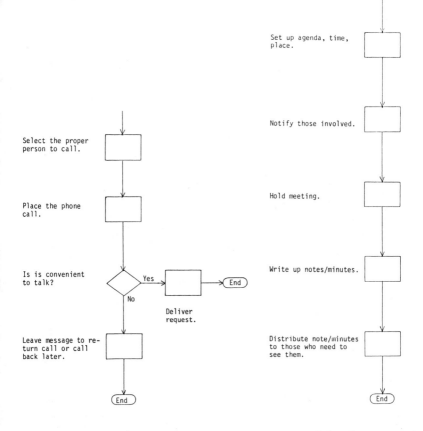

Select the proper person to call.

Place the phone call.

Is is convenient to talk?

Yes

End

No

Deliver request.

Leave message to return call or call back later.

End

Set up agenda, time, place.

Notify those involved.

Hold meeting.

Write up notes/minutes.

Distribute note/minutes to those who need to see them.

End

Figure A.2 Phone Call

Figure A.3 Meeting

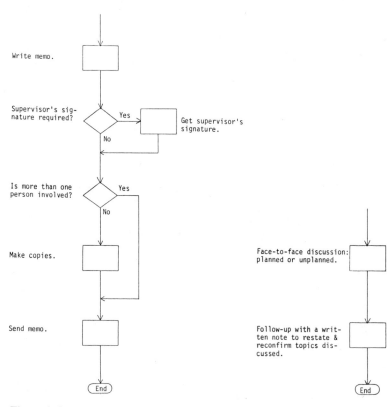

Figure A.4 Memo

Figure A.5 Face-to-Face Contact

Name Index

T

W

Y

Z

Company Index

Subject Index

About the Author

Phillip G. Clampitt is Associate Professor in the Information and Computing Science program at the University of Wisconsin-Green Bay. He holds a joint appointment in the Communication and the Arts program and has taught courses in the business school. He has published in a variety of journals including the *Management Communication Quarterly, Journal of Business Communication,* and *Journal of Broadcasting.* He has consulted with over 50 corporations including TWA, FMC Corporation, Associated Kellogg Bank, Krueger International, and Dean Foods. He is the founder of MetaComm, a consulting firm that specializes in conducting communication assessments and management training.